The Lotus Guide to Learning 1-2-3

Includes Release 2

Lotus Books
Cambridge, Massachusetts

Addison-Wesley Publishing Company, Inc.

Reading, Massachusetts · Menlo Park, California · New York · Don Mills, Ontario · Wokingham, England
Amsterdam · Bonn · Sydney · Singapore · Tokyo · Madrid · San Juan

This book is part of the *Lotus Learning Series.*

This book has been prepared by the staff of Lotus Books™.

Cover Design: Celia Miller
Cover Illustration: Kathleen Mahoney
Illustrations: Glenna Lang

Limitation Of Liability

Copyright

Library of Congress Cataloging-in-Publication Data
Main entry under title:

The Lotus guide to learning 1-2-3.

Includes index.
1. Lotus 1-2-3 (Computer program) 2. Business—
Data processing. I. Lotus Books.
HF5548.4.L67L69 1985 650.'028'55369 85-20078
ISBN 0-201-16687-9

J-DO-898
Tenth Printing, May 1988

Table of Contents

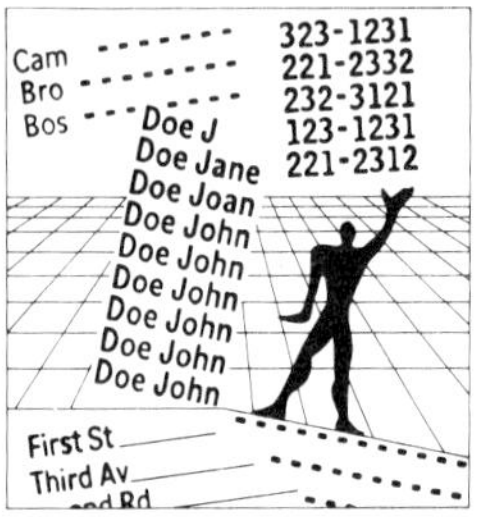

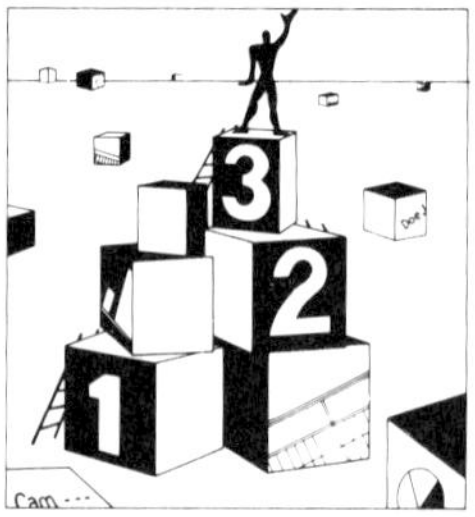

How To Use This Book

This book is a hands-on guide for the new 1-2-3 user. It is designed to introduce 1-2-3 and the functionality of each of its work environments. You'll learn by building simple files and keystroking your way through some basic tasks: creating a worksheet and entering and manipulating data; drawing a bar graph and a pie chart from the worksheet data you entered; generating and manipulating a database; and automating the program with keyboard macros.

This book is written for 1-2-3 Release 2. Users of Release 1a will find the book useful, but should be aware that Release 2 contains some new features that are explained here.

The *Guide* is not a substitute for the 1-2-3 manuals, but it will familiarize you with 1-2-3 so that you can be up and working productively while exploring the manuals at your own pace.

You cannot expect to master 1-2-3 all at once, but you can work while you are learning. You will be surprised at how quickly you will able to use 1-2-3 to accomplish some sophisticated tasks.

The *Lotus Guide to Learning 1-2-3* is comprised of seven chapters:

1. Getting Started
2. How 1-2-3 Works
3. Worksheet
4. Graphics
5. Database
6. Macros
7. 1-2-3 Tips

Chapter 1, "Getting Started," describes the preliminary steps you must take before using 1-2-3 and discusses the conventions used in the *Guide*. It then gives detailed instructions for starting 1-2-3 and configuring it for the *Guide*'s exercises.

Chapter 2, "How 1-2-3 Works," explains the basic 1-2-3 structure and terminology. You will learn how to move among the different work environments and how to use the uniform, menu-driven command structure of 1-2-3. It also teaches you how to do certain operations common to all work environments, such as creating, retrieving and saving files.

Chapters 3 through 6 deal with the individual 1-2-3 work environments. Start with either Worksheet or Database. The Graphics chapter uses a sample file created in the Worksheet chapter. The Macros chapter uses a file created in the Database chapter.

Clear explanations with keystroke directions and liberal screen illustrations and diagrams direct you throughout the *Guide*. The important point is to go at your own pace and enjoy yourself while you're learning. That's what this book is designed for.

1

Getting Started

The 1-2-3 Release 2 program is a fully integrated software package that provides all the tools you need to increase productivity and make decisions effectively. 1-2-3 is comprised of three work environments, each of which provides important elements. They are:

- *worksheets* to calculate numbers, test assumptions, and analyze results
- *graphs* drawn from numeric data, to illustrate and analyze trends
- *databases* to organize and manage information

With 1-2-3, you never have to switch programs or disks to move among the three work environments; you can go from worksheet to database to graphics and back.

The 1-2-3 worksheet and database functions can be used independently with excellent results. Used in conjunction with graphics, however, they comprise a powerful productivity tool. You can, for example, enter information into a database, move to a worksheet and calculate the latest numeric information for the database, and then graph that information in any one of a number of different graphic formats.

Before you begin using this *Guide*, there are some steps you must take to prepare.

Preliminary Steps

Checklist

1. Check the *1-2-3 Reference Manual* to make sure your hardware is capable of running 1-2-3.
2. Gather all the materials necessary for the exercises:
   - the 1-2-3 **disks**

   - the **function-key template** that comes with the 1-2-3 package; this is a molded piece of plastic that fits over the computer's function keys and indicates the special uses of those keys in 1-2-3
   - a **data disk**—a blank, formatted disk on which to save the sample files you'll create during the exercises

     New disks must be formatted before they can be used. Formatting checks the condition of the disk and prepares the disk to store information. Formatting is done with the Disk Operating System, called DOS (the program that contains basic commands that operate the computer).

     The Disk Operating System is discussed in the *1-2-3 Reference Manual.*
3. Make a copy of each of the 1-2-3 disks—these are called **backups**.

Starting 1-2-3

Once you have completed the preliminary steps outlined above, you are ready to work with 1-2-3. The procedure for starting up the program differs for a computer with two disks and a hard-disk computer. Read the section pertaining to your computer system.

Computer with Two Disks

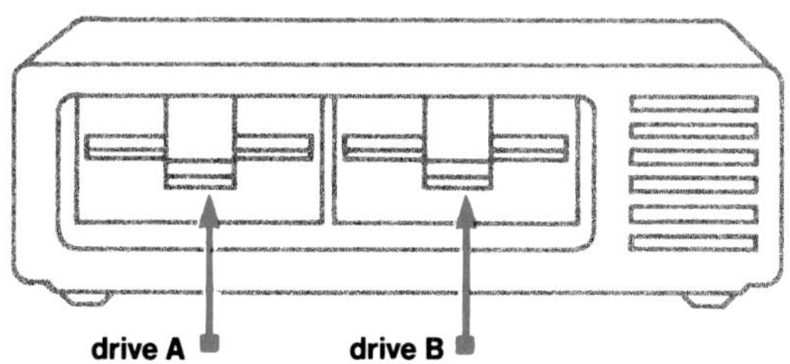

Whenever you start 1-2-3, you must first load the Disk Operating System (DOS) into the computer's memory.

You know that DOS is loaded when messages appear on the screen asking you to type in the date and then the time. After you answer the prompts, you'll see A> on the screen. This is called the DOS **prompt**. At this point you can start 1-2-3. If you have any questions about loading DOS, consult your DOS manual.

Note: Special clock boards are available that automatically enter the date and time when DOS is loaded.

The steps that follow assume that the computer is on, DOS is loaded into the computer's memory, and the date and time have been entered at the prompt. The DOS prompt A> should be on the screen.

1. Insert the 1-2-3 Program Disk in drive A and close the door.
2. Insert the data disk in drive B and close the door.
3. With A> on the screen:

   Type: lotus [↵]

4. The Access System menu appears on the screen. From here you can choose one of the following: the 1-2-3 Program; the PrintGraph Program (to print a graph); the Translate Utility (to read files from certain other programs); the Install Program (to indicate the type of printer and other additional equipment); A View of *1-2-3*; or Exit back to DOS. The pointer is highlighting *1-2-3,* the selection you want.

   Press: ↵

   Note: You can bypass the Access System menu and go directly into 1-2-3 by typing *123* instead of *lotus.*

5. The 1-2-3 logo and copyright notice appear on the screen. It takes a few seconds for the 1-2-3 program to be loaded into the computer's memory.

Hard-Disk Computer

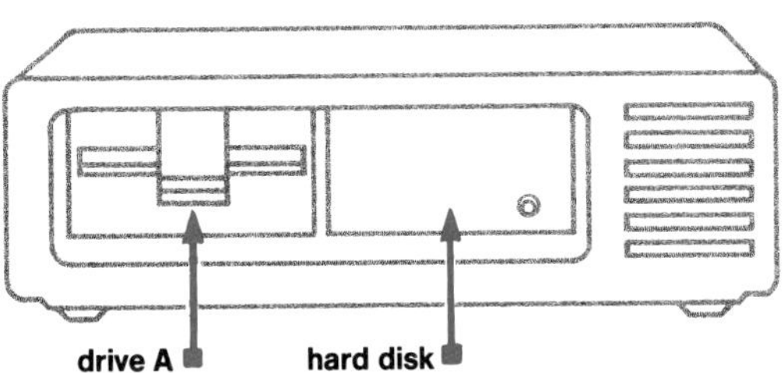

Whenever you start 1-2-3, you must first load the Disk Operating System (DOS) into the computer's memory. Most people with a hard-disk computer use the hard disk (and not the disk drive) as the main source on the computer. In this case, the DOS program is copied directly onto the hard disk so that it is loaded into the computer's memory automatically when the computer is turned on.

A hard disk has a main directory (called the **root directory**) that lists all the programs and files containing data that are stored on the hard disk. Most people also create subdirectories into which specific programs and files are copied. You name a subdirectory when you create it. For example, you might create a subdirectory to hold all the 1-2-3 disks and name that subdirectory 1-2-3. If the hard disk contains subdirectories, all the subdirectory names are listed in the root directory. DOS is usually copied into the root directory.

If DOS is copied onto the hard disk, you'll know that it is loaded into the computer's memory because after you turn the computer on messages appear on the screen asking you to type in the date and then the time. After you answer the prompts, you'll see C> on the screen. This is called the DOS **prompt**. At this point you can start 1-2-3. If you have any questions about copying DOS onto the hard disk or creating subdirectories consult your DOS manual.

Note: Special clock boards are available that automatically enter the date and time when DOS is loaded.

The steps that follow assume that the computer is on, DOS is installed on the hard disk, all the 1-2-3 disks have been copied onto the hard disk, the hard disk is drive C, and the date and time were entered at the prompt when the computer was turned on.

1. Complete the procedure in the booklet (in the 1-2-3 package) entitled *How to Start 1-2-3 Directly from a Hard Disk.* If you do not complete this procedure, each time you start 1-2-3 you must insert the 1-2-3 System Disk in drive A and close the door, even though 1-2-3 is on the hard disk.

2. Be sure the C> prompt is displayed on the monitor, AND that you are in the directory into which you copied the 1-2-3 disks.

   a. If you have A> or B> on the monitor:

      Type: C: [↵]

   b. If 1-2-3 is in a subdirectory, then:

      Type: CD\subdirectory name [↵]

      Note: Be sure to type the specific subdirectory name you created.

3. With the C> prompt on the screen:

   Type: lotus [↵]

4. The Access System menu appears on the screen. From here you can choose one of the following: the 1-2-3 program; the PrintGraph program (to print a graph); the Translate Utility (to read files from certain other programs); A View of 1-2-3; or you can Exit back to DOS. The pointer is highlighting *1-2-3,* the selection you want.

   Press: [↵]

   Note: You can bypass the Access System menu and go directly into 1-2-3 by typing *123* instead of *lotus.*

5. The 1-2-3 logo and copyright notice appear on the screen. It takes a few seconds for the 1-2-3 program to be loaded into the computer's memory.

The 1-2-3 Install Program

Installing 1-2-3 is a simple process. The Install Program presents a series of screens and you select "yes" or "no" in response to the questions on the screen. When you have specified the kind of basic equipment you have (and any additional equipment), 1-2-3 collects the necessary drivers in a special file called a **driver set.**

You do not need to install 1-2-3 to start using the program. However, installing the program enables you to view and print graphs and to print the worksheet files saved on your disk. The Install Program collects information from you about your hardware and from it creates a file called a driver set. A driver set allows 1-2-3 to communicate with your particular combination of hardware. The completed driver set is copied onto the 1-2-3 disks.

The Install procedure uses two disks that come with the 1-2-3 package: the Utility Disk and Install Library Disk.

The finished driver set must have a name. 1-2-3 automatically names the driver set Lotus unless you specify otherwise. Using another name is necessary only if you want to create more than one driver set. (For example, someone may want to be able to run 1-2-3 on a hard-disk computer at the office and on a two-disk computer at home.)

Most first-time users need only one driver set; in this case the name that 1-2-3 gives it is adequate. You can create additional driver sets at any time in the future (you can also change or edit a driver set at any time). The completed driver set is copied onto the 1-2-3 disks.

The Computer Keyboard

The computer keyboard has five sections.

1. The Typewriter Section

   The typewriter section works just like a standard typewriter keyboard. Letter and number keys are in their usual places. Holding the Shift key down and typing a letter key at the same time produces a capital letter. (The Shift key often has an upward arrow rather than the word shift on the keytop.)

2. The Pointer-Movement Keys

   To the right of the typewriter section are four keys, each of which has an arrow on the keytop. These keys are used to move the pointer. (The **pointer**, sometimes called the **cursor**, is a highlighted block that marks your position on the screen.)

   There is a set of keys combined with or next to the arrow keys used to move the pointer in large jumps. These keys are labeled with names that vary from one computer to another.

3. Special Keys

   On either side of the typewriter section, there are a number of keys unique to the computer, such as the Control (Ctrl) key. The names of these keys vary from one computer to another.

   Also included in this section are some standard typewriter keys, such as the Tab, Shift, and Backspace keys.

4. The Return Key

   The Return key often has a left-facing bent arrow on the keytop. It is also called the Enter key or the Carriage Return key on some computers.

   The Return key is actually part of the special keys section, but it is treated separately here because it has particular importance. The Return key is similar to the key on an electric typewriter that makes the move from the end of one line to the beginning of the next. It does that in 1-2-3, but it also does much more.

   In many instances, you press the Return key after selecting a command or typing data to register (or enter) your action with 1-2-3. It is probably the most frequently used key on the computer keyboard.

5. Function Keys

   Most computers have a set of keys called function keys. They vary in number from ten to twenty depending on the computer, and are frequently labeled F1, F2, and so on. These keys are assigned specific functions by the software being used. In 1-2-3, they do such things as recalculate the worksheet and call up Help screens.

   Since there are 12 1-2-3 functions, there are often more 1-2-3 functions than there are function keys on some computers.

   Note: Computers with more than 12 function keys usually use some of the function keys to perform functions that other computers assign to the special keys.

The Keystroking Exercises

The *Guide* teaches by leading you through keystroking sequences. Each sequence is preceded by one or more paragraphs that explain what you are about to do and what will happen on the screen.

To avoid confusion, read this text first. Wait until you reach the actual keystroke directions to begin typing.

In the keystroking sequences, keytops showing words or symbols as they appear on the keyboard are used to represent the Arrow keys and other pointer-movement keys, the special keys, and the Return key. The function keys are represented by keytops marked with the function name (not F1, F2, etc.). Thus, you should use the function key template to familiarize yourself with the particular function performed by each function key.

In the text of the *Guide*, all of the keys are referred to by name. Even those keys that have a symbol on the keytop are called by their name and not the symbol. For example, the name Return is used in text to refer to the Return key; in a keystroking direction you will see a keytop with the bent arrow symbol.

The Keystroke Terminology

The following terminology is used in the *Guide*'s keystroking directions:

Press: This means to strike or press a key. It is used primarily with Arrow keys, special keys, function keys, and the Return key.

Press: [▶]

Type: Type also means to strike or press a key. It is used primarily with the standard typewriter keys.

Type: 60000

Move to: This directs you to reposition the cursor or pointer to a certain place on the screen. This is usually done with the Arrow keys.

Move to: cell D3 *(on a worksheet)*

Note: Do not confuse this direction with the 1-2-3 Move command.

Select: This directs you to select a specific command from a menu.

A **menu** is a list of commands that appears in a line across the top of the screen. As you will discover in the next chapter, there are two ways to select a command: (1) press the first letter of the command name (no two commands in any menu begin with the same first letter), or (2) move the pointer until it highlights (sits on) the command you want, and then press the Return key.

Use either method to select a command when doing the exercises. A *Select:* direction is always written as follows:

Select: File

To select File you can either move the pointer to the word File on the menu and then press Return, or you can simply type F (in which case you neither have to move the pointer nor press Return). If you use the first method, be sure to press Return; it does not appear in the keystroke direction.

Many commands on a menu bring up a submenu from which you choose another command. Selecting the first command replaces the menu with the submenu. In the *Guide*, all the commands in such a sequence are listed on different lines in the keystroking direction. The commands for saving an existing file involve such a sequence. The keystroke directions look like this:

Select: File
Save

Again, if you choose to select these commands by moving the pointer, you have to press Return after highlighting each. If you type F and then S, you do not need to press Return.

There are occasions when a keystroking direction tells you to press Return. When you see this, do press Return.

Sample Keystrokes

The following keystroke directions are representative:

Move to: cell A3
Type: Salary
Press: [↵]
Move to: cell A5
Type: 22700
Press: [↵]

These directions say: move the cell pointer to cell A3 on the worksheet; type in the word Salary; press the Return key to enter "Salary" in A3; move the cell pointer to cell A5; type the number "22700" and press Return to enter the number in cell A5.

Suppose this is an existing file to which you are making changes. The following keystrokes direct you to save the amended file.

Press: [/]
Select: File
Save
Press: [↵]
Select: Replace

These directions say: press the slash key to call up the menu; select the commands File and Save; press the Return key (1-2-3 displays the name of the current file—this accepts it); select Replace (to save the amended file).

Now that you are familiar with the basics of 1-2-3 terminology and the conventions used in the keystroking exercises, go to the next chapter to learn some basics about how 1-2-3 works.

2

How 1-2-3 Works

This chapter introduces the basics of 1-2-3 and its command structure. It also explores methods for manipulating worksheet files—saving, retrieving, and amending them. As in all the chapters in the book, you learn by actually keystroking through some simple tasks.

Before You Start

You should begin this and every other chapter by starting 1-2-3. Remember, the 1-2-3 Program Disk must always be in drive A when you start the program, unless you have completed the procedure that allows you to start 1-2-3 directly from a hard disk. (See Chapter 1, page 10).

During the course of working through this book, you will be creating a number of files. In some cases, the files you create in one chapter will be used in other chapters, so you will want to save the files—on a data disk if you have a computer with two disk drives, and in the root directory or in a special subdirectory if you have a hard-disk computer. (Be sure to use a blank, formatted disk for the data disk.)

Each chapter begins with the following reminder:

For a computer with two disk drives:

- 1-2-3 should be set up to save files on a disk in drive B.
- The data disk should be in drive B.
- The Program Disk should be in drive A.

For a hard-disk computer:

- 1-2-3 should be set up to save files in the root directory or in a subdirectory.
- All the 1-2-3 disks should be copied in the root directory or in their own subdirectory on the hard disk.

The first step is to review some terminology. Start up 1-2-3 if you haven't already done so. Instructions are in Chapter 1.

The 1-2-3 Worksheet

When you start 1-2-3, the screen displays a blank worksheet.

Look at the screen. The worksheet is bordered by a row of letters across the top and by a column of numbers down the left side. The horizontal rows and vertical columns form a pattern of boxes called cells. All data are entered into cells.

The 1-2-3 worksheet is very large: it has 256 columns (labeled A-IV) and 8,192 rows (numbered 1-8192). Obviously, you can't see an entire worksheet of this size on the screen at one time. The screen provides a window that displays a small portion of the worksheet.

The 1-2-3 Main Menu

1-2-3 is a menu-driven program. When you press the Slash (/) key, the main menu appears on the second line of the control panel above the worksheet. The menu offers a variety of commands for use in the different work environments. All commands are complete English words; there are no codes, no abbreviations, and no computer jargon. 1-2-3 leads you through a command sequence by displaying clear explanations of each command on the third line of the control panel, directly below the menu.

Press: /

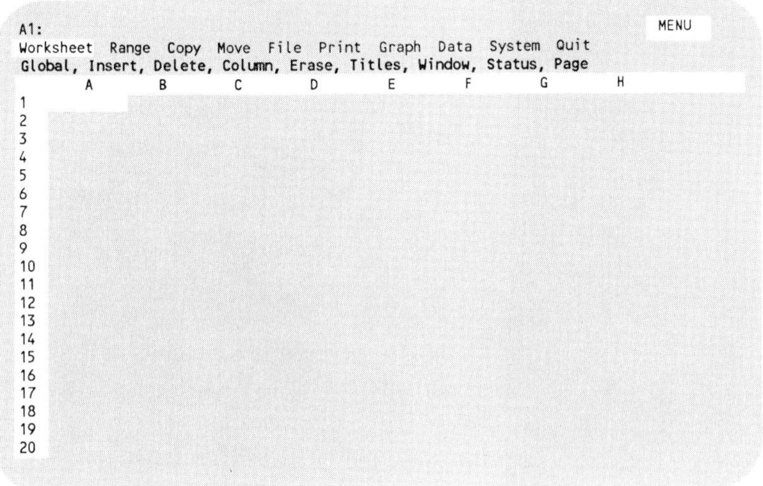

The main 1-2-3 menu is displayed on the second line of the control panel. The information on the third line explains the 1-2-3 menu item currently highlighted. The explanation changes each time the pointer highlights a different command in the second line. The Right and Left keys move the pointer along the command menu.

Many commands lead to submenus that offer further options. When the pointer is resting on such a command, you will see the submenu options listed on the third line of the control panel. For example, when Worksheet is highlighted on the second line, the third line lists the Worksheet submenu commands (Global, Insert, and so on).

Notice that the pointer works with a circular movement. Pressing the Right key when the last command on the right is highlighted brings the pointer back to the first command on the left, in this case, Worksheet. Try it.

Press: [▶] *(ten times)*

You can make a selection from a menu in either of two ways: (1) move the pointer to a command (with the Arrow keys), and then press the Return key; or (2) type the first letter of the command you want to use. If you type the first letter of the command, you do not need to move the pointer nor do you need to press Return. As you become proficient with 1-2-3 you'll find that typing the first letter of the command is quicker. Make a selection by typing the first letter of Worksheet.

Type: W

Worksheet Submenu

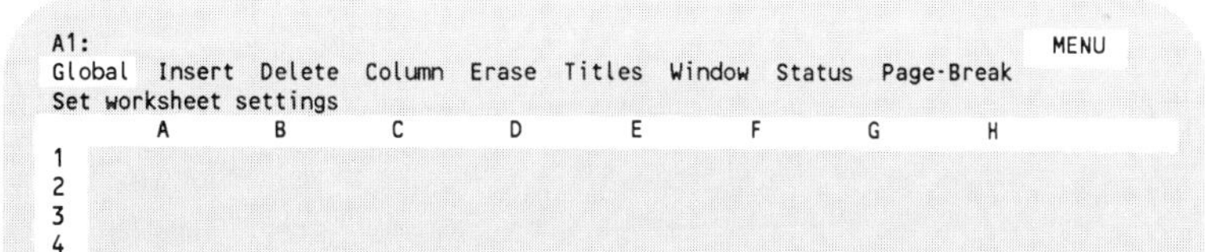

The Worksheet submenu, previously displayed in the third line of the control panel, appears on the second line.

Note: The keystroke directions in this book simply tell you to *Select:* a command. You can use either of the above methods to make the selection. However, if you choose to use the Arrow key to highlight the command, don't forget to press Return. All Return keystrokes that appear in the directions are for other purposes and should not be confused with selecting a command.

It is not uncommon to call up a menu by mistake or to decide not to complete a command once you are already in the command sequence. The Escape key takes you backwards through a command sequence, replacing the current menu with the one previous to it. Try it.

Press: [ESC] *(twice)*

The first time you press Escape, the Worksheet submenu is replaced by the main menu; the second time, the main menu disappears, leaving the line blank.

The uniformity of the 1-2-3 command structure and the clarity of its commands make the program simple to use. You'll be surprised at how quickly you'll find yourself issuing commands by typing letters without even looking up at the menu.

Files

All the work you do with 1-2-3 is done in the worksheet window on the screen. You then permanently save the contents of each worksheet in a file on a disk. That file contains your work, and it's available at any time for you to use and change as necessary. Electronic files are similar to traditional file folders; a disk containing electronic files is analogous to a filing cabinet containing folders.

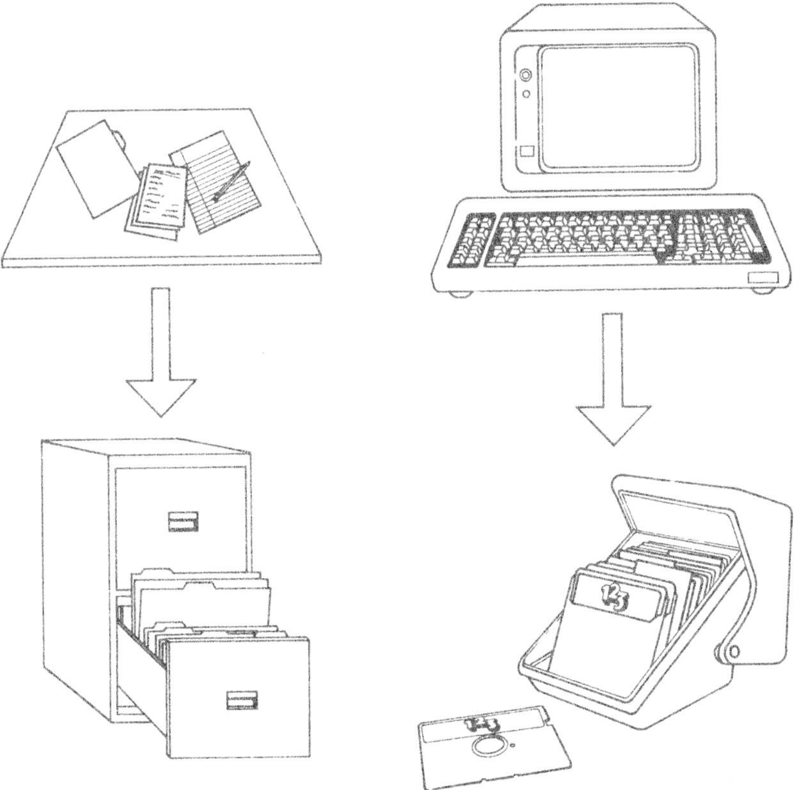

As you have seen, whenever you start up 1-2-3 it displays a blank worksheet. 1-2-3 always assumes that you want to start a new worksheet. In many instances, of course, you will actually want to work on an existing worksheet saved in a file. The following section explains how to name and save files, and then how to retrieve them.

Saving Files

You should already have a blank worksheet on your screen. You are going to enter a number in that worksheet, and then save the worksheet in a file.

Type: 1000
Press: [↵]

In order to save a worksheet in a file, you must first specify a file name of up to eight characters. There is a .WK1 extension at the end of all 1-2-3 worksheet file names. 1-2-3 automatically adds this extension; you don't have to type it.

Press: [/]
Select: File
Save

The prompts you see on the control panel above the window when saving a file are slightly different for a computer with two disk drives and a hard-disk computer.

- On a computer with two disk drives, you will see the following on the control panel:

  Enter save file name: B:*.wk1

  The B: indicates that the file will be saved on the disk in drive B. The name of the file will appear to the right of the B: as you type it. The Return key then enters the name. Name the file One.

  Type: One [↵]

- On a hard-disk computer you will see the following on the control panel:

  Enter save file name: C:\123*.wk1

  This example assumes that the default drive is a subdirectory named 123 on the hard disk. The C:\123*.wk1 indicates that the file will be saved in the subdirectory named 123 on the hard disk. As you type the name of the file, it will appear to the right of the second backslash (\ ). The Return key then enters the name. Name the file One.

Type: One [↵]

After you type the name, the mode indicator changes to WAIT while the worksheet is saved in a file (this won't take long because the worksheet is a small one).

Notice that the worksheet named One remains on the screen after you save it.

Retrieving Files

Retrieving an existing file is a simple, straightforward process using the File Retrieve command. In this example you will erase the curren worksheet (the file named One) from the screen, and then recover it by retrieving the file. Start by erasing the worksheet.

Press: [/]
Select: Worksheet
Erase
Yes

Now issue the command that will retrieve the file named One from the disk and make it the current worksheet.

Press: [/]
Select: File
Retrieve

1-2-3 responds with a prompt in the second line of the control panel asking you to identify the file to retrieve.

- On a computer with two disk drives:

  Name of file to retrieve: B:*.wk?

- On a hard-disk computer:

  Name of file to retrieve: C:\123*.wk?

The files stored on the disk are listed on the third line of the control panel. At this point the only file listed is ONE.WK1. It is the only file on the disk.

To select the file to be retrieved, simply highlight the name and press Return. ONE.WK1 is already highlighted, so just press the Return key.

Press: [↵]

The mode indicator flashes WAIT, the red light on the disk drive flashes, and the file named ONE.WK1 appears on the screen. (You can tell it is the same file because the 1000 that you entered is now back on the screen.)

Saving an Amended File

Whenever you finish working on any file, new or old, be sure to save the latest version of it before you retrieve another file or end the work session. The worksheet currently on the screen is always erased from the screen when you retrieve another file or leave 1-2-3.

When you select the File Save command for a file that has been saved once already, 1-2-3 still displays the save prompt on the second line of the control panel, but now it lists the current name of the file as well. A small blinking cursor is positioned right after the name. You have two options at this point: you can change the file name or you can save the amended file under the old name.

To change the name of the file, type a new name (without the .WK1 extension), and then press Return. This results in two files: the old file with the old name, and a new file with any changes you have made and a new name.

Usually, however, you will not want to change the name of the file—you will want to save the changes to the existing file. In this case, you simply press Return when the old file name appears. 1-2-3 then gives you two options:

Cancel Replace

Selecting Cancel aborts the File Save operation; the new file is not saved at all (you can repeat the procedure to save it). The file currently stored under that name is left intact. Selecting Replace saves the amended worksheet on the screen by writing over the old version of the file.

Replacing the file simply means saving the existing file with the changes. Try it now with the file named One. First, add some data to distinguish the new file.

Press: [▼]

Type: 5000 [↵]

Now save the revised file. You will accept the name offered (One), and then instruct 1-2-3 to replace the existing file with the revised one.

Press: [/]
Select: File
Save
Press: [↵]
Select: Replace

There's an important point to keep in mind here. While working on a file, all the work you do is stored in the temporary memory of the computer (called random access memory, or RAM). None of the changes are permanent until you save them on disk. Thus it is a good idea to save your work periodically—don't wait until you have completed all the desired changes to the worksheet, unless you have very few changes to make. Since saving a file in 1-2-3 takes only a few seconds and leaves the current file on the screen, periodic saves will take little time. Develop the habit of saving your work every 10 to 15 minutes.

Some Final Notes on Retrieving Files

This section describes the process for retrieving files when there is more than one file on the disk. It gives you more practice in the fundamental skills of saving and retrieving files.

The first step is to create a new worksheet and save it under the file named Two. Begin by erasing the worksheet currently on the screen.

Press: [/]
Select: Worksheet
Erase
Yes

A blank worksheet appears on the screen. Enter some data and save the file. When you select the commands to save this file, you'll notice that the the name of the first file you created appears in the third line of the control panel. Again, you will simply type in the new file name.

Type: 2000 [↵]
Press: [/]
Select: File
Save
Type: Two [↵]

You've now created two separate files, named One and Two. At this point, erase the current worksheet and take the time to create and save four more small files on the same disk. Type a number on each worksheet to distinguish one file from the next (try 3000, 4000, 5000 and 6000) and name them Three, Four, Five, and Six respectively. It's important here that you create a total of six files.

When you have created the six files, select the File Retrieve command so you can see the list of files on the screen.

Press: [/]
Select: File
Retrieve

You should see the following in the control panel (this is for a computer with two disk drives; only the drive letter is different for a hard-disk computer):

```
Name of file to retrieve: B:\*.wk?
FIVE.WK1  FOUR.WK1  ONE.WK1  SIX.WK1  THREE.WK1
```

Notice two things: First, 1-2-3 lists the files in alphabetical order (rather than in the order in which they were saved). Second, 1-2-3 lists only five file names on the screen at one time—however, there are six files on the disk.

You will frequently have more than six files on a disk or in a subdirectory on the hard disk. In order to see all the file names, you use the Right and Left keys to move along the line.

Press: [▶] *(five times)*

Once the pointer is highlighting the last file name on the right, pressing the Right key one more time causes the first line of file names to be replaced by a second line. In this case, the second line contains only one file name.

Selecting the file to retrieve is somewhat like selecting a command from a menu. You use the Right and Left keys to move the pointer along the file names. To make a selection, you press the Return key when the pointer is resting on the file you want to retrieve.

You can also type the name of the file you want to retrieve. However, note that you cannot simply type the first letter of the file (as you can when selecting a command). You must type the full name of the file.

The 1-2-3 Help Facility

1-2-3's Help facility provides detailed information about how the program works and how to use it. Pressing the Help key while you are working on a worksheet brings up a Help screen that deals with the specific activity you are doing at the moment. If you want additional help, highlight a topic mentioned on the Help screen and you will see another screen on that topic.

To use the Help facility on a computer with two disk drives, you must have the System Disk in drive A. Keep your data disk in drive B.

To use the Help facility on a hard-disk computer, you must have the Help files in the same directory on the hard disk as the one that contains the files from the 1-2-3 Program Disk.

Initial Settings

1-2-3 has numerous initial settings that control the operation and format of the overall program. The worksheet, for example, has columns of a specific predetermined width, and it will automatically recalculate related numbers if you make a change in the worksheet.

You can change these initial settings to your own default settings in order to customize 1-2-3 to your hardware, your general work needs, and the requirements of specific projects.

You can view the status of many of the initial settings and any of your own default settings on the status screen. The status screen can be called up at any time while you are working on a worksheet. For more information on initial settings and the status screen, see the Tips Chapter.

3

Worksheet

A spreadsheet is a structure for numeric or financial calculations. It is an integral tool for all business operations. A traditional spreadsheet is a ledger whose columns and rows intersect to form a pattern of boxes, each of which holds a value. Many values on a spreadsheet depend on other values entered elsewhere on the spreadsheet. Thus, making a change to one value requires that you change all other values related to it.

For example, a ledger containing the operating expenses of a company is a spreadsheet. One column contains the salary figures of all employees; the total of that column represents the total compensation paid by the company. That total is then entered in another column detailing monthly expenditures. If the salary of an employee or, as is frequently the case, a number of employees changes, you must go back and recalculate the entire column. You must also recalculate any figure that uses the total compensation.

PAYROLL

	NAME	1 REGULAR PAY	2 FEDERAL TAX	3 STATE TAX	4 FICA	5 DEDUCTIONS	6 NET PAY	
1	Haunton, Lee	500 00	62 24	21 24	35 25	11 00	370 27	1
2	Jones, Doris	650 00	97 50	32 50	45 76	65	467 74	2
3	Levitt, David	650 00	80 93	27 63	45 76	11 00	484 68	3
4	Pinto, Maria	375 00	56 25	18 75	26 40	3 00	270 60	4
5	Seaver, Helen	575 00	71 58	24 43	40 48	11 00	427 51	5
6	Tan, Chiaw	500 00	62 24	21 24	35 25	11 00	370 27	6
7	Tobias, Albert	825 00	123 75	41 25	58 08	3 00	598 92	7
8	Wagner, Suzi	915 00	156 06	55 08	64 63	11 00	628 23	8
9	Williams, Carol	425 00	52 91	18 06	29 92	65	317 61	9
10	Yang, Shin-Chan	500 00	75 00	25 00	35 20	3 00	361 80	10
11								11
12	Total	5915 00	838 46	285 18	416 73	77 00	4297 63	12

While retaining the basic format of the ledger, the electronic worksheet not only makes the maintenance of the worksheet easier but also allows sophisticated operations that would be quite demanding if done manually. The boxes formed by the electronic worksheet's column and row structure are called **cells**. Related numbers entered in different cells are dynamically linked together—when you change a value, all other values related to it change automatically and instantly. In the case of the payroll ledger, you would only have to enter the corrected salary figure in its proper cell, and all the related numbers would adjust immediately. This linkage gives the worksheet increased power and flexibility, and lets you experiment with your figures.

Before You Start

For a computer with two disk drives:

- 1-2-3 should be set up to save files on a disk in drive B.
- The data disk should be in drive B.
- The Program Disk should be in drive A.

For a hard-disk computer:

- 1-2-3 should be set up to save files in the root directory or in a subdirectory.
- All the 1-2-3 disks should be copied in the root directory or in their own subdirectory on the hard disk.

The 1-2-3 Electronic Worksheet

As you move through the examples in this chapter, you will learn the basics of the 1-2-3 electronic worksheet. The keystrokes and commands for setting up and maintaining a worksheet are one of the first steps.

When you start the program, 1-2-3 automatically displays a blank worksheet. However, if you begin this chapter after having read another one, or if you've experimented with 1-2-3, the screen may contain data. Clear the screen and create a new worksheet.

Press: [/]
Select: Worksheet
Erase
Yes

A blank worksheet is displayed on the screen. READY appears in the upper-right corner. This is one of several mode indicators.

The Worksheet Window

The 1-2-3 worksheet has numbers down the left side of the window and letters across the top. The highlighted rectangle on the screen is called the **pointer**; it marks the current cell on the worksheet.

The cell address of the current cell is always displayed on the first line of the control panel, which is at the upper-left corner of the screen above the window. The current cell is cell A1. Whenever you create a new worksheet, the pointer is positioned at the intersection of column A and row 1.

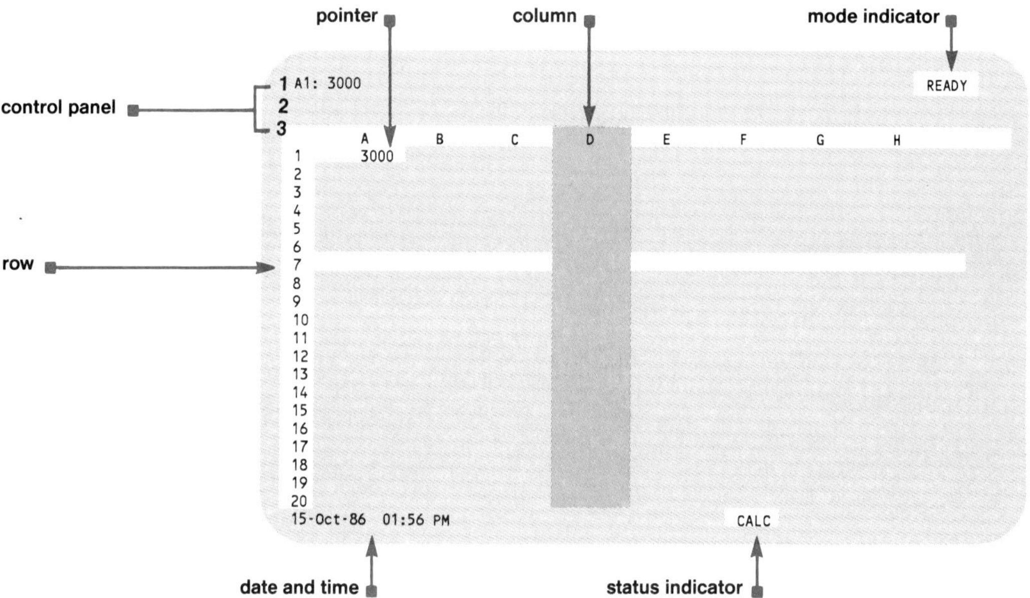

Parts of the Worksheet

Columns	256 columns labeled A through IV.
Rows	8,192 rows labeled 1 through 8192.
Cells	Rectangular boxes formed by the intersection of a column and a row. A cell is identified by its cell address, made up of the column letter plus the row number—for example, the cell in the upper-left corner of the worksheet has the cell address A1.
Pointer	The highlighted area that marks the current cell.
Control panel	The area across the top of the screen at the left side, consisting of the first line, the second line, and the third line.
First line	The line that indicates the current cell's address and contents.
Second line	The line that displays menus items and prompts. Also, an entry is displayed here as you type it into a cell or edit it.
Third line	The line that displays submenus and descriptions of menu items highlighted in the second line. Prompts are also displayed here.
Mode indicator	The box that shows the current mode of operation. The mode indicator changes as you work to show, for example, that you are entering a value or a label, editing an entry, or making an error. Since the worksheet is now ready to receive data, the mode indicator reads READY.
Status indicator	The box that shows the status of the worksheet. Status indicators include CALC, which shows that the program is in manual recalculation mode, and CAPS, which indicates that the Caps Lock key is on.
Date/time	The 1-2-3 clock normally displays the current date and time. You can suppress the display or adjust it to an international format.

Moving Around the Worksheet

Working in the worksheet involves moving from one cell to another and entering labels or values. There are a number of ways to move around the worksheet quickly and efficiently.

First, you can move the pointer one cell at a time with the Arrow keys. Experiment with the Arrow keys now. Watch the screen to see their effects.

Press: Each of the Arrow keys a few times

You'll notice that 1-2-3 buzzes each time the pointer hits the edge of the worksheet.

Second, you can use the Goto key, which allows you to make larger jumps. After pressing the Goto key, type a cell address and press the Return key. (Cell addresses can be typed using uppercase or lowercase letters.)

Press: GOTO

Type: Z75 ↵ *(note the position of the pointer)*

```
Z75:                                                READY

       Z       AA      AB      AC      AD      AE      AF      AG
75
76
77
78
79
80
81
82
83
84
85
86
87
88
89
90
91
92
93
94
```

Press: HOME

Various other keys, known as pointer-movement keys, enable you to move the pointer around the worksheet by cell, window, and blocks of data. You're going to enter some data into the worksheet and experiment with the pointer-movement keys. The pointer should be in cell A1. If it is not, press the Home key.

Data that you type is entered into the cell occupied by the pointer. However, the data does not appear in the cell as you are typing. Instead, as you type, the entry appears in the second line of the control panel. When you're done, you insert the completed entry into the cell by pressing the Return key. The pointer remains on the cell.

Type: 3000 [↵]

You can also enter data and move the pointer to a contiguous cell with any one of the Arrow keys. Unlike Return, the Arrow keys enter the data into the cell and move the pointer to the next cell. Try it.

Press: [▶]

Type: 4000 [▶]

5000 [▶]

6000 [↵]

```
D1: 6000                                                        READY

      A       B       C       D       E       F       G       H
1     3000    4000    5000    6000
2
3
4
5
6
7
8
9
10
11
12
13
14
15
16
17
18
19
20
```

The Page Up and Page Down keys move the pointer up and down one window height.

Press: [PAGE DOWN]
[PAGE UP]

The Ctrl key can be used in conjunction with the right and left Arrow keys to move the screen right and left one window width. (In the keystroke instructions in this book, those keys linked with a hyphen must be pressed simultaneously; for example, hold down Ctrl, press the Arrow key, then release both keys.)

Press: [CTRL] - [▶]
[CTRL] - [◀]

Worksheet Movement Keys

The following lists all the keys and key combinations you can use to move around the worksheet. Keys linked with a hyphen must be pressed simultaneously.

[◀] [▶] [▲] [▼]	Move the pointer one cell in each direction.
[PAGE UP]	Moves up one window height.
[PAGE DOWN]	Moves down one window height.
[CTRL] - [▶]	Moves right one window width.
[CTRL] - [◀]	Moves left one window width.
[HOME]	Moves to the upper-left corner of the worksheet.
[END] [HOME]	Moves to the last cell into which you've entered information.
[END] [▶] [END] [◀] [END] [▲] [END] [▼]	If the pointer is on a blank cell, it moves in the direction of the arrow either to the first filled cell or to the edge of the worksheet. If the pointer is on a filled cell, it moves either to the last filled cell before a blank cell or to the edge of the worksheet. When you press the End key, the word END appears in the status indicator; the word disappears when you press an Arrow key to complete the command.
[GOTO]	Moves to the cell address you specify.

Special Keys

In addition to the pointer-movement keys, some other keys have special uses which may be helpful while building a worksheet.

NUM LOCK — Number Lock allows you to use the numeric keypad to type numbers; it disables the Arrow keys. Press the Number Lock key once to turn Number Lock on, and again to turn it off. Notice that NUM appears in the status indicator when Number Lock is on.

CAPS LOCK — Caps Lock capitalizes lowercase letters and makes capital letters lowercase. It affects only letters being typed in, and it does not replace the Shift key. Press once to turn Caps Lock on, and again to turn it off. Notice that CAPS appears in the status indicator when Caps Lock is on.

SCROLL LOCK — When Scroll Lock is on, the Arrow keys move the window one column or row at a time. When Scroll Lock is off, the Arrow keys move the pointer. Press once to turn Scroll Lock on, and again to turn it off. SCROLL appears in the status indicator when Scroll Lock is on.

Menu Commands

Pressing the slash key calls up the main menu of commands. (You cannot enter data when a menu is displayed above the window; to remove a menu press the Escape key.)

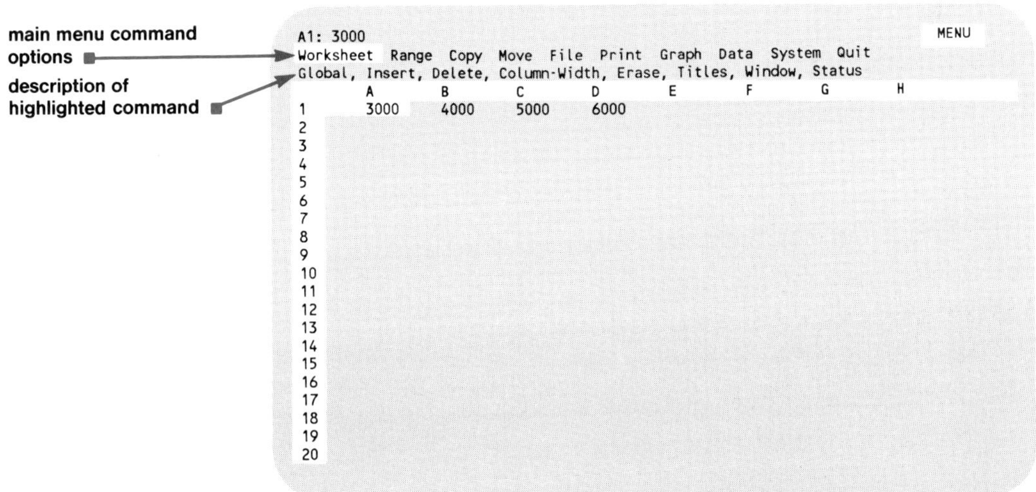

Notice that the mode indicator reads MENU when you press the slash key.

The main menu contains commands that control various aspects of the 1-2-3 program. Four of these commands are used to manipulate worksheet data: Worksheet, Range, Copy, and Move. Both Worksheet and Range have submenus with their own sets of commands. In addition, Graph and Data call up the graphics and database applications. Print controls all the specifications involved in printing a document. The remaining commands manage 1-2-3 system functions: File contains commands to manipulate files; System takes you back to the DOS prompt; and Quit exits the program.

When the pointer is highlighting a command on the second line of the control panel, a description of that command appears on the third line, below. Move the pointer along the list of commands and look at the different descriptions. Notice that many of them refer to ranges. A range is one of the fundamental concepts in the worksheet work environment.

Ranges

A **range** is a cell or a group of contiguous cells in the worksheet. It can be one cell, a single row or column of cells, or a block of cells composed of many rows and columns. A range, however, must be a rectangular block. The data you just entered, for example, occupy the range of cells from A1 to D1. 1-2-3 prompts define a range with the notation A1..D1.

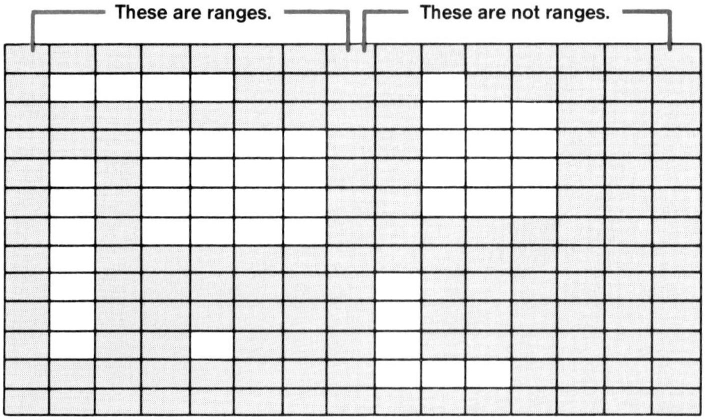

These are ranges.

These are not ranges.

Ranges are one of the significant benefits of an electronic worksheet. They can be used to copy or move sections of the worksheet; to format an entire area quickly; and to erase, print, and name a group of cells.

You are going to copy data in the A1..D1 range to another section of the worksheet. Copying is a two-step process in which you first indicate the range to be copied FROM and then indicate the place you want it copied TO. Prompts on the second line of the control panel guide you through the process.

Select: Copy (*the pointer should be on cell A1*)

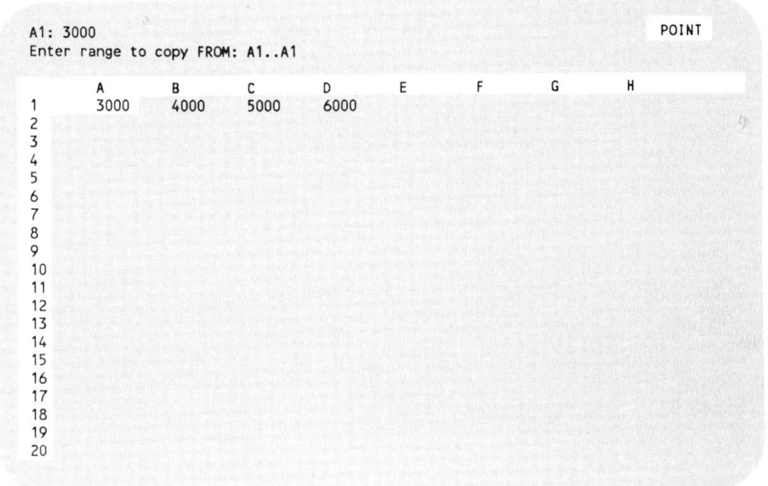

Notice that the mode indicator reads POINT and the second line of the control panel displays a prompt asking you to indicate the range of cells to copy. The notation A1..A1 appears beside the prompt; it shows the current position of the pointer (which is also a one-cell range). The second cell address in the notation will change when you highlight the range to be copied.

There are two ways to indicate a range: (1) type the cell addresses that comprise the range, or (2) expand the highlight so that all the cells in the range are highlighted. In order to expand the highlight, you must first anchor the range. You can tell if the range is anchored by looking at the notation beside the prompt. A cell address (A1) means the range is not anchored, while a notation of a range (A1..A1) shows it is anchored. The range is automatically anchored for several commands, including the Copy command.

Note: If the range is anchored in the wrong place, press the Escape key to release the range, then reposition the pointer, and press the period key to reanchor the range.

Expand the highlight to complete the Copy command.

Press: [▶] *(three times)*

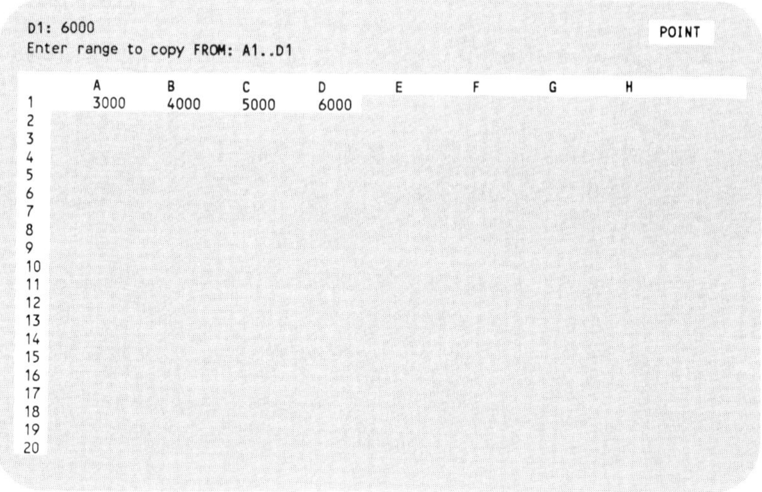

Press: [↵]

```
A1: 3000                                                      POINT
Enter range to copy TO: A1

        A       B       C       D       E       F       G       H
1       3000    4000    5000    6000
2
3
4
5
6
7
8
9
10
11
12
13
14
15
16
17
18
19
20
```

Pressing Return confirms the specified range. The second line of the control panel then displays a second prompt asking you to indicate where you want the range copied to. Notice that the notation beside the second prompt is a cell address (A1). This means that the range is not anchored. Move the pointer to the place on the worksheet where you want to copy the range. You do not have to specify a full range equal in size to that occupied by the data to be copied; you only need to indicate the first cell of the range that will contain the data.

Before copying a range, make sure there is no data in the area where you want the data to be copied. The Copy command will write over any data that is already there.

Move to: cell A5

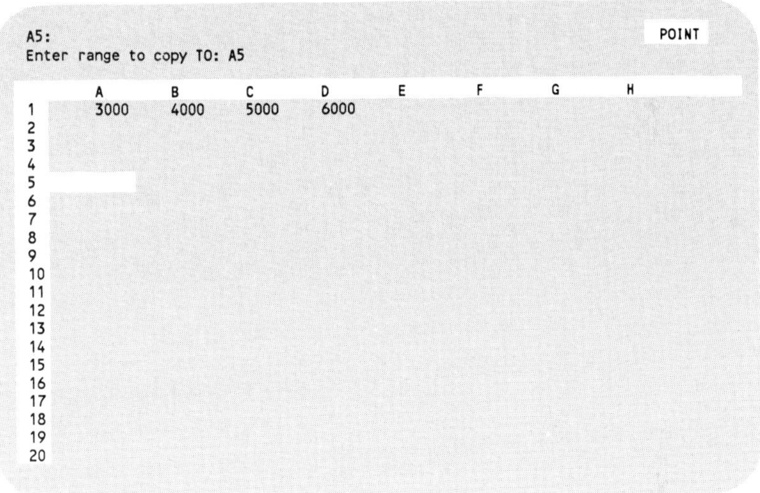

Press: ↵

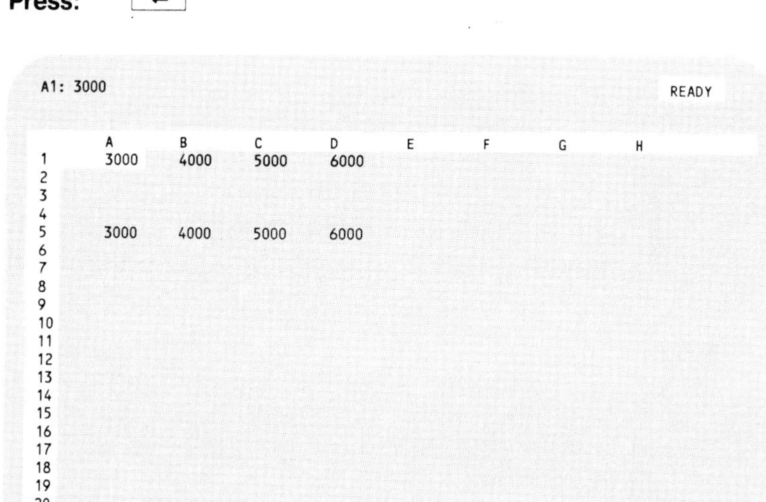

Pressing Return completes the second step. It also activates the Copy command.

Now erase all the data from the worksheet. Unlike copying, erasing is a one-step process: you indicate the range to be erased and then press Return. A prompt on the control panel guides you. This time you'll type the range rather than point to it. (You only need to type one period between the two cell addresses.)

Press: [/]
Select: Range
Erase
Type: a1.d5

```
A1: 3000                                                          EDIT
Enter range to erase: a1.d5

        A        B        C        D        E        F        G        H
1       3000     4000     5000     6000
2
3
4
5       3000     4000     5000     6000
6
7
8
9
10
11
12
13
14
15
16
17
18
19
20
```

Press: [↵]

Note: To erase the worksheet, you can also press the slash key and select Worksheet, Erase, and Yes.

Creating a Worksheet

You've already seen how to enter data in a worksheet, learned about ranges, and used two worksheet commands. In this section you'll learn more about the basic worksheet moves and commands by building an income statement. The sample income statement is similar to one that a company might use to analyze product sales and expenses.

First, look at the various parts of the completed income statement.

Income Statement
July-1-86 July-31-86

000's omitted	PROD.1	PROD.2	PROD.3	TOTAL
Gross Sales	$100	$200	$200	$500
Sales Allowance	$20	$80	$60	$160
Net Sales	$80	$120	$140	$340
Cost of Goods Sold	$30	$60	$70	$160
Gross Margin	$50	$60	$70	$180
Marketing/G&A Expenses	$35	$30	$30	$95
EBIT	$45	$30	$40	$85
Interest	$1	$2	$2	$5
Taxes	$7	$14	$19	$40
Net Income	$7	$14	$19	$40
% Total Net Sales	24%	35%	41%	100%

The Income Statement

Sales	Revenue for sales of products 1, 2, and 3
Sales Allowance	Discounts, returns, transportation costs, and other items that affect sales income
Net Sales	Gross Sales minus Sales Allowance
Cost of Goods Sold	The amount it costs to manufacture each product
Gross Margin	Net Sales minus Cost of Goods Sold
Marketing/G&A	Marketing, General and Administrative. For example, advertising, rent, salaries, and utilities
EBIT	Earnings Before Interest and Taxes—that is, Gross Margin minus Marketing/G&A Expenses
Interest	Interest on loans, for example
Taxes	Federal, state, and local taxes
Net Income	Earnings Before Interest and Taxes minus Interest and Taxes—the actual profit that this company makes on its products
% Total Net Sales	The percentage of Net Sales that each product's sales represent—for example, Product 1's $80,000 is 24% of the total sales

Notice that the data are interrelated. Many of the values result from adding or subtracting two or more other values. For example, Net Sales equals Gross Sales minus Sales Allowance ($80,000 = $100,000 - $20,000 for Product 1). The interrelation of data is the most essential characteristic of the worksheet; the electronic worksheet's ability to recalculate automatically those interrelated values when any single value is changed is its most singular advantage. The illustration shows those values that must be entered manually and those that 1-2-3 calculates automatically.

	A	B	C	D	E
1		Income Statement			
2		July-1-86	July-31-86		
3					
4	000's omitted	PROD.1	PROD.2	PROD.3	TOTAL
5	============	============	============	============	============
6	Gross Sales	$100	$200	$200	$500
7	Sales Allowance	$20	$80	$60	$160
8	Net Sales	$80	$120	$140	$340
9	Cost of Goods Sold	$30	$60	$70	$160
10	Gross Margin	$50	$60	$70	$180
11	Marketing/G&A Expenses	$35	$30	$30	$95
12	EBIT	$15	$30	$40	$85
13	Interest	$1	$2	$2	$5
14	Taxes	$7	$14	$19	$40
15	Net Income	$7	$14	$19	$40
16					
17	% Total Net Sales	24%	35%	41%	100%
18					
19					
20	labels			data	

= data automatically calculated by 1-2-3

Think of a worksheet as being comprised of two parts: a basic structure and the numbers you enter into that structure. The basic structure is designed for a specific purpose, such as an income statement, an expense report, or a general ledger. It includes labels that describe the kind of information available, formatting specifications that control the worksheet's physical appearance (column width, how numbers are displayed, and so forth), and formulas that tell the computer how to calculate the values in certain cells.

The numeric data from which 1-2-3 automatically calculates any formulas are entered into this structure.

Entering Data on the Worksheet

There are two kinds of worksheet entries: labels and values. In most cases, **labels** are letters or words; they can be titles, captions that describe what is in a column or row, or special characters. **Values** can be numbers or they can be formulas that calculate numbers.

1-2-3 distinguishes between a label entry and a value entry by the first character. Since labels are usually words and values numbers, 1-2-3 assumes that an entry beginning with a letter is a label and one beginning with a number is a value. For example, Net Sales and Total are labels; 100 and 80 are values.

Certain entries, however, such as those that begin with symbols, can be ambiguous. The following rules apply:

- 1-2-3 will interpret the entry as a value if the first character is one of the following:

  0 1 2 3 4 5 6 7 8 9 + - (. @ # $

- 1-2-3 will interpret the entry as a label if the first character is not one of the characters listed above.

Note: In some cases, a label may begin with a number (i.e., 4th Quarter); a formula in a value can begin with a letter (i.e., A3+A4). See "Special Entries" later in this chapter for information about these exceptions.

Entering Labels

Begin the Income Statement by entering the first label in the worksheet. As you enter the label, you'll notice that the mode indicator reads LABEL.

Move to: cell A5

Type: Gross Sales [↵]

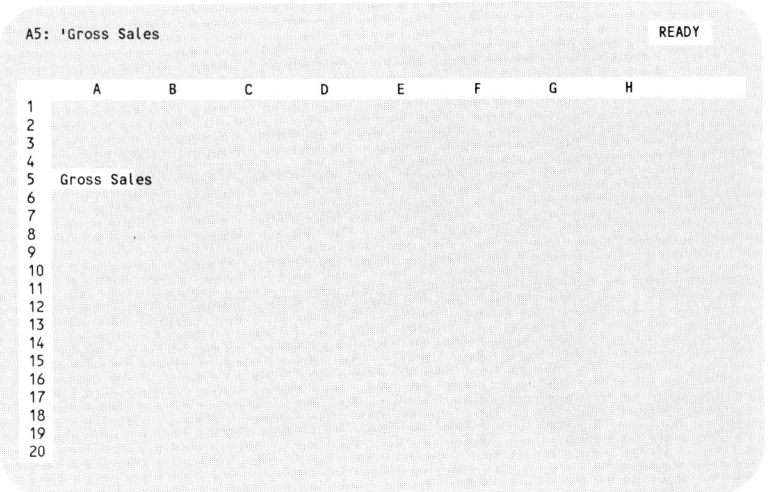

Now look at the first line of the control panel:

A5: 'Gross Sales

1-2-3 recognizes that the entry is a label and automatically puts an apostrophe (') before it. This symbol, one of a number of **label prefixes**, indicates that this entry is a label, aligned at the left side of the cell.

Note: If you make a mistake while typing the entry, use the Backspace or Delete key to remove the error, and then retype the entry. If you notice the mistake after pressing Return, correct it by moving the pointer to the cell, typing the correct entry, and pressing Return. (You'll see more about editing entries below.)

Enter the remaining labels in column A. Remember, you can press the Down key instead of the Return key to enter the label in the cell and move the pointer to the cell below. Follow the keystrokes for the next three labels.

Move to: cell A6

Press: [SPACE BAR] *(two times)*

Type: Sales Allowance [▼]

Net Sales [▼]

Press: [SPACE BAR] *(two times)*

Type: Cost of Goods Sold [▼]

Copy the rest of the labels from the illustration below into column A. Remember to leave two blank spaces (press the spacebar twice) at the beginning of labels that are indented.

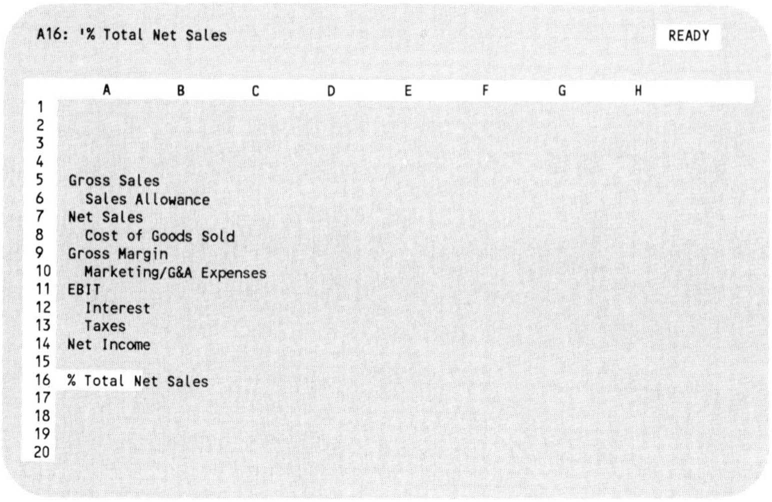

```
A16: '% Total Net Sales                                          READY

        A         B         C         D         E         F         G         H
 1
 2
 3
 4
 5   Gross Sales
 6     Sales Allowance
 7   Net Sales
 8     Cost of Goods Sold
 9   Gross Margin
10     Marketing/G&A Expenses
11   EBIT
12     Interest
13     Taxes
14   Net Income
15
16   % Total Net Sales
17
18
19
20
```

Widening a Column

Some of the labels run over into columns B and C. Column widths can be adjusted to fit any data you need to enter. Widen column A before entering the rest of the labels.

Move to: any cell in column A

Press: [/]

Select: Worksheet
Column
Set-Width

Type: 24 [↵]

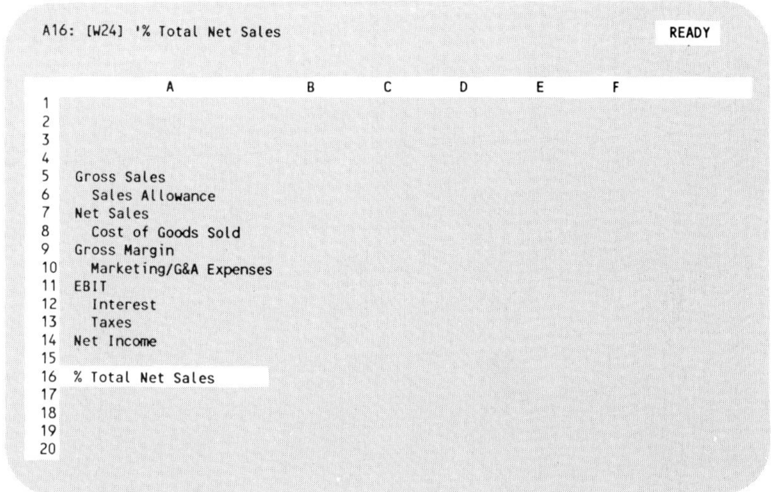

Column A went from nine to twenty-four spaces wide, and the pointer has expanded to fill the wider column. Notice that the other columns did not change; they remain nine spaces wide.

The width of column A is now set at a number other than the initial setting. 1-2-3 indicates the exact width with a message in the first line of the control panel. Notice that [W24] follows the cell address on that line.

Enter the column labels in row 4.

Move to: cell B4

Type: PROD.1 [▶]
PROD.2 [▶]
PROD.3 [▶]
TOTAL [↵]

Enter the title and date. (The dates will run together. You'll fix them later.)

Move to: cell B1

Type: Income Statement [▼]

July-2-86 [▶]

Aug-1-86 [↵]

```
C2: 'Aug-1-86                                                    READY

            A              B        C        D        E        F
1                          Income Statement
2                          July-2-86Aug-1-86
3
4                          PROD.1   PROD.2   PROD.3   TOTAL
5   Gross Sales
6     Sales Allowance
7   Net Sales
8     Cost of Goods Sold
9   Gross Margin
10    Marketing/G&A Expenses
11  EBIT
12    Interest
13    Taxes
14  Net Income
15
16  % Total Net Sales
17
18
19
20
```

This title contains more characters than the cell can display, so the label overflows into cell C1. This type of entry is called a long label. 1-2-3 stores the long label only in cell B1, leaving cell C1 blank. You can see this by moving the pointer back to B1 and C1 and looking at the first line of the control panel.

Entering Values

The labels have been entered and the basic structure of the worksheet is complete. The next step is to enter the values. Enter Gross Sales values for Products 1, 2, and 3. You'll notice that the mode indicator will read VALUE as soon as you start to type a value.

Move to: cell B5

Type: 100 [►]

200 [►]

200 [↵]

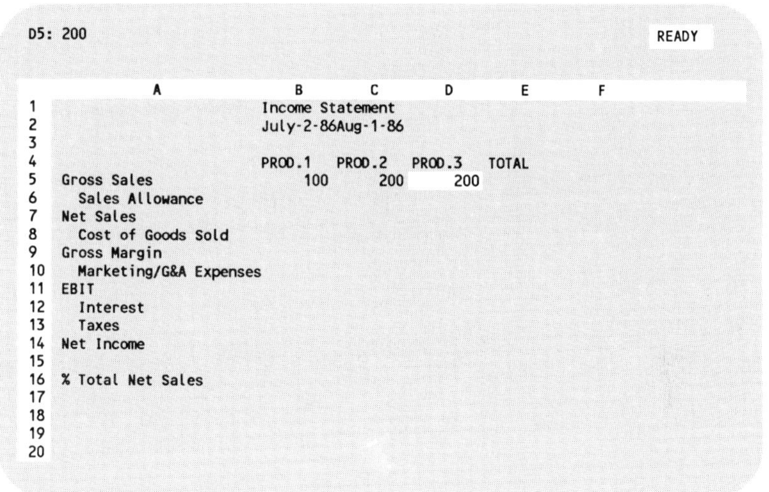

The worksheet now contains both labels and values. 1-2-3's initial settings cause labels to align on the left side of the cell and values on the right side.

Enter the Sales Allowance values for Products 1, 2, and 3.

Move to: cell B6

Type: 20 [►]

80 [►]

60 [↵]

Finally, enter the following data. (The blank rows will be filled in later.)

```
D13: 19                                                          READY

              A                  B       C        D        E        F
1                           Income Statement
2                           July-2-86Aug-1-86
3
4                           PROD.1   PROD.2   PROD.3   TOTAL
5    Gross Sales               100      200      200
6      Sales Allowance          20       80       60
7    Net Sales
8      Cost of Goods Sold       30       60       70
9    Gross Margin
10     Marketing/G&A Expenses   35       30       30
11   EBIT
12     Interest                  1        2        2
13     Taxes                     7       14       19
14   Net Income
15
16   % Total Net Sales
17
18
19
20
```

When you're finished, your screen should look like the one pictured above.

Editing Data

There are two ways to edit entries on the worksheet. First, you can move the pointer to the cell that contains an entry you want to change, type a new entry, and press Return or an Arrow key. This method is the best choice for replacing an entire entry.

Second, you can use the Edit key, which is the best way to make a minor change in a long entry. The Edit key lets you edit the entry in the second line on the control panel. In this example, you are going to use the Edit key to change the dates. The mode indicator will read EDIT.

Move to: cell B2

Press: [EDIT]

[◄] *(four times)*

[DELETE]

Type: 1 [↵]

```
B2: 'July-1-86                                                    READY

                      A             B        C        D        E        F
1                                   Income Statement
2                                   July-1-86Aug-1-86
3
4                                   PROD.1   PROD.2   PROD.3   TOTAL
5    Gross Sales                        100      200      200
6      Sales Allowance                   20       80       60
7    Net Sales
8      Cost of Goods Sold                30       60       70
9    Gross Margin
10     Marketing/G&A Expenses            35       30       30
11   EBIT
12     Interest                           1        2        2
13     Taxes                              7       14       19
14   Net Income
15
16   % Total Net Sales
17
18
19
20
```

The corrected label is entered. Edit the other date the same way.

Move to: cell C2

Press: EDIT

HOME

▶

DELETE *(four times)*

Type: July-3 ↵

```
C2: 'July-31-86                                                        READY

              A                     B         C         D         E         F
1                                   Income Statement
2                                   July-1-86July-31-86
3
4                                   PROD.1    PROD.2    PROD.3    TOTAL
5   Gross Sales                        100       200       200
6     Sales Allowance                   20        80        60
7   Net Sales
8     Cost of Goods Sold                30        60        70
9   Gross Margin
10    Marketing/G&A Expenses            35        30        30
11  EBIT
12    Interest                           1         2         2
13    Taxes                              7        14        19
14  Net Income
15
16  % Total Net Sales
17
18
19
20
```

The Edit Command Keys

Use the following keys when editing entries:

EDIT	Lets you start editing; the mode indicator reads EDIT. Pressing Return turns editing off and returns the mode indicator to READY.
↵	Replaces the original entry with the edited one.
ESC	Lets you stop editing and leaves the original entry intact.
BACKSPACE	Erases the character to the left and moves left.
DELETE	Erases the character the cursor is on.

The following keys have special functions when you are in the Edit mode.

HOME	Moves to the first character of the entry. (If your entry is a label, the first character will be an apostrophe or other prefix.)
END	Moves to the last character of the entry.
◄ ►	Move one space at a time.

Changing the Appearance of the Worksheet

1-2-3 offers flexibility in adapting the worksheet for both appearance and functionality. The worksheet is readily adjustable, as you saw above when you widened a column. Other structural changes are equally simple.

Inserting a Row

A blank row is easily inserted into the worksheet. Insert one between the rows with the Product and Gross Sales labels. Begin by placing the pointer in the row below where you want the new row to appear.

Move to: any cell in row 5

Press: [/]

Select: Worksheet
Insert
Row

Press: [↵]

```
A5: [W24]                                                          READY

                  A                B        C        D        E        F
1                                  Income Statement
2                                  July-1-86July-31-86
3
4                                  PROD.1   PROD.2   PROD.3   TOTAL
5
6    Gross Sales                      100      200      200
7      Sales Allowance                 20       80       60
8    Net Sales
9      Cost of Goods Sold              30       60       70
10   Gross Margin
11     Marketing/G&A Expenses          35       30       30
12   EBIT
13     Interest                         1        2        2
14     Taxes                            7       14       19
15   Net Income
16
17   % Total Net Sales
18
19
20
```

Notice that each cell in the worksheet below the new row now has a new cell address. Gross Sales, for example, was in A5 and is now in A6. This simple example shows how an electronic worksheet makes automatic adjustments; 1-2-3 can do even more. For instance, if the worksheet contains a formula that refers to a certain range and you insert or delete a row or column within that range, all the cell addresses in the formulas change to reflect the new row/column relationships.

Drawing a Double Line

You can draw lines or borders to separate sections of the worksheet by typing a repeating character in one cell and then copying it to a range of cells. A repeating character is specified by typing a backslash (\) before the character; after you press Return the character will repeat across the entire cell. Then copy the contents of the cell to the appropriate range. A repeated equal sign (=) makes a double line. The underscore (_), dash (-), and asterisk (*) are among the other characters that can be used.

Draw a double line across the top of the Income Statement in the new row.

Move to: cell A5
Type: \= [↵]
Press: [/]
Select: Copy
Press: [↵] *(to accept the range A5..A5)*
Move to: cell B5 *(the start of the range to be copied to)*
Press: [.] *(period key—to anchor the range)*
Move to: cell E5 *(to specify the range B5..E5)*
Press: [↵]

```
A5: [W24] \=                                                         READY

                    A             B        C        D        E        F
 1                             Income Statement
 2                             July-1-86July-31-86
 3
 4                             PROD.1   PROD.2   PROD.3   TOTAL
 5  ==========================================================
 6  Gross Sales                     100      200      200
 7    Sales Allowance                20       80       60
 8  Net Sales
 9    Cost of Goods Sold             30       60       70
10  Gross Margin
11    Marketing/G&A Expenses         35       30       30
12  EBIT
13    Interest                        1        2        2
14    Taxes                           7       14       19
15  Net Income
16
17  % Total Net Sales
18
19
20
```

Centering Labels

Centered labels can improve the appearance of the worksheet. A choice of three label prefixes determines the placement of the label within a cell. The apostrophe is 1-2-3's initial setting. 1-2-3 automatically places an apostrophe before a label and aligns the label on the left side of the cell. When you change the position of the label within the cell using the Range Label command, the prefix changes. A double quotation mark (") indicates that the label is aligned on the right side of the cell. A caret (^) shows the label is centered in the cell.

You can change label prefixes manually, one at a time. Or you can change the alignment of all the labels in a range with a single command. (You can even change the initial setting from the apostrophe to any label prefix you want.)

Center the product column labels by using the Label command. The label prefix will change from an apostrophe (') to a caret (^).

Move to: cell B4

Press: [/]

Select: Range
Label
Center

Press: [END]
[▶]
[↵]

```
B4: ^PROD.1                                                    READY

              A               B       C       D       E       F
 1                          Income Statement
 2                          July-1-86July-31-86
 3
 4                            PROD.1  PROD.2  PROD.3   TOTAL
 5  ===========================================================
 6  Gross Sales                  100     200     200
 7    Sales Allowance             20      80      60
 8  Net Sales
 9    Cost of Goods Sold          30      60      70
10  Gross Margin
11    Marketing/G&A Expenses      35      30      30
12  EBIT
13    Interest                     1       2       2
14    Taxes                        7      14      19
15  Net Income
16
17  % Total Net Sales
18
19
20
```

The Label command instantly centers all the labels in row 4. Move the pointer through them and look at the first line of the control panel. The new prefix appears before each label.

Changing Column Widths

You are going to change the column widths on the Income Statement from nine to eleven to make the worksheet easier to read. The worksheet will display the wider columns as you enter the new settings.

Move to: cell B4

Press: [/]

Select: Worksheet
Global
Column-Width

Press: [▶] *(two times)*

```
B4: ^PROD.1                                                        POINT
Enter global column width (1..240): 11

              A                   B          C          D          E
1                          Income Statement
2                          July-1-86  July-31-86
3
4                            PROD.1     PROD.2     PROD.3     TOTAL
5    ====================================================================
6    Gross Sales                  100        200        200
7      Sales Allowance             20         80         60
8    Net Sales
9      Cost of Goods Sold          30         60         70
10   Gross Margin
11     Marketing/G&A Expenses      35         30         30
12   EBIT
13     Interest                     1          2          2
14     Taxes                        7         14         19
15   Net Income
16
17   % Total Net Sales
18
19
20
```

Notice that the prompt in the second line of the control panel changes as you widen columns B, C, D, and E with the Right Arrow key. You can type in the new column width instead of pressing arrows, but using the Arrow key lets you see the effect of the change immediately. For example, notice that the date labels in row 2 are now separated. Stop when Enter global column width (1..240): reads 11.

Press: [↵]

Note: The width of column A did not change. This is because earlier you set the width of this column manually with the Set-Width command from the Worksheet menu. That command sets individual column widths and takes precedence over global commands that control the entire worksheet.

If you decide at a later point that you want to change the global column width, you simply use the Global Column-Width command again.

Special Entries

1-2-3 automatically identifies each entry you type as a label or value by looking at the first character. Sometimes, however, the first character is misleading. For example, you may want to enter a label that begins with a number, such as 1st Product.

In order to use this kind of label, you manually type a label prefix before the first character: '1st Product. This tells the program that the entry is a label. The prefix does not appear in the cell, but you will see it on the first line of the control panel when the pointer is in the cell.

All of the values entered on the Income Statement represent numbers in the thousands, but the last three zeros have been left out. You indicate this abbreviation by entering 000's omitted—a label that begins with a number—at the top of the Income Statement. Try entering it without the prefix:

Move to: cell A4

Type: 000's omitted [↵]

```
A4: [W24]                                                          EDIT
000's omitted

              A                B          C          D          E
 1                          Income Statement
 2                          July-1-86  July-31-86
 3
 4                             PROD.1     PROD.2     PROD.3     TOTAL
 5  ===================================================================
 6  Gross Sales                   100        200        200
 7    Sales Allowance              20         80         60
 8  Net Sales
 9    Cost of Goods Sold           30         60         70
10  Gross Margin
11    Marketing/G&A Expenses       35         30         30
12  EBIT
13    Interest                      1          2          2
14    Taxes                         7         14         19
15  Net Income
16
17  % Total Net Sales
18
19
20
```

The computer beeps and the mode indicator reads EDIT. The initial 0 tells 1-2-3 the entry is a value, but the program does not accept a value that contains alphabetical characters.

Try it again with a label prefix. Keep your eye on the mode indicator; once you have typed the apostrophe, the indicator will read LABEL.

Press: [ESC] *(twice)*

Type: '000's omitted [↵]

```
A4: [W24] '000's omitted                                          READY

               A               B          C          D          E
1                            Income Statement
2                            July-1-86  July-31-86
3
4   000's omitted            PROD.1     PROD.2     PROD.3     TOTAL
5   ===================================================================
6   Gross Sales                  100        200        200
7     Sales Allowance             20         80         60
8   Net Sales
9     Cost of Goods Sold          30         60         70
10  Gross Margin
11    Marketing/G&A Expenses      35         30         30
12  EBIT
13    Interest                     1          2          2
14    Taxes                        7         14         19
15  Net Income
16
17  % Total Net Sales
18
19
20
```

Saving the File

You've created the basic structure of the worksheet and entered some data. Before proceeding, save what you've done. Develop the habit of saving your work every 15 minutes or so.

When saving a file that has been previously named and saved, 1-2-3 provides the file name; you only need to press Return. New files, however, need to be given file names. Name this file Income.

Press: /

Select: File
Save

Any files you've already created will be listed on the third line of the control panel. In the second line, you'll see the prompt Enter save file name: B:*.wk1. (This applies to a computer with two disk drives. If you have a hard-disk computer, the prompt will read C:*.WK1.) Simply type in the file name.

Type: Income

```
A4: [W24] '000's omitted                                              EDIT
Enter save file name: B:\Income

              A                 B         C          D          E
1                         Income Statement
2                         July-1-86  July-31-86
3
4   000's omitted              PROD.1    PROD.2     PROD.3     TOTAL
5   ================================================================
6   Gross Sales                   100       200        200
7     Sales Allowance              20        80         60
8   Net Sales
9     Cost of Goods Sold           30        60         70
10  Gross Margin
11    Marketing/G&A Expenses       35        30         30
12  EBIT
13    Interest                      1         2          2
14    Taxes                         7        14         19
15  Net Income
16
17  % Total Net Sales
18
19
20
```

Press: ↵

The disk drive light goes on while the file is being saved.

Formulas

Formulas are another important element of the worksheet. They perform both simple and sophisticated mathematical operations. Formulas enable 1-2-3 to recalculate all related values to reflect whatever changes you make.

Formulas contain references to particular cells (indicated by their cell addresses) and specify the mathematical operations to be performed on the values within those cells. 1-2-3 looks at the values in each of the cells listed in the formula when it performs a calculation.

This section explains how to enter formulas and provides an introduction to 1-2-3's powerful built-in formulas, called @functions ("at" functions).

Entering a Formula

You enter a formula on the worksheet just as you would any other entry—by typing it in a cell. A formula is a value; however, they often contain cell references, and so many times they begin with the plus sign (+) to indicate that a formula follows (for example, +A1+B7, +C3/5.2).

The basic way to create a formula is to enter a cell address or a value, then a mathematical operator, then another address or value, and so on. This is similar to the way a formula is entered on a calculator.

The most frequently used mathematical operators are:

+ add
- subtract
* multiply
/ divide

A formula can be entered in two ways: (1) by pointing to the cells to be included (as you'll do in this example), or (2) by typing the formula. (The Edit and Goto keys do not function while you are pointing to cells in a formula.)

A formula being entered appears in the second line of the control panel. When you press Return or an Arrow key, the result of the formula appears in the cell on the worksheet.

You are going to enter a formula for the Total Gross Sales for Products 1, 2, and 3. It will add the values in cells B6, C6, and D6. Begin by moving the pointer to the cell that will contain the formula.

Move to: cell E6
Type: +
Move to: cell B6 *(the mode indicator reads POINT)*
Type: + *(the cell marker moves back to cell E6)*
Move to: cell C6
Type: +
Move to: cell D6
Press: ↵

```
E6: +B6+C6+D6                                                    READY

              A                   B         C         D          E
1                              Income Statement
2                              July-1-86  July-31-86
3
4   000's omitted               PROD.1    PROD.2    PROD.3     TOTAL
5   =================================================================
6   Gross Sales                    100       200       200        500
7     Sales Allowance               20        80        60
8   Net Sales
9     Cost of Goods Sold            30        60        70
10  Gross Margin
11    Marketing/G&A Expenses        35        30        30
12  EBIT
13    Interest                       1         2         2
14    Taxes                          7        14        19
15  Net Income
16
17  % Total Net Sales
18
19
20
```

The value 500 appears in cell E6, and the formula +B6+C6+D6 appears in the first line of the control panel.

Note: To look at any formula stored on the worksheet, move the pointer to the cell containing the formula. While a value may be displayed in the cell, the formula itself appears in the first line of the control panel. You can edit a formula as you would any other entry—type over it or use the Edit key.

@Functions

In addition to standard arithmetical calculations, 1-2-3 can perform many special-purpose calculations. Each of these begins with the "at" character (@); thus they are called **@functions** ("at functions"). The various @functions make it easy to build sophisticated calculations in the worksheet.

An @function is made up of three parts:

1. The at symbol (@), which must appear as the first character
2. The name of the function, typed in either uppercase or lowercase letters
3. One or more arguments enclosed in parentheses (the **argument** specifies the data the function works on and can be anything from a single value to a range of cells, depending on the particular function).

For example:

@SUM(A1..A10)	The argument, A1..A10, is the range of cells that will be added by the @SUM function
@SQRT(16)	The argument, 16, is what the @SQRT function will find the square root of

You just calculated Total Gross Sales by pointing to each cell and building the formula cell by cell. Now you are going to enter a similar formula with the function @SUM. The function will add the Sales Allowances for Products 1, 2, and 3 to calculate the Total in cell E7.

Move to: cell E7

Type: @sum(b7.d7) *(the period in the formula tells 1-2-3 that this is a range)*

Press: ↵

```
E7: @SUM(B7..D7)                                              READY

              A               B         C         D         E
1                         Income Statement
2                         July-1-86  July-31-86
3
4    000's omitted          PROD.1    PROD.2    PROD.3     TOTAL
5    ==============================================================
6    Gross Sales               100       200       200        500
7      Sales Allowance          20        80        60        160
8    Net Sales
9      Cost of Goods Sold       30        60        70
10   Gross Margin
11     Marketing/G&A Expenses   35        30        30
12   EBIT
13     Interest                  1         2         2
14     Taxes                     7        14        19
15   Net Income
16
17   % Total Net Sales
18
19
20
```

The number 160 appears in cell E7, and the formula appears in the first line of the control panel.

The @functions have a number of advantages that provide great flexibility.

- You can use a range in a formula. For example, instead of individually typing ten numbers you want to add, use the function @SUM and a range: @SUM(A1..A10).
- They perform advanced calculations of many kinds:

  Mathematical: @COS......the cosine of a number
  @EXP......e raised to a number
  @SQRT.....the square root of a number

  Statistical: @AVG......the average of a list
  @STD......the standard deviation of a list
  @VAR......the variance of a list

  Financial: @FV.......the future value of a series of payments at a certain interest rate
  @PMT......a loan payment, based on the specified principal and interest

Note: These are only a few of the advanced calculations 1-2-3 can perform using @functions.

- You can use logical arithmetic, that is, make an entry depend on certain conditions. For example, the Logical function @IF(A1>5,300,0) means that if the value in A1 is greater than 5, put 300 in the cell containing the formula; if the value is not greater than 5, put 0 in the cell.
- Other kinds of @functions help you do such things as look up a value in a table, convert a number into a string (String functions), or change a date into a serial number (Date and Time functions).

Note: These functions are described in detail in the *1-2-3 Reference Manual.*

Copying a Formula

Copy is one of the most frequently used worksheet commands. You've seen how it can copy the contents of a cell or a range of cells to another place on the worksheet. (The Move command works in a similar way, except that it also erases the original.)

Copy works differently when copying cells that contain formulas. Rather than copying the value displayed in the cell, it copies the formula displayed in the control panel. Copying formulas instead of typing them individually in every place they are needed saves time and keystrokes.

Note: The Range Value command copies cell values (the results of formulaic calculations) rather than formulas.

Remember, copying is a two-step process: (1) point to where you want to copy FROM, and (2) point to where you want to copy TO.

On the Income Statement, you are going to use the same formula to calculate Total Net Sales (adding the three cells to the left of the Total column) that you used to obtain Total Sales Allowances. Instead of typing the formula over again, copy it from cell E7 to cell E8.

Move to: cell E7

Press: [/]

Select: Copy

```
E7: @SUM(B7..D7)                                                    POINT
Enter range to copy FROM: E7..E7

            A                B           C           D           E
1                        Income Statement
2                        July-1-86   July-31-86
3
4    000's omitted          PROD.1      PROD.2      PROD.3      TOTAL
5    ==================================================================
6    Gross Sales               100         200         200         500
7      Sales Allowance          20          80          60         160
8    Net Sales
9      Cost of Goods Sold       30          60          70
10   Gross Margin
11     Marketing/G&A Expenses   35          30          30
12   EBIT
13     Interest                  1           2           2
14     Taxes                     7          14          19
15   Net Income
16
17   % Total Net Sales
18
19
20
```

The prompt on the control panel reads: Enter range to copy FROM: E7..E7. Since you're copying the one-cell range marked by the pointer, you don't need to point to a range.

Press: ↵

The new prompt on the second line of the control panel reads Enter range to copy TO: E7.

Press: ▼

↵

```
E7: @SUM(B7..D7)                                                  READY

             A                  B         C          D          E
1                        Income Statement
2                        July-1-86  July-31-86
3
4   000's omitted           PROD.1     PROD.2     PROD.3      TOTAL
5   ==================================================================
6   Gross Sales                100        200        200        500
7     Sales Allowance           20         80         60        160
8   Net Sales                                                     0
9     Cost of Goods Sold        30         60         70
10  Gross Margin
11    Marketing/G&A Expenses    35         30         30
12  EBIT
13    Interest                   1          2          2
14    Taxes                      7         14         19
15  Net Income
16
17  % Total Net Sales
18
19
20
```

Move to cell E8 and look at the first line of the control panel; 1-2-3 has copied the formula. (You'll see in a moment why the two formulas look different.) The number 0 appears in cell E8 because you haven't entered values in cells B8, C8, or D8. When you do fill in the values, 1-2-3 will display a value other than 0 in cell E8.

Relative Cell Addresses

Look at the original formula in cell E7. Now look at the copy you made in cell E8. They are different because 1-2-3 automatically adjusted the cell addresses in the formula to reflect the different position of the copied formula. Such adjustable cell addresses are called **relative cell addresses**.

1-2-3 reads the original formula, @SUM(B7..D7), as "Add the contents of the three cells immediately to the left and place the answer here." When you copied the formula to E8, its meaning, "Add the contents of the three cells immediately to the left...," stayed the same relative to its new location. Those cells are now B8, C8, and D8; thus the copied formula reads @SUM(B8..D8).

1-2-3 considers all cell addresses in formulas to be relative cell addresses unless you specify otherwise. This means that a copied formula performs the same operation no matter where it is placed. (The alternative to a relative cell address is called an **absolute cell address**; it is discussed later in this chapter.)

Copying a Formula to a Range

You just copied a formula to a single cell. You can also copy one formula to many cells by specifying a range in the second step of the Copy process.

Copy the formula in cell E8 down the entire Total column on the Income Statement.

Move to: cell E8

Press: [/]

Select: Copy

Press: [↵]

```
E8: @SUM(B8..D8)                                                    POINT
Enter range to copy TO: E8

              A                   B         C         D         E
1                            Income Statement
2                            July-1-86  July-31-86
3
4   000's omitted              PROD.1    PROD.2    PROD.3     TOTAL
5   ==============================================================
6   Gross Sales                   100       200       200       500
7     Sales Allowance              20        80        60       160
8   Net Sales                                                     0
9     Cost of Goods Sold           30        60        70
10  Gross Margin
11    Marketing/G&A Expenses       35        30        30
12  EBIT
13    Interest                      1         2         2
14    Taxes                         7        14        19
15  Net Income
16
17  % Total Net Sales
18
19
20
```

After accepting E8..E8 as the range to copy FROM, the prompt Enter range to copy TO: E8 appears.

Move to: cell E9
Press: [.] *(to anchor the range)*
Move to: cell E15

```
E15:                                                              POINT
Enter range to copy TO: E9..E15

            A               B           C          D          E
1                         Income Statement
2                         July-1-86  July-31-86
3
4   000's omitted          PROD.1     PROD.2     PROD.3     TOTAL
5   ================================================================
6   Gross Sales               100        200        200        500
7     Sales Allowance          20         80         60        160
8   Net Sales                                                    0
9     Cost of Goods Sold       30         60         70
10  Gross Margin
11    Marketing/G&A Expenses   35         30         30
12  EBIT
13    Interest                  1          2          2
14    Taxes                     7         14         19
15  Net Income
16
17  % Total Net Sales
18
19
20
```

Press: [↵]

When the formula has been copied, zeros will appear in some cells of the Total Column because you have not yet entered all the values. Move the pointer up and down the Total column while looking at the first line of the control panel, and you'll see that the formula has been copied with relative cell addresses.

Each formula adds the values in the three cells immediately to its left.

@SUM (B9..D9)
@SUM (B10..D10)
@SUM (B11..D11)
@SUM (B12..D12)
@SUM (B13..D13)
@SUM (B14..D14)
@SUM (B15..D15)

```
E8: @SUM(B8..D8)                                                  READY

            A               B           C          D          E
1                         Income Statement
2                         July-1-86  July-31-86
3
4   000's omitted          PROD.1     PROD.2     PROD.3     TOTAL
5   ================================================================
6   Gross Sales               100        200        200        500
7     Sales Allowance          20         80         60        160
8   Net Sales                                                    0
9     Cost of Goods Sold       30         60         70        160
10  Gross Margin                                                 0
11    Marketing/G&A Expenses   35         30         30         95
12  EBIT                                                         0
13    Interest                  1          2          2          5
14    Taxes                     7         14         19         40
15  Net Income                                                   0
16
17  % Total Net Sales
18
19
20
```

Complete the Income Statement

Enter the remaining data for the Income Statement according to the following directions. Notice what happens to the Total column as you add new information in each row.

Enter a formula for Net Sales for Product 1: Gross Sales minus Sales Allowances.

Move to: cell B8

Type: +b6-b7 [↵]

```
B8: +B6-B7                                                          READY

              A                  B          C          D          E
 1                          Income Statement
 2                          July-1-86   July-31-86
 3
 4   000's omitted              PROD.1     PROD.2     PROD.3     TOTAL
 5   ====================================================================
 6   Gross Sales                   100        200        200        500
 7     Sales Allowance              20         80         60        160
 8   Net Sales                      80                                80
 9     Cost of Goods Sold           30         60         70        160
10   Gross Margin                                                      0
11     Marketing/G&A Expenses       35         30         30         95
12   EBIT                                                              0
13     Interest                      1          2          2          5
14     Taxes                         7         14         19         40
15   Net Income                                                        0
16
17   % Total Net Sales
18
19
20
```

Copy the Net Sales formula for Products 2 and 3.

Press: [/]
Select: Copy
Press: [↵] *(for the FROM range)*
Move to: cell C8 *(for the TO range)*
Press: [.] *(to anchor the range)*
Move to: cell D8 *(to highlight the range)*
Press: [↵]

```
B8: +B6-B7                                                     READY

              A                   B        C        D        E
1                              Income Statement
2                              July-1-86  July-31-86
3
4   000's omitted                PROD.1    PROD.2    PROD.3    TOTAL
5   ==================================================================
6   Gross Sales                    100      200      200       500
7     Sales Allowance               20       80       60       160
8   Net Sales                       80      120      140       340
9     Cost of Goods Sold            30       60       70       160
10  Gross Margin                                                 0
11    Marketing/G&A Expenses        35       30       30        95
12  EBIT                                                         0
13    Interest                       1        2        2         5
14    Taxes                          7       14       19        40
15  Net Income                                                   0
16
17  % Total Net Sales
18
19
20
```

Enter a formula to compute the Gross Margin for Product 1: Net Sales minus Cost of Goods Sold.

Move to: cell B10

Type: +b8-b9 [↵]

Copy: the formula to cells C10 and D10 *(as you did above)*

```
B10: +B8-B9                                                        READY

           A                  B          C          D          E
1                        Income Statement
2                        July-1-86  July-31-86
3
4    000's omitted          PROD.1     PROD.2     PROD.3     TOTAL
5    ==================================================================
6    Gross Sales                100        200        200        500
7      Sales Allowance           20         80         60        160
8    Net Sales                   80        120        140        340
9      Cost of Goods Sold        30         60         70        160
10   Gross Margin                50         60         70        180
11     Marketing/G&A Expenses    35         30         30         95
12   EBIT                                                          0
13     Interest                   1          2          2          5
14     Taxes                      7         14         19         40
15   Net Income                                                    0
16
17   % Total Net Sales
18
19
20
```

You are going to enter a formula to compute EBIT: Gross Margin minus Marketing/G&A Expenses. The formula is basically the same as the one for Net Sales and for Gross Margin: subtract the cell one row above from the cell two rows above. Enter this formula in range B12..D12 by copying it from row 10 (Gross Margin).

Move to: cell B10
Press: [/]
Select: Copy
Press: [↵] *(for the FROM range)*
Move to: cell B12 *(for the TO range)*
Press: [.] *(to anchor the range)*
Move to: cell D12 *(to highlight the range)*
Press: [↵]

```
B10: +B8-B9                                                      READY

              A                  B          C          D          E
1                              Income Statement
2                              July-1-86  July-31-86
3
4   000's omitted               PROD.1     PROD.2     PROD.3     TOTAL
5   =================================================================
6   Gross Sales                    100        200        200        500
7     Sales Allowance               20         80         60        160
8   Net Sales                       80        120        140        340
9     Cost of Goods Sold            30         60         70        160
10  Gross Margin                    50         60         70        180
11    Marketing/G&A Expenses        35         30         30         95
12  EBIT                            15         30         40         85
13    Interest                       1          2          2          5
14    Taxes                          7         14         19         40
15  Net Income                                                        0
16
17  % Total Net Sales
18
19
20
```

Enter the formula to compute Net Income for Product 1: EBIT minus Interest plus Taxes.

Move to: cell B15
Type: +b12-(b13+b14) [↵]

Notice how parentheses are used to group the different parts of the formula. Any calculations inside parentheses take place first.

Copy the formula to cells C15 and D15.

Press: [/]
Select: Copy
Press: [↵]
Move to: cell C15
Press: [.]
Move to: cell D15
Press: [↵]

B15: +B12-(B13+B14) READY

	A	B	C	D	E
1		Income Statement			
2		July-1-86	July-31-86		
3					
4	000's omitted	PROD.1	PROD.2	PROD.3	TOTAL
5	==========	==========	==========	==========	==========
6	Gross Sales	100	200	200	500
7	Sales Allowance	20	80	60	160
8	Net Sales	80	120	140	340
9	Cost of Goods Sold	30	60	70	160
10	Gross Margin	50	60	70	180
11	Marketing/G&A Expenses	35	30	30	95
12	EBIT	15	30	40	85
13	Interest	1	2	2	5
14	Taxes	7	14	19	40
15	Net Income	7	14	19	40
16					
17	% Total Net Sales				
18					
19					
20					

Save the worksheet file again. You named it the first time you saved it, so now you only need to accept the file name when it is displayed. 1-2-3 indicates that a file with that name already exists and asks if you want to replace it—that is, replace the saved file with the altered worksheet containing data you've added or changed.

Press: [/]
Select: File
Save
Press: [↵]
Select: Replace

Absolute Cell Addresses

All the formulas entered and copied to this point have relative cell addresses. The addresses changed when you copied a formula from one location on the worksheet to another.

There are instances, however, when you do not want to copy a formula using relative cell addresses. For example, you have yet to enter formulas to calculate the % Total Net Sales. These figures will show each product's proportion of the month's total net sales.

To obtain the percentage of the total net sales for Product 1, you would divide that Product's net sales in cell B8 ($80,000) by the total net sales in cell E8 ($340,000). The percentage for Product 2 would be obtained by dividing its net sales in cell C8 ($120,000) by the total net sales in cell E8. The same pattern would be followed for Product 3. You would put the following formulas in cells B17, C17, and D17 to calculate each product's percentage of the total net sales:

For Product 1....+B8/E8
For Product 2....+C8/E8
For Product 3....+D8/E8

Notice that the first cell address in each formula is different but that the second is the same for each formula. If you were to enter the first formula in cell B17 and then copy it to cells C17 and D17 (as you did earlier), the result would look like this:

A8: [W24] 'Net Sales READY

	A	B	C	D	E
1		Income Statement			
2		July-1-86	July-31-86		
3					
4	000's omitted	PROD.1	PROD.2	PROD.3	TOTAL
5	=========================	==========	==========	==========	==========
6	Gross Sales	100	200	200	500
7	Sales Allowance	20	80	60	160
8	Net Sales	80	120	140	340
9	Cost of Goods Sold	30	60	70	160
10	Gross Margin	50	60	70	180
11	Marketing/G&A Expenses	35	30	30	95
12	EBIT	15	30	40	85
13	Interest	1	2	2	5
14	Taxes	7	14	19	40
15	Net Income	7	14	19	40
16					
17	% Total Net Sales	+B8/E8	+C8/F8	+D8/G8	
18					
19					
20					

Each formula divides the value located nine cells above it by the value three cells to the right of the first value.

The diagram above shows that the second cell addresses in the formulas for Products 2 and 3 are not what you want. They refer to cells that are three cells to the right of the first cell, and in this case, these are blank. Since cell addresses in formulas are interpreted to be relative, copying the formula to another cell changes the cell addresses relative to the location of the original formula.

To type a formula with an absolute cell address, use the Abs key to indicate that a cell address remains the same (absolute) whenever the formula is copied. The Abs key places a dollar sign ($) before both the column letter and the row number in the cell address.

A8: [W24] 'Net Sales READY

	A	B	C	D	E
1		Income Statement			
2		July-1-86	July-31-86		
3					
4	000's omitted	PROD.1	PROD.2	PROD.3	TOTAL
5	==========================	==========	==========	==========	==========
6	Gross Sales	100	200	200	500
7	Sales Allowance	20	80	60	160
8	Net Sales	80	120	140	340
9	Cost of Goods Sold	30	60	70	160
10	Gross Margin	50	60	70	180
11	Marketing/G&A Expenses	35	30	30	95
12	EBIT	15	30	40	85
13	Interest	1	2	2	5
14	Taxes	7	14	19	40
15	Net Income	7	14	19	40
16					
17	% Total Net Sales	+B8/$E$8	+C8/$E$8	+D8/$E$8	
18					
19					
20					

Each formula divides the value located nine cells above it by the value in cell E8.

Enter the necessary formula with the absolute cell address in cell B17.

Move to: cell B17
Type: + *(signaling a value)*
Move to: cell B8
Type: / *(indicating "divided by")*
Move to: cell E8
Press: ABS *(making E8 an absolute cell address)*
↵

```
B17: +B8/$E$8                                                     READY

                 A                  B          C          D          E
 1                               Income Statement
 2                               July-1-86  July-31-86
 3
 4   000's omitted                  PROD.1     PROD.2     PROD.3     TOTAL
 5   ====================================================================
 6   Gross Sales                       100        200        200        500
 7     Sales Allowance                  20         80         60        160
 8   Net Sales                          80        120        140        340
 9     Cost of Goods Sold               30         60         70        160
10   Gross Margin                       50         60         70        180
11     Marketing/G&A Expenses           35         30         30         95
12   EBIT                               15         30         40         85
13     Interest                          1          2          2          5
14     Taxes                             7         14         19         40
15   Net Income                          7         14         19         40
16
17   % Total Net Sales           0.23529411
18
19
20
```

The answer, 0.23529411, appears in cell B17. Notice that the Abs key inserted a $ before E and before 8 in the first line of the control panel. This means that the cell address E8 in this formula will remain E8 no matter where the formula is moved. (The cell address B8 will change—it is still a relative cell address.)

Copy this formula across the rest of the % Total Net Sales row.

Move to: cell B17
Press: [/]
Select: Copy
Press: [↵] *(for the FROM range)*
Move to: cell C17
Press: [.]
Move to: cell E17 *(to expand the highlight)*
Press: [↵]

```
B17: +B8/$E$8                                                      READY

                 A              B          C          D          E
1                           Income Statement
2                           July-1-86  July-31-86
3
4    000's omitted             PROD.1     PROD.2     PROD.3      TOTAL
5    ===================================================================
6    Gross Sales                  100        200        200        500
7      Sales Allowance             20         80         60        160
8    Net Sales                     80        120        140        340
9      Cost of Goods Sold          30         60         70        160
10   Gross Margin                  50         60         70        180
11     Marketing/G&A Expenses      35         30         30         95
12   EBIT                          15         30         40         85
13     Interest                     1          2          2          5
14     Taxes                        7         14         19         40
15   Net Income                     7         14         19         40
16
17   % Total Net Sales     0.23529411 0.35294117 0.41176470          1
18
19
20
```

The formula with the absolute cell address (referring to cell E8) has been copied. Use the Arrow keys to look at the formula in each cell. Notice that the first cell address in each formula (B8, C8, D8) has changed—without a $ symbol it remains a relative cell address—but that the second, absolute cell address ($E$8) has stayed the same.

Formatting Values in Cells

All the values entered in the Income Statement are currency, but they are displayed in the cells as unformatted numbers. Values within cells can be formatted; you can add dollar signs, insert commas, or round off decimal places. As you would expect, you can format one cell or a range of cells. The following list contains the options available with the Format command.

Fixed	Rounds to a fixed number of decimal places: 1125.62
Scientific	Exponential notation: 1.13E+03
Currency	Dollars and cents: $1,125.62
, (Punctuated)	Adds commas to long numbers: 1,125.62; places negative values in parentheses
General	No fixed number of decimal places: 1125.621 (the initial setting format)
Percent	Multiplies by 100 and adds a % sign: .42 = 42%
Date	Formats into one of several date formats: for example, DD-MMM-YY (01-Sep-87)
Other	Three other formats: +/- (pictograph); Text (formula displayed in the cell); Hidden (cell entries hidden)
Reset	Returns to the global default format (General, if not changed).

Note: Formatting a value only changes the way it is displayed. The value itself is not changed.

With most formats, you are asked to choose the number of decimal places you'd like displayed. 1-2-3 can display up to 15 decimal places. No matter how many decimal places are displayed, however, 1-2-3 always remembers the number at maximum precision. Although it appears to have rounded off the number, 1-2-3 still knows the value up to 15 decimal places and will use that value in calculations.

You are going to format the cells in the bottom row of the Income Statement to display their contents as percentages with no decimal places.

Move to: cell B17
Press: [/]
Select: Range
Format
Percent
Type: 0 [↵] *(for 0 decimal places)*
Move to: cell E17 *(to highlight the range)*
Press: [↵]

```
B17: (P0) +B8/$E$8                                             READY

          A                  B          C          D          E
1                          Income Statement
2                          July-1-86  July-31-86
3
4   000's omitted            PROD.1     PROD.2     PROD.3     TOTAL
5   ================================================================
6   Gross Sales                 100        200        200        500
7     Sales Allowance            20         80         60        160
8   Net Sales                    80        120        140        340
9     Cost of Goods Sold         30         60         70        160
10  Gross Margin                 50         60         70        180
11    Marketing/G&A Expenses     35         30         30         95
12  EBIT                         15         30         40         85
13    Interest                    1          2          2          5
14    Taxes                       7         14         19         40
15  Net Income                    7         14         19         40
16
17  % Total Net Sales           24%        35%        41%       100%
18
19
20
```

Look at the first line of the control panel as you move through the cells in the bottom row of the Income Statement. Notice that (P0) now appears before the contents of the cell shown on the control panel. This means the format is "Percent, 0 decimal places."

Now format the Total column for currency with no decimal places (dollar values only).

Move to: cell E6

Press: [/]

Select: Range
Format
Currency

Type: 0 [↵] *(for 0 decimal places)*

Move to: cell E15

Press: [↵]

```
E6: (C0) +B6+C6+D6                                                        READY

                A                   B          C          D          E
1                             Income Statement
2                             July-1-86  July-31-86
3
4   000's omitted                PROD.1     PROD.2     PROD.3      TOTAL
5   ====================================================================
6   Gross Sales                     100        200        200       $500
7     Sales Allowance                20         80         60       $160
8   Net Sales                        80        120        140       $340
9     Cost of Goods Sold             30         60         70       $160
10  Gross Margin                     50         60         70       $180
11    Marketing/G&A Expenses         35         30         30        $95
12  EBIT                             15         30         40        $85
13    Interest                        1          2          2         $5
14    Taxes                           7         14         19        $40
15  Net Income                        7         14         19        $40
16
17  % Total Net Sales               24%        35%        41%       100%
18
19
20
```

The values in the Total column now appear as currency with no decimal places.

The Help Facility

You can call up a Help screen at any point (even in the middle of a command sequence). Each Help message is tailored to what is currently on the screen. Pressing Escape will return you to the worksheet.

Note: Remember, to use Help on a computer with two disk drives, the System Disk must be in drive A; on a hard-disk computer, the Help files must be copied into the same subdirectory as the 1-2-3 Program Disk.

Naming a Range

You've seen how frequently ranges are used in the worksheet work environment. Instead of typing or highlighting a range, you can specify a **range name** for that range of cells. Naming a range of cells makes a worksheet much easier to use. For example, it is easier to use a name like Total to refer to the cells in a range than it is to remember that cells E6 through E15 comprise the range.

After creating a range name, you can use the name with any command that calls for a range, from copying and moving to formatting and graphing. When prompted to specify a range, simply type the name. Range names are created with the Range Name command. They are automatically saved with the worksheet so they remain available for future work sessions (unless you choose to delete them).

Creating a Range Name

First you'll give the name Net-Sales to the cells in the Net Sales row (B8..D8). The two-step process is similar to that you've used with other worksheet commands. At the first prompt `Enter name:` you will type the name of the range. (Range names can be up to 15 characters long, and should not contain any spaces.)

Move to: cell B8

Press: [/]

Select: Range
Name
Create

Type: Net-Sales [↵]

When you see Enter range: B8..B8, highlight the range to be named Net-Sales.

Press: [▶] *(two times to move to cell D8)*

```
D8: +D6-D7                                                              POINT
Enter name: Net-Sales                    Enter range: B8..D8

              A                 B          C          D          E
1                               Income Statement
2                               July-1-86  July-31-86
3
4   000's omitted              PROD.1     PROD.2     PROD.3      TOTAL
5   ===================================================================
6   Gross Sales                   100        200        200      $500
7     Sales Allowance              20         80         60      $160
8   Net Sales                      80        120        140      $340
9     Cost of Goods Sold           30         60         70      $160
10  Gross Margin                   50         60         70      $180
11    Marketing/G&A Expenses       35         30         30       $95
12  EBIT                           15         30         40       $85
13    Interest                      1          2          2        $5
14    Taxes                         7         14         19       $40
15  Net Income                      7         14         19       $40
16
17  % Total Net Sales             24%        35%        41%      100%
18
19
20
```

Press: [↵]

Name a second range that includes the cells in the Gross Margin row.

Move to: cell B10

Press: [/]

Select: Range
Name
Create

```
B10: +B8-B9                                                       FILES
Enter name:
NET-SALES
               A                  B         C         D          E
1                            Income Statement
2                            July-1-86  July-31-86
3
4   000's omitted               PROD.1    PROD.2    PROD.3     TOTAL
5   ==================================================================
6   Gross Sales                    100       200       200      $500
7     Sales Allowance               20        80        60      $160
8   Net Sales                       80       120       140      $340
9     Cost of Goods Sold            30        60        70      $160
10  Gross Margin                    50        60        70      $180
11    Marketing/G&A Expenses        35        30        30       $95
12  EBIT                            15        30        40       $85
13    Interest                       1         2         2        $5
14    Taxes                          7        14        19       $40
15  Net Income                       7        14        19       $40
16
17  % Total Net Sales              24%       35%       41%      100%
18
19
20
```

Look at the third line of the control panel. Below the prompt **Enter name**: you'll see NET-SALES. Each range name you create will now be listed when you select the Range Name Create command. When there are more names than fit the width of the control panel, use the Arrow keys to see the complete list. The names will disappear when you type in a range name.

Type: Gross-Margin [↵]

Press: [▶] *(two times)*

[↵]

Name a third range that includes all the product data in columns B, C, and D.

Move to: cell B6

Press: [/]

Select: Range

Name

Create

Two range names are now listed on the control panel.

Type: Products [↵]

Press: [▶] *(two times)*

[END]

[▼]

```
D15: +D12-(D13+D14)                                              POINT
Enter name: Products                Enter range: B6..D15

              A                  B        C        D         E
1                          Income Statement
2                          July-1-86  July-31-86
3
4    000's omitted           PROD.1    PROD.2    PROD.3    TOTAL
5    ==============================================================
6    Gross Sales                100       200       200      $500
7      Sales Allowance           20        80        60      $160
8    Net Sales                   80       120       140      $340
9      Cost of Goods Sold        30        60        70      $160
10   Gross Margin                50        60        70      $180
11     Marketing/G&A Expenses    35        30        30       $95
12   EBIT                        15        30        40       $85
13     Interest                   1         2         2        $5
14     Taxes                      7        14        19       $40
15   Net Income                   7        14        19       $40
16
17   % Total Net Sales          24%       35%       41%      100%
18
19
20
```

Press: [↵]

Using a Range Name for Copying

Now that you have named these ranges, they can be used wherever they are required. For example, using a range name can save time when copying.

To see how this copying with range names works, first erase the Gross Margin data. (Remember that this row contains formulas that were copied from the Net Sales row.)

Move to: cell B10

Press: [/]

Select: Range

Erase

Move to: cell D10

Press: [↵]

Some of the values in the worksheet change to reflect the loss of data (rows 12 and 15 show negative values). Now you'll replace the original formulas in the Gross Margin row by copying them from the Net Sales row. Instead of indicating the FROM and TO ranges by highlighting them on the worksheet, you will use the range names. At the Copy command prompts, you will type in the range names for the Net Sales and Gross Margin ranges.

Press: [/]

Select: Copy

Type: Net-Sales [↵] *(to indicate the FROM range)*
Gross-Margin [↵] *(to indicate the TO range)*

```
B10: (C0)                                                          EDIT
Enter range to copy TO: Gross-Margin

            A                B          C          D          E
1                         Income Statement
2                         July-1-86  July-31-86
3
4   000's omitted            PROD.1     PROD.2     PROD.3     TOTAL
5   =================================================================
6   Gross Sales                $100       $200       $200       $500
7     Sales Allowance           $20        $80        $60       $160
8   Net Sales                   $80       $120       $140       $340
9     Cost of Goods Sold        $30        $60        $70       $160
10  Gross Margin                                                  $0
11    Marketing/G&A Expenses    $35        $30        $30        $95
12  EBIT                      ($35)      ($30)      ($30)      ($95)
13    Interest                  $1         $2         $2         $5
14    Taxes                     $7        $14        $19        $40
15  Net Income                ($43)      ($46)      ($51)     ($140)
16
17  % Total Net Sales           24%        35%        41%       100%
18
19
20
```

The formulas will be copied from the Net Sales to the Gross Margin range and will recalculate with the related values. The worksheet should look just as it did before you erased the range.

Using a Range Name for Formatting

Range names can also be used with Format commands. On the Income Statement, you'll format all of the cells under the Products columns for currency. Since your range has been named, this procedure is quick.

Press: [/]

Select: Range
Format
Currency

Type: 0 [↵] *(for 0 decimal places)*
Products [↵]

```
B10: (C0) +B8-B9                                                    READY

            A                  B          C          D          E
1                              Income Statement
2                              July-1-86  July-31-86
3
4   000's omitted                PROD.1     PROD.2     PROD.3     TOTAL
5   ==================================================================
6   Gross Sales                   $100       $200       $200       $500
7     Sales Allowance              $20        $80        $60       $160
8   Net Sales                      $80       $120       $140       $340
9     Cost of Goods Sold           $30        $60        $70       $160
10  Gross Margin                   $50        $60        $70       $180
11    Marketing/G&A Expenses       $35        $30        $30        $95
12  EBIT                           $15        $30        $40        $85
13    Interest                      $1         $2         $2         $5
14    Taxes                         $7        $14        $19        $40
15  Net Income                      $7        $14        $19        $40
16
17  % Total Net Sales              24%        35%        41%       100%
18
19
20
```

The cells are now formatted for dollars.

Using a Range Name in Formulas

Range names can also be used in a formula. Earlier you entered this formula for Net Sales: @SUM(B8..D8). The range of cells in B8..D8 is the same range you named Net-Sales. Thus the formula can be written: @SUM(NET-SALES).

Move to: cell E8

```
E8: (C0) @SUM(NET-SALES)                                              READY

              A                   B          C          D          E
1                           Income Statement
2                           July-1-86  July-31-86
3
4   000's omitted             PROD.1     PROD.2     PROD.3      TOTAL
5   ================================================================
6   Gross Sales                 $100       $200       $200       $500
7     Sales Allowance            $20        $80        $60       $160
8   Net Sales                    $80       $120       $140       $340
9     Cost of Goods Sold         $30        $60        $70       $160
10  Gross Margin                 $50        $60        $70       $180
11    Marketing/G&A Expenses     $35        $30        $30        $95
12  EBIT                         $15        $30        $40        $85
13    Interest                    $1         $2         $2         $5
14    Taxes                       $7        $14        $19        $40
15  Net Income                    $7        $14        $19        $40
16
17  % Total Net Sales            24%        35%        41%       100%
18
19
20
```

Look at the first line of the control panel. When you named the range earlier, 1-2-3 automatically changed the formula by replacing the cell addresses B8..D8 with the range name NET-SALES. If you move to cell E10, you will see that 1-2-3 also substituted the range name GROSS-MARGIN for the cell addresses B10..D10. If you decide to delete the range names, 1-2-3 will reinsert the cell references in the formulas.

Creating a Range Name Table

You've already named three ranges on the Income Statement: Net Sales, Gross Margin, and Products. On a large worksheet you might name several ranges to help copy formulas or identify sections of the worksheet that you refer to regularly.

One way of locating a range that you have saved is by using the Goto key.

Press: GOTO

Type: Net-Sales

```
E8: (C0) @SUM(NET-SALES)                                              EDIT
Enter address to go to: Net-Sales

              A                B           C           D           E
1                          Income Statement
2                          July-1-86  July-31-86
3
4    000's omitted           PROD.1      PROD.2      PROD.3      TOTAL
5    ===================================================================
6    Gross Sales               $100        $200        $200        $500
7      Sales Allowance          $20         $80         $60        $160
8    Net Sales                  $80        $120        $140        $340
9      Cost of Goods Sold       $30         $60         $70        $160
10   Gross Margin               $50         $60         $70        $180
11     Marketing/G&A Expenses   $35         $30         $30         $95
12   EBIT                       $15         $30         $40         $85
13     Interest                  $1          $2          $2          $5
14     Taxes                     $7         $14         $19         $40
15   Net Income                  $7         $14         $19         $40
16
17   % Total Net Sales          24%         35%         41%        100%
18
19
20
```

Press: ↵

The pointer moves to the first cell in the named range.

A second way is to use the Range Name Create command. When the second line of the control panel reads `Enter name:` an alphabetical list of the existing range names will be displayed on the third line. The first range name is highlighted; if you press Return, 1-2-3 will display another prompt that will give the cell location of that range, and the entire range will be highlighted.

Press: [/]
Select: Range
Name
Create
Press: [↵]

```
D10: (C0) +D8-D9                                                    POINT
Enter name: GROSS-MARGIN              Enter range: B10..D10

         A                   B         C         D         E
1                     Income Statement
2                     July-1-86  July-31-86
3
4   000's omitted          PROD.1    PROD.2    PROD.3     TOTAL
5   ===============================================================
6   Gross Sales              $100      $200      $200      $500
7     Sales Allowance         $20       $80       $60      $160
8   Net Sales                 $80      $120      $140      $340
9     Cost of Goods Sold      $30       $60       $70      $160
10  Gross Margin              $50       $60       $70      $180
11    Marketing/G&A Expenses  $35       $30       $30       $95
12  EBIT                      $15       $30       $40       $85
13    Interest                 $1        $2        $2        $5
14    Taxes                    $7       $14       $19       $40
15  Net Income                 $7       $14       $19       $40
16
17  % Total Net Sales          24%       35%       41%      100%
18
19
20
```

Press: [↵]

An even better way of keeping track of range names—especially when there are many of them—is to create a range name table. Then you can see the names and locations of all the range names in a file at one time.

A range name table is written on the worksheet. It takes two columns: one for the range names and one for the cell addresses. When deciding where to locate the table, be sure to go far enough beyond the worksheet data you've already entered so that you have sufficient room to continue the worksheet. You should also widen the first column of the table so that it is large enough to hold the range names.

You're going to create a range name table of the three ranges you've named for the Income Statement. Move to a blank area of the worksheet and widen the first column.

Move to: cell G1
Press: [/]
Select: Worksheet
Column
Set-Width
Type: 20 [↵]

Next you use the Range Name Table command and press Return at the prompt Enter range: G1..G1. This accepts cell G1 as the upper-left corner of the range to contain the table.

Press: [/]
Select: Range
Name
Table
Press: [↵]
[▶]

```
H1: 'B10..D10                                                    READY

          C          D          E       F          G               H
 1   ement                                    GROSS-MARGIN    B10..D10
 2   July-31-86                               NET-SALES       B8..D8
 3                                            PRODUCTS        B6..D15
 4     PROD.2     PROD.3      TOTAL
 5   ================================
 6         $200       $200       $500
 7          $80        $60       $160
 8         $120       $140       $340
 9          $60        $70       $160
10          $60        $70       $180
11          $30        $30        $95
12          $30        $40        $85
13           $2         $2         $5
14          $14        $19        $40
15          $14        $19        $40
16
17          35%        41%       100%
18
19
20
```

A table of all of the named ranges for this worksheet appears in columns G and H. Notice that the table is in alphabetical order and contains the upper-left and lower-right cell address for each range.

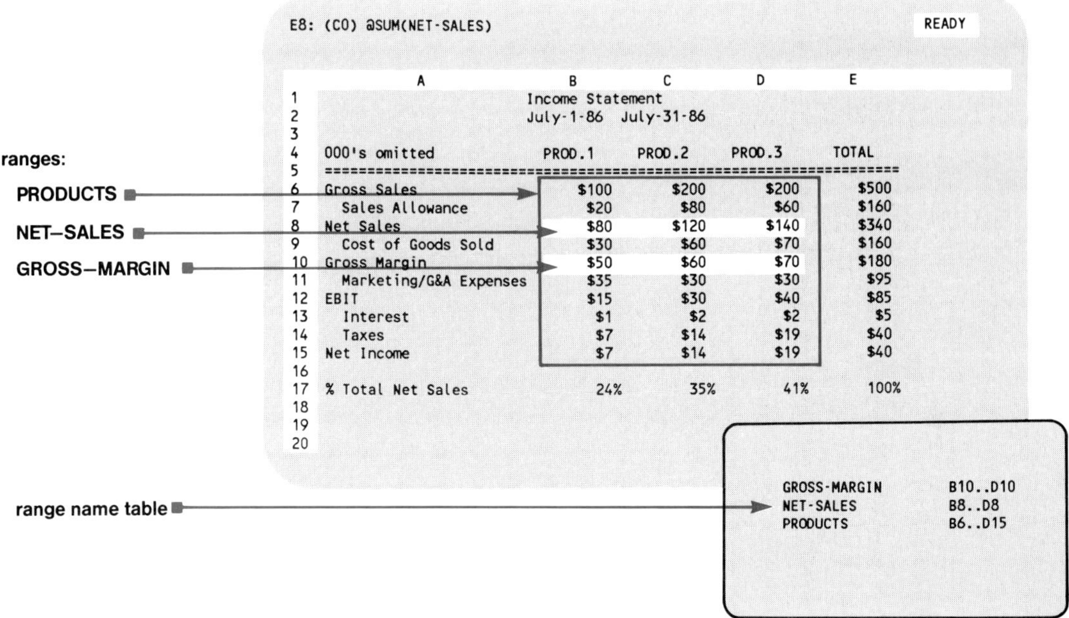

Press Home to return to the upper-left corner of the worksheet.

Note: Once you have created the table, you can see it at any time. If you give the table itself a range name (such as Table), you can see it by pressing Goto and typing the name.

Using Range Transpose

The Range Transpose command changes a column to a row or a row to a column. This command is extremely helpful when building a detailed worksheet involving labels or values that you have already typed.

For example, you could create a small worksheet below the Income Statement to show total costs for each product over a three-month period. On this expenses worksheet, the labels PROD.1, PROD.2, and PROD.3 need to run down the side of the worksheet rather than across the top.

Create the expenses sheet below the Income Statement. First, title it and add monthly labels.

Move to: cell A21
Type: Monthly Expenses [▶]
June [▶]
July [▶]
August [↵]

```
D21: 'August                                                        READY

         A                 B          C          D          E
2                       July-1-86  July-31-86
3
4   000's omitted          PROD.1     PROD.2     PROD.3     TOTAL
5   ==============================================================
6   Gross Sales               $100       $200       $200       $500
7     Sales Allowance          $20        $80        $60       $160
8   Net Sales                  $80       $120       $140       $340
9     Cost of Goods Sold       $30        $60        $70       $160
10  Gross Margin               $50        $60        $70       $180
11    Marketing/G&A Expenses   $35        $30        $30        $95
12  EBIT                       $15        $30        $40        $85
13    Interest                  $1         $2         $2         $5
14    Taxes                     $7        $14        $19        $40
15  Net Income                  $7        $14        $19        $40
16
17  % Total Net Sales          24%        35%        41%       100%
18
19
20
21  Monthly Expenses      June       July       August
```

Next you copy the product labels from the Income Statement to the Monthly Expenses worksheet. Following the procedure you've used before, you first indicate the range you want to copy, and then where you want to copy it to. Follow the prompts.

Move to: cell B4 *(the beginning of the range to be transposed)*
Press: [/]
Select: Range
Transpose
Press: [▶] *(two times)*
[↵]
Move to: cell A22
Press: [↵]
Move to: cell A24

```
A24: [W24] ^PROD.3                                                        READY

                 A                   B          C          D          E
5   ==================================================================
6   Gross Sales                      $100       $200       $200       $500
7     Sales Allowance                 $20        $80        $60       $160
8   Net Sales                         $80       $120       $140       $340
9     Cost of Goods Sold              $30        $60        $70       $160
10  Gross Margin                      $50        $60        $70       $180
11    Marketing/G&A Expenses          $35        $30        $30        $95
12  EBIT                              $15        $30        $40        $85
13    Interest                         $1         $2         $2         $5
14    Taxes                            $7        $14        $19        $40
15  Net Income                         $7        $14        $19        $40
16
17  % Total Net Sales                 24%        35%        41%       100%
18
19
20
21  Monthly Expenses        June       July       August
22            PROD.1
23            PROD.2
24            PROD.3
```

When you move the pointer down to see rows 23 and 24, you can see that the labels are transposed from column labels to row labels. Notice that the label prefix (the caret) has been copied with the labels as well, causing them to be centered in column A.

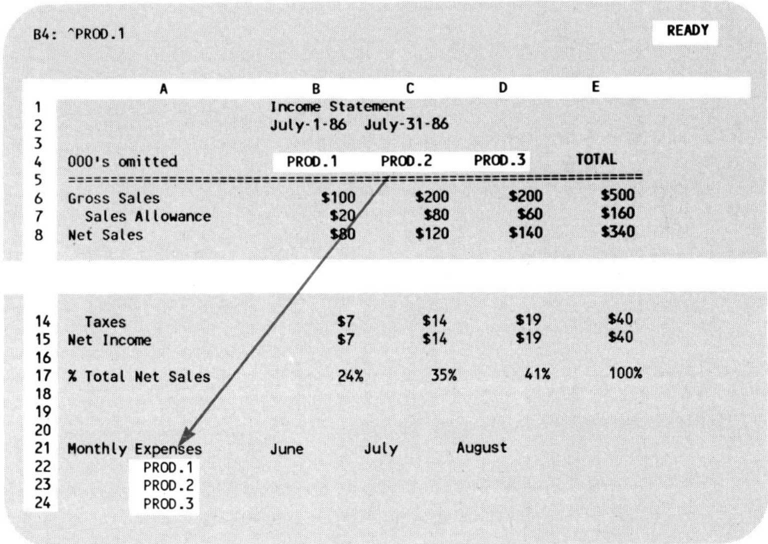

```
B4: ^PROD.1                                                               READY

                 A                   B          C          D          E
1                               Income Statement
2                               July-1-86  July-31-86
3
4   000's omitted                  PROD.1     PROD.2     PROD.3     TOTAL
5   ==================================================================
6   Gross Sales                      $100       $200       $200       $500
7     Sales Allowance                 $20        $80        $60       $160
8   Net Sales                         $80       $120       $140       $340

14    Taxes                            $7        $14        $19        $40
15  Net Income                         $7        $14        $19        $40
16
17  % Total Net Sales                 24%        35%        41%       100%
18
19
20
21  Monthly Expenses        June       July       August
22            PROD.1
23            PROD.2
24            PROD.3
```

The row of labels is changed to a column of labels.

Splitting the Screen

If a worksheet is longer than twenty rows or wider than eight columns, it is too large to fit on one screen. You can move around the worksheet to view it quickly and easily using the movement keys, but 1-2-3 also has a feature which allows you to see two separate sections of the worksheet on the screen at the same time.

Using the Window command, you can create a second window on the screen that contains a range of cells from any area of the worksheet. This feature enables you to keep track of more than one area at once; you can see the effects of changes in one range on cells in another.

In the Monthly Expenses worksheet you just created, the range of transposed labels starts in row 22. This means the area is out of view when you're looking at the entire Income Statement. Here you will create another window on the screen that will allow you to view both the majority of the Income Statement and the Monthly Expenses worksheet at the same time.

Press: HOME *(to place row 1 at the top of the screen)*

Move to: cell A16

Press: /

Select: Worksheet
Window

The Window menu offers you the choice of either a horizontal or a vertical window (as well as synchronized or unsynchronized windows, options which are covered below). The highlight is on Horizontal, and the third line of the control panel reads Split the screen horizontally at the current row.

Select: Horizontal

```
A15: [W24] 'Net Income                                              READY

                  A                B         C         D         E
 1                          Income Statement
 2                          July-1-86  July-31-86
 3
 4  000's omitted             PROD.1    PROD.2    PROD.3    TOTAL
 5  =================================================================
 6  Gross Sales                 $100      $200      $200      $500
 7    Sales Allowance            $20       $80       $60      $160
 8  Net Sales                    $80      $120      $140      $340
 9    Cost of Goods Sold         $30       $60       $70      $160
10  Gross Margin                 $50       $60       $70      $180
11    Marketing/G&A Expenses     $35       $30       $30       $95
12  EBIT                         $15       $30       $40       $85
13    Interest                    $1        $2        $2        $5
14    Taxes                       $7       $14       $19       $40
15  Net Income                    $7       $14       $19       $40
                  A                B         C         D         E
16
17  % Total Net Sales            24%       35%       41%      100%
18
19
```

A new row of column labels appears between rows 15 and 16, separating the two windows. Notice that the bottom row is now row 19.

The pointer is currently in the top window. You can move the pointer between the two windows with the Window key. Move the pointer to the bottom window and scroll down.

Press: [WINDOW]

Move to: cell A24 *(using* [▼])

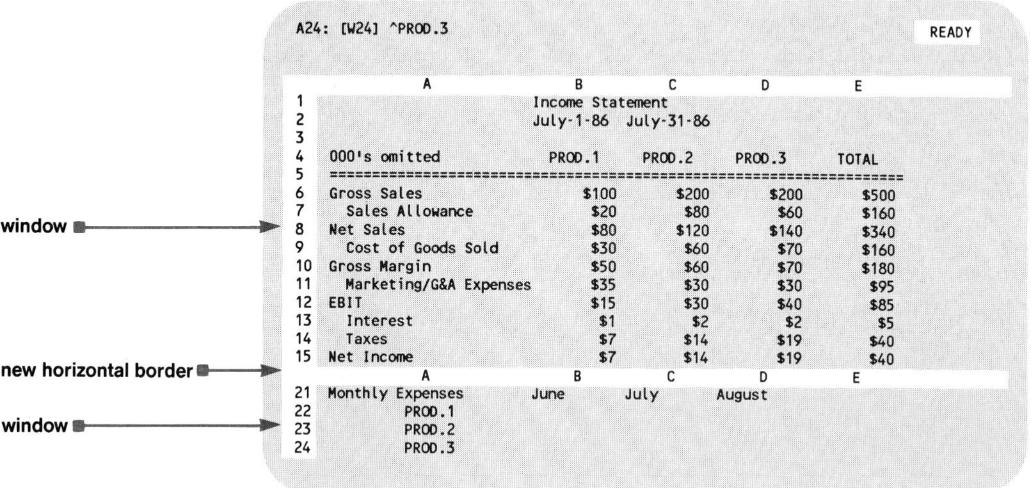

The range containing the Monthly Expenses labels is now visible on the screen.

Experiment with the Window key and the Arrow keys to see how you can move between and around the two windows. Notice that when the screen moves right or left, both windows scroll together.

You can opt to make the two windows scroll separately. Use the Sync and Unsync (Synchronized and Unsynchronized) commands to control this feature.

Move to: any cell in column A

Press: [/]

Select: Worksheet
Window
Unsync

No difference is immediately visible, but now when you scroll one window to the right or left, the other window remains stationary.

Press: [▶] *(several times, until the pointer in either window is in column G)*

```
G23: [W20]                                                        READY

                 A                 B          C          D          E
 1                              Income Statement
 2                              July-1-86  July-31-86
 3
 4   000's omitted              PROD.1     PROD.2     PROD.3     TOTAL
 5   ==============================================================
 6   Gross Sales                     $100       $200       $200       $500
 7     Sales Allowance                $20        $80        $60       $160
 8   Net Sales                        $80       $120       $140       $340
 9     Cost of Goods Sold             $30        $60        $70       $160
10   Gross Margin                     $50        $60        $70       $180
11     Marketing/G&A Expenses         $35        $30        $30        $95
12   EBIT                             $15        $30        $40        $85
13     Interest                        $1         $2         $2         $5
14     Taxes                           $7        $14        $19        $40
15   Net Income                        $7        $14        $19        $40
            C          D          E          F             G
21   July       August
22
23
24
```

When you are through moving around the two windows, clear them from the screen.

Press: [/]

Select: Worksheet
Window
Clear

Range Erase

The Range Erase command is used to remove parts of the worksheet that you no longer need. The command erases the cell contents of the specified range, but it leaves the cell formats intact.

In this example, the range of transposed labels is no longer necessary. Use the Range Erase command to replace the labels with blank cells.

Move to: cell A21

Press: [/]

Select: Range
Erase

The second line of the control panel reads Enter range to erase: A21..A21. Highlight the range.

Press: [▼] *(three times)*
[▶] *(three times)*

```
D24:                                                          POINT
Enter range to erase: A21..D24

              A                   B        C        D        E
5  =================================================================
6  Gross Sales                  $100     $200     $200     $500
7    Sales Allowance             $20      $80      $60     $160
8  Net Sales                     $80     $120     $140     $340
9    Cost of Goods Sold          $30      $60      $70     $160
10 Gross Margin                  $50      $60      $70     $180
11   Marketing/G&A Expenses      $35      $30      $30      $95
12 EBIT                          $15      $30      $40      $85
13   Interest                     $1       $2       $2       $5
14   Taxes                        $7      $14      $19      $40
15 Net Income                     $7      $14      $19      $40
16
17 % Total Net Sales             24%      35%      41%     100%
18
19
20
21 Monthly Expenses        June     July     August
22         PROD.1
23         PROD.2
24         PROD.3
```

Press: 

Text Editing

The 1-2-3 worksheet has features that enable you to do a small amount of text editing on the worksheet screen. You can enter a few lines of text to document portions of the worksheet or include a memo.

As you have seen, 1-2-3 allows a label to be longer than the cell in which it is entered. The label overflows into adjacent cells, provided they are blank. The Range Justify command acts on the label, breaking the lines so they fit into a range of any width you specify.

Write a short memo at the bottom of the Income Statement. When you enter the sentence into cell A23 do not press Return until you reach the end of the sentence. Then use the Range Justify command to fit the sentence into a block across columns A and B.

Move to: cell A21

Type: Memo to All Departments [↵]

Press: [▼] *(twice)*

Type: All products are currently showing a profit, but we should keep an eye on product 1. [↵]

```
A23: [W24] 'All products are currently showing a profit, but we should keepREADY

              A                 B          C          D          E
4   000's omitted            PROD.1     PROD.2     PROD.3      TOTAL
5   ================================================================
6   Gross Sales                $100       $200       $200       $500
7     Sales Allowance           $20        $80        $60       $160
8   Net Sales                   $80       $120       $140       $340
9     Cost of Goods Sold        $30        $60        $70       $160
10  Gross Margin                $50        $60        $70       $180
11    Marketing/G&A Expenses    $35        $30        $30        $95
12  EBIT                        $15        $30        $40        $85
13    Interest                   $1         $2         $2         $5
14    Taxes                      $7        $14        $19        $40
15  Net Income                   $7        $14        $19        $40
16
17  % Total Net Sales            24%        35%        41%       100%
18
19
20
21  Memo to All Departments
22
23  All products are currently showing a profit, but we should keep an eye on pr
```

The sentence extends across the screen, and the last characters are not visible.

Press: [/]

Select: Range

Justify

The second line of the control panel will read Enter justify range: A23..A23. You want the text to extend across columns A and B.

Press: [▶] *(to expand the highlight to cell B23)*

[↵]

[▼] *(twice)*

```
A25: [W24] 'eye on product 1.                                    READY

          A                   B          C          D          E
6   Gross Sales              $100       $200       $200       $500
7     Sales Allowance         $20        $80        $60       $160
8   Net Sales                 $80       $120       $140       $340
9     Cost of Goods Sold      $30        $60        $70       $160
10  Gross Margin              $50        $60        $70       $180
11    Marketing/G&A Expenses  $35        $30        $30        $95
12  EBIT                      $15        $30        $40        $85
13    Interest                 $1         $2         $2         $5
14    Taxes                    $7        $14        $19        $40
15  Net Income                 $7        $14        $19        $40
16
17  % Total Net Sales          24%        35%        41%       100%
18
19
20
21  Memo to All Departments
22
23  All products are currently showing
24  a profit, but we should keep an
25  eye on product 1.
```

The text is broken into three lines that spread across columns A and B. If you move the cursor down column A, you will see that there are now three labels, located in cells A23, A24, and A25. To edit the text, you would move to one of those cells and press the Edit key.

What-If Calculations

Changing Sample Values

If the electronic worksheet's automatic recalculation is the key to greater efficiency, its use in what-if scenarios is the key to better decision making. The two examples that follow illustrate the what-if potential of 1-2-3.

1. What if Gross Sales for Product 1 increased by 12%? What effect would this have on Net Income?

Move to: cell B6

Type: 100*112% ↵ *(to increase the amount by 12%)*

```
B6: (C0) 100*1.12                                                    READY

              A                  B          C          D          E
1                            Income Statement
2                            July-1-86  July-31-86
3
4   000's omitted              PROD.1     PROD.2     PROD.3     TOTAL
5   ================================================================
6   Gross Sales                  $112       $200       $200      $512
7     Sales Allowance             $20        $80        $60      $160
8   Net Sales                     $92       $120       $140      $352
9     Cost of Goods Sold          $30        $60        $70      $160
10  Gross Margin                  $62        $60        $70      $192
11    Marketing/G&A Expenses      $35        $30        $30       $95
12  EBIT                          $27        $30        $40       $97
13    Interest                     $1         $2         $2        $5
14    Taxes                        $7        $14        $19       $40
15  Net Income                    $19        $14        $19       $52
16
17  % Total Net Sales              26%        34%        40%      100%
18
19
20
```

Notice how all the values related to the contents of cell B6 are instantly updated to reflect the change you made. Net Income, in cell B15, has increased from $7 in the original to $19 in this scenario. Compare other values in the original against the new version.

2. What if Marketing/G&A expenses for Product 1 could be lowered by $2,000 and taxes decreased by 30%? What effect would this have on Net Income?

Move to: cell B11
Type: 33 ↵ *(to lower the amount by $2,000)*
Move to: cell B14
Type: 7*70% ↵ *(to lower the amount by 30%)*

```
B14: (C0) 7*0.7                                                          READY

              A                  B          C          D          E
1                            Income Statement
2                            July-1-86  July-31-86
3
4   000's omitted              PROD.1     PROD.2     PROD.3      TOTAL
5   ==================================================================
6   Gross Sales                  $112       $200       $200       $512
7     Sales Allowance             $20        $80        $60       $160
8   Net Sales                     $92       $120       $140       $352
9     Cost of Goods Sold          $30        $60        $70       $160
10  Gross Margin                  $62        $60        $70       $192
11    Marketing/G&A Expenses      $33        $30        $30        $93
12  EBIT                          $29        $30        $40        $99
13    Interest                     $1         $2         $2         $5
14    Taxes                        $5        $14        $19        $38
15  Net Income                    $23        $14        $19        $56
16
17  % Total Net Sales             26%        34%        40%       100%
18
19
20
```

Notice how these changes affect other values on the worksheet. Net Income has now increased from the original value of $7 to a new value of $23—a significant change.

Restoring Original Values

Before going on, restore the original values to the worksheet.

Move to: cell B6
Type: 100 ↵
Move to: cell B11
Type: 35 ↵
Move to: cell B14
Type: 7 ↵

Creating and Saving Worksheets

Worksheets are often printed in reports and used in presentations. And a report or presentation might involve what-if scenarios. Thus, you could conceivably want different versions of the same worksheet.

This is easy with 1-2-3. Any time you change values on a worksheet, you can save the changed version of the worksheet under a new name (thereby creating a different file). For example, if you were to save the Income Statement with the changes entered above, you could use the name Income2 to differentiate it from the original version.

Printing the Worksheet

Before you print a worksheet (or anything else), you should save the file so that all the latest changes are saved. Problems can occur because of the simplest errors or oversights and the final version of the worksheet may be lost.

Save the file.

Press: [/]
Select: File
Save
Press: [↵]
Select: Replace

The Print Menu

Printing the worksheet is a simple task. Before you print, however, you may want to change some of 1-2-3's print settings. For example, your worksheet may be much wider than your paper. To take care of this, you could set wider margins or choose to print only a portion of the worksheet at a time. The Print menu determines these and other printing specifications for all 1-2-3 applications.

Note: If the data in the print range is wider than the paper you're printing on, 1-2-3 automatically prints the data that extends beyond the right margin on a separate page.

Before you start, make sure the printer is turned on and ready. Call up the Print menu.

Press: [/]

Select: Print

1-2-3 offers you two choices at this point: You can send the output to the printer or to a print file. In this case you want to send it to the printer. (A print file can be saved and accessed later in DOS or other software programs.)

Select: Printer

```
B14: (C0) 7                                                          MENU
Range  Line  Page  Options  Clear  Align  Go  Quit
Specify a range to print
             A                  B         C         D         E
1                            Income Statement
2                            July-1-86  July-31-86
3
4    000's omitted              PROD.1    PROD.2    PROD.3     TOTAL
5    ====================================================================
6    Gross Sales                  $100      $200      $200      $500
7      Sales Allowance             $20       $80       $60      $160
8    Net Sales                     $80      $120      $140      $340
9      Cost of Goods Sold          $30       $60       $70      $160
10   Gross Margin                  $50       $60       $70      $180
11     Marketing/G&A Expenses      $35       $30       $30       $95
12   EBIT                          $15       $30       $40       $85
13     Interest                     $1        $2        $2        $5
14     Taxes                        $7       $14       $19       $40
15   Net Income                     $7       $14       $19       $40
16
17   % Total Net Sales              24%       35%       41%      100%
18
19
20
```

The Print menu appears. It offers you a number of choices about the appearance and format of the printout. The only option that **must** be specified is the range to be printed.

Range — Specifies the range of the worksheet that will be printed. This must be specified even if you want to print all the data on the worksheet.

Line, Page — Each advances the paper one line or one page, respectively.

Options — Contains a number of choices about the appearance of the printout.

- Header, Footer — Specify a header or footer to be printed on each page.

Margins	Sets left, right, top, and bottom margins to fit the dimensions of the worksheet and the paper size.
Borders	Specifies border columns and/or rows.
Setup	Establishes a printer setup string.
Page-Length	Specifies the number of lines per page. This allows you to print on shorter or longer paper.
Other	This option contains two separate commands: you can opt to print the formulas on a worksheet; you can choose to ignore the print settings.

Clear	Resets some or all of the print settings.
Align	Resets the alignment of the paper to the top of the page.
Go	Begins the printing process.
Quit	Returns 1-2-3 to the READY mode.

Specify the range of the worksheet you want to print. You will be printing the entire Income Statement.

Select: Range
Move to: cell A1
Press: .
Move to: cell E25

E25:
Enter Print range: A1..E25 POINT

	A	B	C	D	E
6	Gross Sales	$100	$200	$200	$500
7	Sales Allowance	$20	$80	$60	$160
8	Net Sales	$80	$120	$140	$340
9	Cost of Goods Sold	$30	$60	$70	$160
10	Gross Margin	$50	$60	$70	$180
11	Marketing/G&A Expenses	$35	$30	$30	$95
12	EBIT	$15	$30	$40	$85
13	Interest	$1	$2	$2	$5
14	Taxes	$7	$14	$19	$40
15	Net Income	$7	$14	$19	$40
16					
17	% Total Net Sales	24%	35%	41%	100%
18					
19					
20					
21	Memo to All Departments				
22					
23	All products are currently showing				
24	a profit, but we should keep an				
25	eye on product 1.				

Press: ↵

Select: Align

Go

```
                        Income Statement
                        July-1-86  July-31-86

000's omitted             PROD.1     PROD.2     PROD.3      TOTAL
=================================================================
Gross Sales                 $100       $200       $200       $500
  Sales Allowance            $20        $80        $60       $160
Net Sales                    $80       $120       $140       $340
  Cost of Goods Sold         $30        $60        $70       $160
Gross Margin                 $50        $60        $70       $180
  Marketing/G&A Expenses     $35        $30        $30        $95
EBIT                         $15        $30        $40        $85
  Interest                    $1         $2         $2         $5
  Taxes                       $7        $14        $19        $40
Net Income                    $7        $14        $19        $40

% Total Net Sales            24%        35%        41%       100%


Memo to All Departments

All products are currently showing
a profit, but we should keep an
eye on product 1.
```

The mode indicator flashes WAIT while the worksheet is printing. After the worksheet is printed, select Quit to remove the print menu. If you want to save the settings you specified, save the file again.

Main Menu Command Structure

Worksheet	Range	Copy	Move	File	Print	Graph	Data	System	Quit
Global	Format			Retrieve	Printer	Type	Fill		No
Insert	Label			Save	File	X	Table		Yes
Delete	Erase			Combine	Range	A	Sort		
Column	Name			Xtract	Line	B	Query		
Erase	Justify			Erase	Page	C	Distribution		
Titles	Protect			List	Options	D	Matrix		
Window	Unprotect			Import	Clear	E	Regression		
Status	Input			Directory	Align	F	Parse		
Page	Value				Go	Reset			
	Transpose				Quit	View			
						Save			
						Options			
						Name			
						Quit			

Worksheet Menu Command Structure

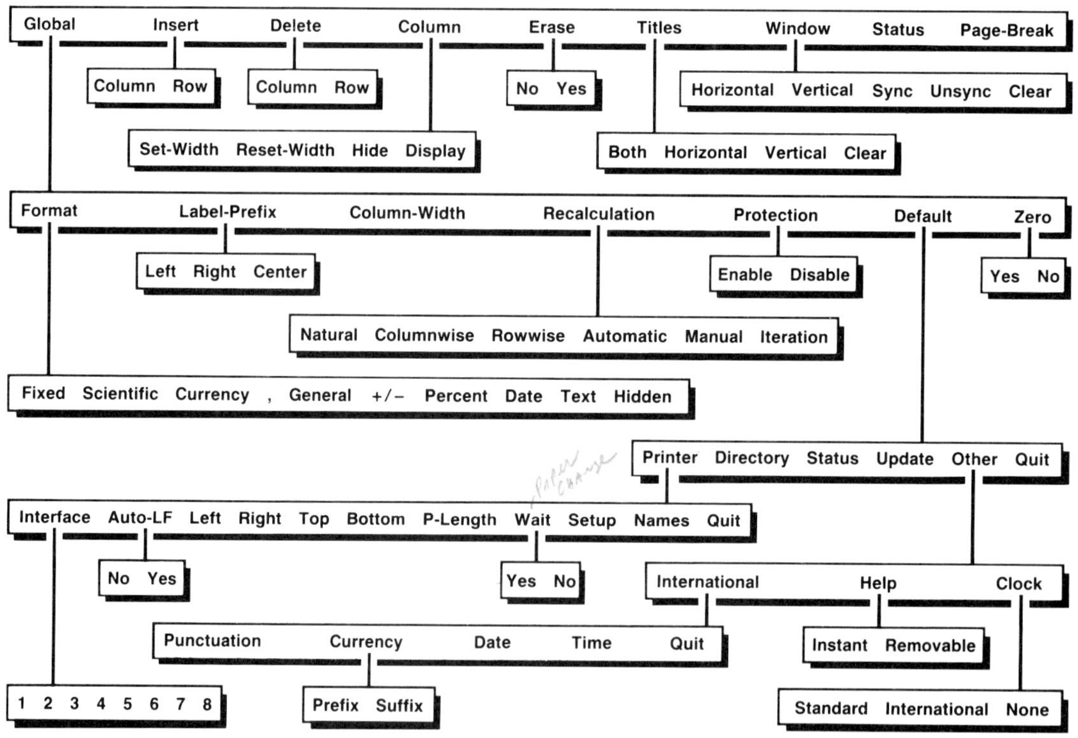

Range Menu Command Structure

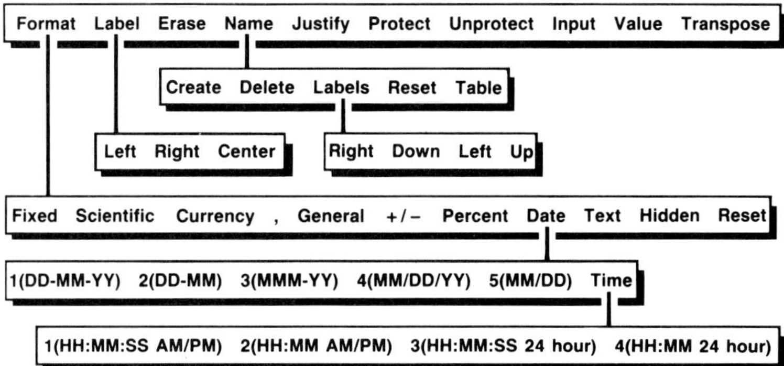

File Menu Command Structure

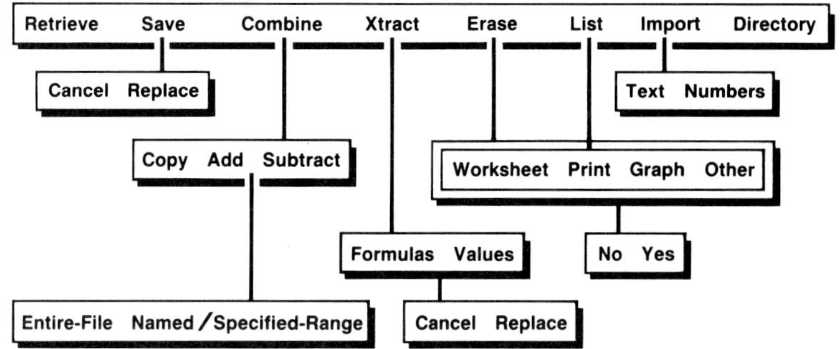

Print Menu Command Structure

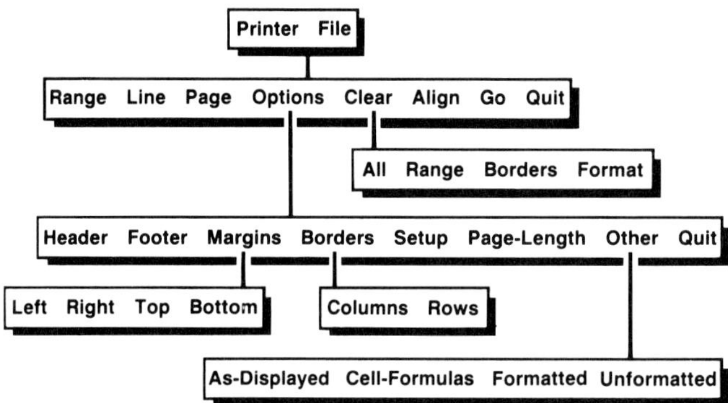

4

Graphics

Business graphics are frequently used in presentations and reports. In many situations a graph can communicate worksheet data more clearly and effectively than the values themselves. A graph can reveal the patterns in rows and columns of values and can illustrate overall trends and projections.

The graphics capability of 1-2-3 lets you draw graphs directly from the data in a worksheet. What's more, the graph is dynamically connected to the worksheet data: Change a number on the worksheet and the graph is instantly redrawn to reflect the change. You can view a graph on the screen as you create it, and you can change it or add to it as necessary. Once a graph is completed, you can print it out on a printer or plot it on a graphics plotter.

The graphics in 1-2-3 offer tremendous flexibility. There are five different types of graphs, and various shading and color options. For printing a graph, 1-2-3 provides a wide selection of colors for the graph and print styles for the titles and legends.

In this chapter you will create a bar graph and a pie chart. You will also explore some of the graphics options: experimenting with different shading patterns, adding titles and legends, and printing the graphs.

Before You Start

For a computer with two disk drives:

- 1-2-3 should be set up to save files on a disk in drive B.
- The data disk should be in drive B.
- The System Disk should be in drive A.

For a hard-disk computer:

- 1-2-3 should be set up to save files in the root directory or a subdirectory.
- All the 1-2-3 disks should be copied in the root directory or in their own subdirectory on the hard disk.

Graphs are drawn from values on a worksheet. The exercises in this chapter use the Income Statement in the file named Income that you created in the worksheet chapter. (If you have not gone through the worksheet chapter, create the worksheet illustrated below and save it under a file named INCOME.)

```
A1: [W24]                                                              READY

              A                B          C          D          E
1                            Income Statement
2                            July-1-86  July-31-86
3
4   000's omitted              PROD.1     PROD.2     PROD.3     TOTAL
5   ==================================================================
6   Gross Sales                  $100       $200       $200       $500
7     Sales Allowance             $20        $80        $60       $160
8   Net Sales                     $80       $120       $140       $340
9     Cost of Goods Sold          $30        $60        $70       $160
10  Gross Margin                  $50        $60        $70       $180
11    Marketing/G&A Expenses      $35        $30        $30        $95
12  EBIT                          $15        $30        $40        $85
13    Interest                     $1         $2         $2         $5
14    Taxes                        $7        $14        $19        $40
15  Net Income                     $7        $14        $19        $40
16
17  % Total Net Sales             24%        35%        41%       100%
18
19
20
```

Graph Types

1-2-3 offers five different types of graphs: line graphs, bar graphs, stacked-bar graphs, pie charts, and XY graphs. All are drawn from the data on a worksheet, but each has a different use.

Line Graph

A line graph displays the values from a row or column on the worksheet as a continuous line. The graph has two axes: X (horizontal) and Y (vertical). The X axis defines a specific period of time. The Y axis is a numbered scale.

A line graph shows how much numeric values have changed over a period of time. It is used to demonstrate trends and projections.

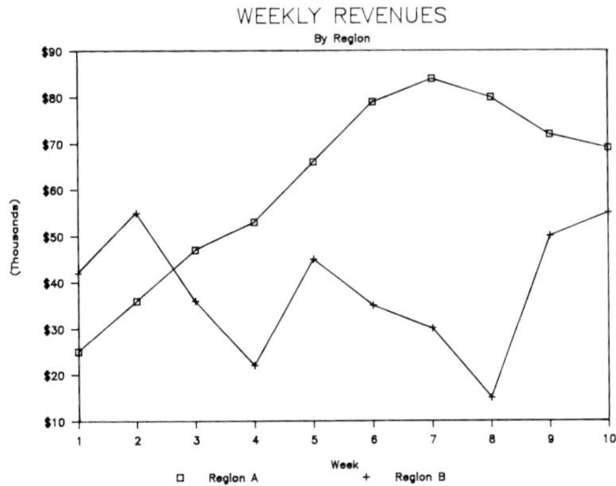

Bar Graph

A bar graph represents numeric values as vertical bars. Each bar reflects the value of a single worksheet cell.

The X axis of a bar graph has labels that identify what each bar represents. Each label can apply to as many as six bars. The Y axis is scaled numerically, according to the worksheet values being represented.

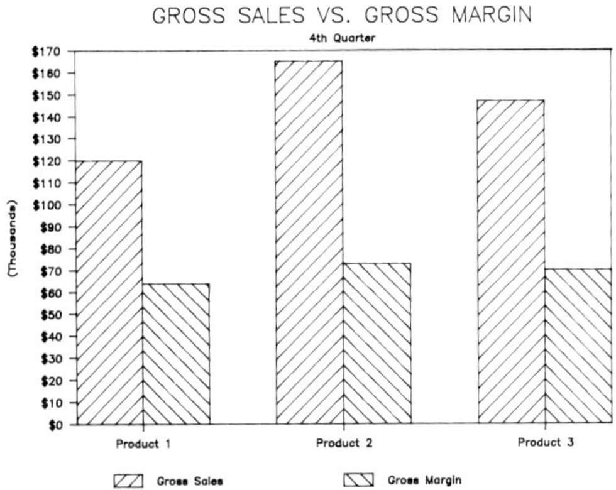

Stacked-Bar Graph

A stacked-bar graph is similar to a bar graph except that related bars are placed on top of each other (stacked) rather than side by side. Up to six bars can be stacked. Each stacked-bar has a label on the X axis. Each part of the stacked-bar represents a cell value on the worksheet. A stacked-bar graph often is used to compare totals for groups of bars.

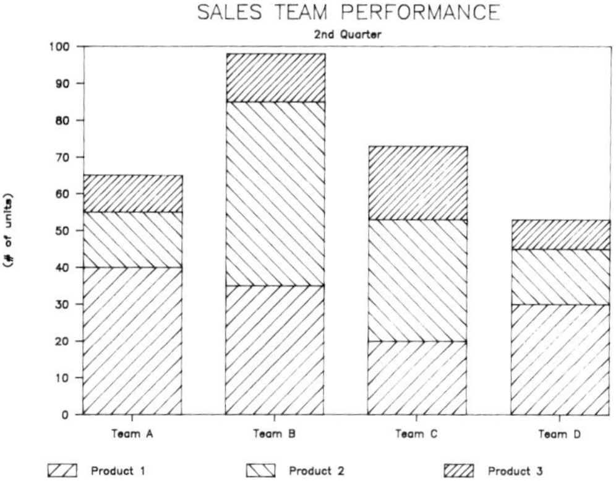

Pie Chart

A pie chart, as its name implies, is a circle divided into slices. Each slice represents a cell value on the worksheet. If one value is twice as large as another, it gets a slice that is twice as large. A pie chart is used to compare parts to the whole. You can "explode" (separate and lift out) one or more slices of the pie for emphasis.

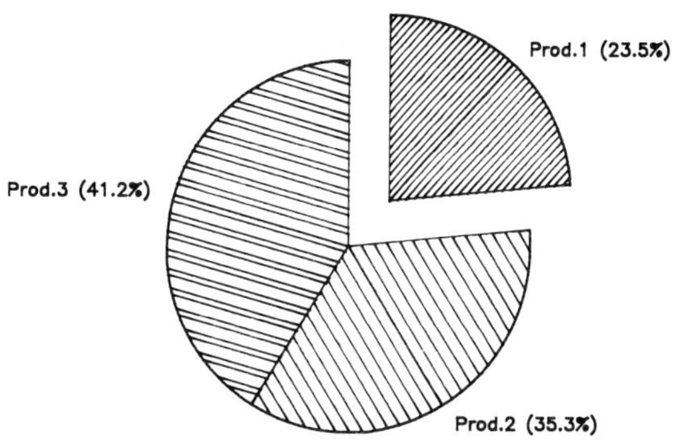

XY Graph

Each point on an XY graph depends on a value from both the X and Y axes. The X value determines how far left or right a point is placed on the graph. The Y value controls the vertical placement of a point. An XY graph is used to plot mathematical formulas and make statistical analyses.

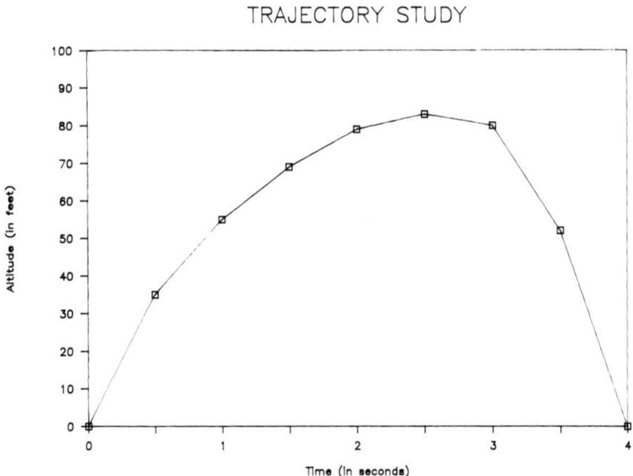

Creating a Graph

You create a graph by using commands from the Graph menu to specify certain characteristics. Each graph has its own series of specifications, covering such characteristics as the type of graph and the worksheet data from which it is to be drawn.

Graph Menu

```
A1: [W24]                                                     MENU
Type  X  A  B  C  D  E  F  Reset  View  Save  Options  Name  Quit
Set graph type
                     A                  B          C          D          E
1
2
3
4
```

Since 1-2-3 is capable of drawing very detailed graphs, there are a number of submenus containing commands used to refine the graphs. These more advanced commands are used after the basic graph is created. You can, for example, choose to add titles, change the numeric formatting for the X and Y axes, and perform other adjustments.

Type Submenu

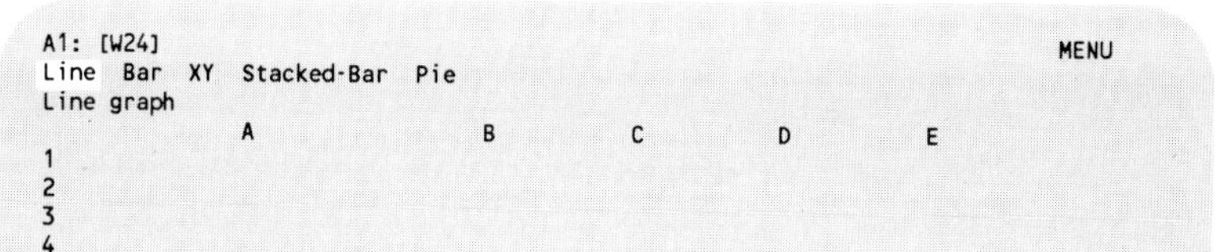

Options Submenu

```
A1: [W24]                                                              MENU
Legend  Format  Titles  Grid  Scale  Color  B&W  Data-Labels  Quit
Specify data-range legends
             A              B         C         D         E
1
2
3
4
```

Once the graph has been created, you can choose to name it and save it. You can then call it up at any time. This allows you to graph the same data from a worksheet in a number of different ways. All graphs are saved with the worksheet file from which they are drawn—so when you retrieve the file, you simply call up a graph by name.

Creating a Bar Graph

You are going to draw a bar graph comparing Net Sales and Net Income for each of three products. Start by retrieving the file INCOME.

Press: [/]

Select: File
Retrieve
INCOME.WK1

Press: [↵]

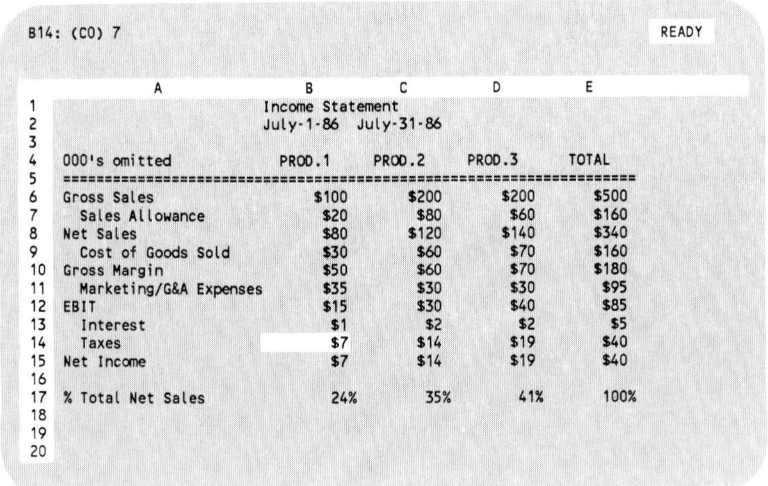

B14: (C0) 7 READY

	A	B	C	D	E
1		Income Statement			
2		July-1-86 July-31-86			
3					
4	000's omitted	PROD.1	PROD.2	PROD.3	TOTAL
5	============	============	============	============	============
6	Gross Sales	$100	$200	$200	$500
7	Sales Allowance	$20	$80	$60	$160
8	Net Sales	$80	$120	$140	$340
9	Cost of Goods Sold	$30	$60	$70	$160
10	Gross Margin	$50	$60	$70	$180
11	Marketing/G&A Expenses	$35	$30	$30	$95
12	EBIT	$15	$30	$40	$85
13	Interest	$1	$2	$2	$5
14	Taxes	$7	$14	$19	$40
15	Net Income	$7	$14	$19	$40
16					
17	% Total Net Sales	24%	35%	41%	100%
18					
19					
20					

The Income Statement appears on the screen, and the mode indicator reads READY.

You will use the following commands in the Graph menu to create the bar graph.

Graph menu

Type	Identifies which of the five types of graphs is to be drawn
X, A-F (Range)	Identify the ranges of the worksheet from which the graph is to be drawn and labeled
Name	Names and creates the graph in the worksheet file

Options submenu

Legend	Adds a legend to identify the different worksheet ranges
Titles	Adds a title to the graph

Selecting the Graph Type

The first step is to specify the type of graph to be drawn. As soon as you make your selection, the Graph menu reappears on the screen.

Press: [/]
Select: Graph
Type
Bar

Specifying Data and Labels

Use the range commands (X, A, B, C, D, E, F) to specify both the worksheet data to be graphed and the labels that describe those data. The commands refer to worksheet ranges. (Remember, a range is a group of one or more cells in a rectangular shape.)

X This option specifies a range of labels that appear along the X axis, or, for a pie chart, next to each slice. For a bar graph, each label identifies a bar or a related group of bars.

A-F These specify ranges of data. You can specify up to six.

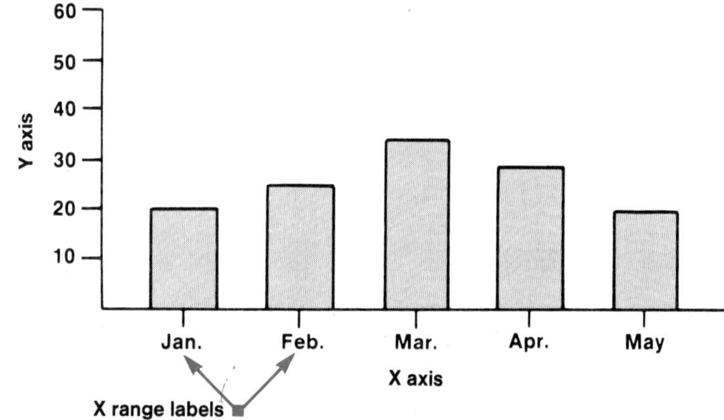

Since the bar graph will compare three products, use the names of the products to identify the bars. After you have invoked the command to select the ranges, point to the worksheet range that contains the product names.

Select: X

Move to: cell B4

Press: [.] *(to anchor the range)*

Move to: cell D4 *(to highlight the range B4..D4)*

```
D4: ^PROD.3                                                          POINT
Enter X axis range: B4..D4

               A                  B          C          D          E
1                           Income Statement
2                           July-1-86  July-31-86
3
4   000's omitted              PROD.1     PROD.2     PROD.3      TOTAL
5   ====================================================================
6   Gross Sales                  $100       $200       $200       $500
7     Sales Allowance             $20        $80        $60       $160
8   Net Sales                     $80       $120       $140       $340
9     Cost of Goods Sold          $30        $60        $70       $160
10  Gross Margin                  $50        $60        $70       $180
11    Marketing/G&A Expenses      $35        $30        $30        $95
12  EBIT                          $15        $30        $40        $85
13    Interest                     $1         $2         $2         $5
14    Taxes                        $7        $14        $19        $40
15  Net Income                     $7        $14        $19        $40
16
17  % Total Net Sales             24%        35%        41%       100%
18
19
20
```

Press: [↵]

When you press Return, the Graph menu reappears. If you want to see the range, select X and the cell addresses will be displayed on the second line of the control panel. Then press Return to see the Graph menu again.

The letters A through F are used to specify up to six ranges of worksheet data to be graphed along the Y axis. Each new data range specified (A-F on the menu) adds another set of bars to the graph. You are going to use the A range to represent the first set of bars, showing Net Sales for each of the three products. Use the Net Sales row from the Income Statement. Again, you will point to the range on the worksheet.

Select: A
Move to: cell B8
Press: [.] *(to anchor the range)*
Move to: cell D8 *(to highlight the range B8..D8)*

```
D8: (C0) +D6-D7                                                    POINT
Enter first data range: B8..D8

            A                  B          C          D          E
 1                        Income Statement
 2                        July-1-86  July-31-86
 3
 4   000's omitted           PROD.1     PROD.2     PROD.3      TOTAL
 5   ================================================================
 6   Gross Sales               $100       $200       $200       $500
 7     Sales Allowance          $20        $80        $60       $160
 8   Net Sales                  $80       $120       $140       $340
 9     Cost of Goods Sold       $30        $60        $70       $160
10   Gross Margin               $50        $60        $70       $180
11     Marketing/G&A Expenses   $35        $30        $30        $95
12   EBIT                       $15        $30        $40        $85
13     Interest                  $1         $2         $2         $5
14     Taxes                     $7        $14        $19        $40
15   Net Income                  $7        $14        $19        $40
16
17   % Total Net Sales          24%        35%        41%       100%
18
19
20
```

Press: [↵]

Viewing the Graph

While creating a graph, you may often want to see what it looks like. The View command lets you do just that. 1-2-3 temporarily replaces the worksheet with a window that displays the graph. You can remove this window and return to the worksheet by pressing the Escape key. You've already entered enough specifications to create a bar graph. Use View to see how the graph looks.

Select: View

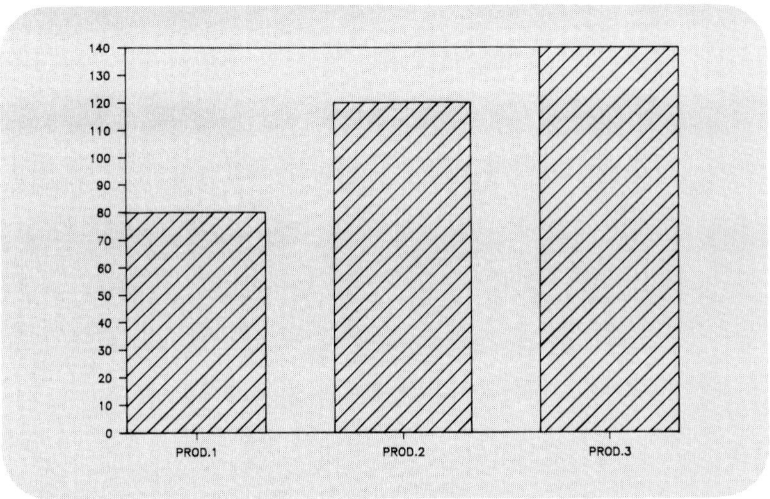

1-2-3 automatically draws a scale on the Y axis. The tick marks are in increments of 10. The top of the scale is 140, the highest Net Sales value. Notice the shading pattern in each bar of the graph.

Note: The graphs in this book have been created with 1-2-3 and printed with the PrintGraph Program. A printed graph differs slightly from one displayed on the screen. The title is larger on the printed version, the increments on the Y axis are often more numerous, and there are other minor differences. Despite these variations in appearance, however, the numbers and the resulting graphic elements are exactly the same in both versions.

Remove the window from the screen.

Press: ESC

Graphing a Second Data Range

You are going to graph a second data range. To compare Net Sales to Net Income for each of the three products in the bar graph, designate the Net Income row on the Income Statement as the B range.

Select: B
Move to: cell B15
Press: [.] *(to anchor the range)*
Move to: cell D15 *(to highlight the range B15..D15)*

```
D15: (C0) +D12-(D13+D14)                                              POINT
Enter second data range: B15..D15

            A                 B           C           D           E
1                        Income Statement
2                        July-1-86   July-31-86
3
4   000's omitted           PROD.1      PROD.2      PROD.3       TOTAL
5   ===================================================================
6   Gross Sales                $100        $200        $200        $500
7     Sales Allowance           $20         $80         $60        $160
8   Net Sales                   $80        $120        $140        $340
9     Cost of Goods Sold        $30         $60         $70        $160
10  Gross Margin                $50         $60         $70        $180
11    Marketing/G&A Expenses    $35         $30         $30         $95
12  EBIT                        $15         $30         $40         $85
13    Interest                   $1          $2          $2          $5
14    Taxes                      $7         $14         $19         $40
15  Net Income                   $7         $14         $19         $40
16
17  % Total Net Sales            24%         35%         41%        100%
18
19
20
```

Press: [↵]

Now view the graph again. You'll see one new bar for each label. Notice that 1-2-3 automatically gives each set of bars different shading patterns.

Select: View

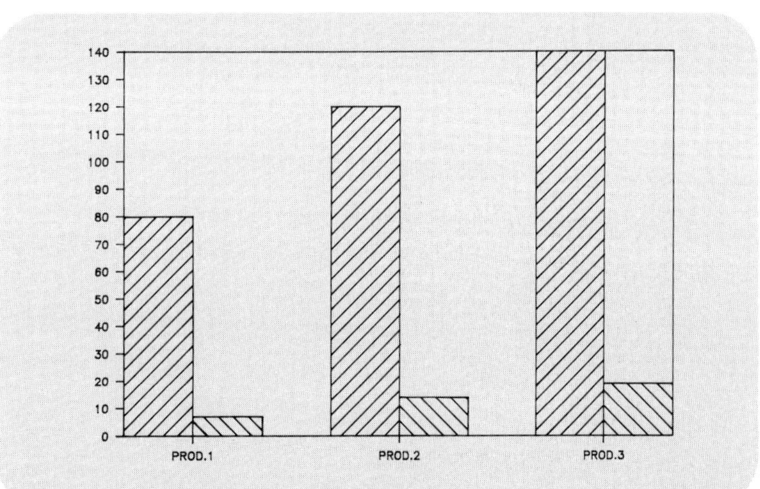

The following diagram illustrates how data from the worksheet are transformed into a bar graph when the ranges are specified.

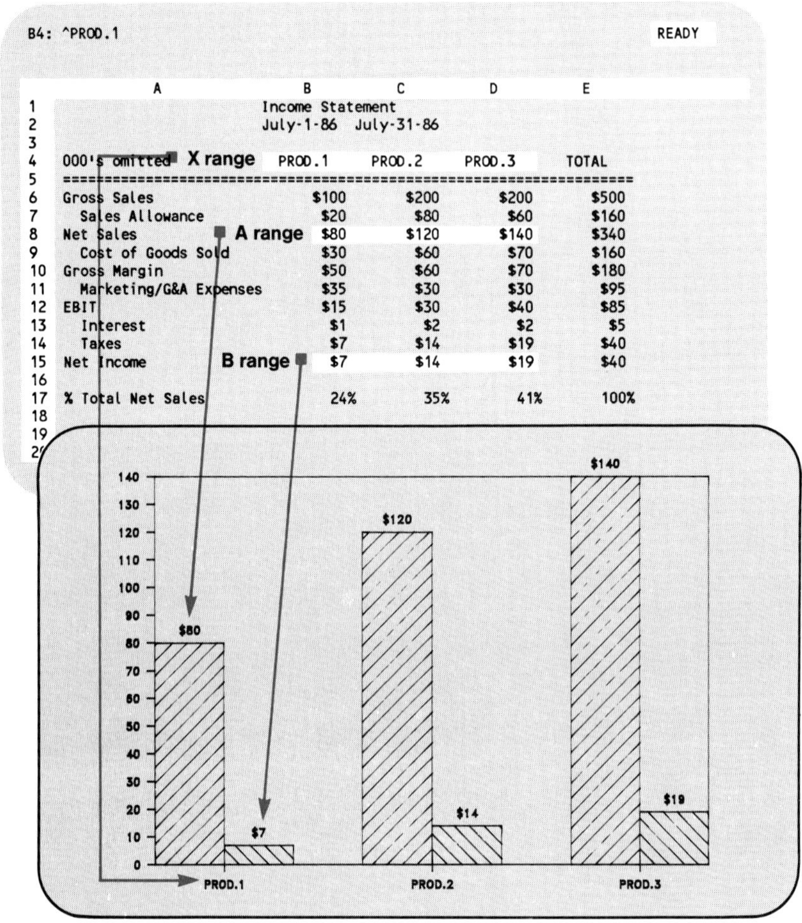

Legends

The Options submenu contains a number of commands that enhance the appearance of a graph and make it easier to understand. Legends are used to identify the A through F ranges. For example, it is not yet clear on the graph what the A and B ranges represent—that is, which is Net Sales and which is Net Income.

You are going to add legends to the graph. First you specify the range to be identified by a legend, and then type in the text of the legend. Name range A Net Sales and range B Net Income. Then view the graph and see how the legends look.

Press: ESC *(to remove the graph from the screen)*

Select: Options

Legend

A

Type: Net Sales

```
B14: (C0) 7                                                            EDIT
Enter legend for A range: Net Sales

              A               B         C          D          E
1                          Income Statement
2                          July-1-86  July-31-86
3
4   000's omitted             PROD.1     PROD.2     PROD.3     TOTAL
5   ================================================================
6   Gross Sales                 $100       $200       $200      $500
7     Sales Allowance            $20        $80        $60      $160
8   Net Sales                    $80       $120       $140      $340
9     Cost of Goods Sold         $30        $60        $70      $160
10  Gross Margin                 $50        $60        $70      $180
11    Marketing/G&A Expenses     $35        $30        $30       $95
12  EBIT                         $15        $30        $40       $85
13    Interest                    $1         $2         $2        $5
14    Taxes                       $7        $14        $19       $40
15  Net Income                    $7        $14        $19       $40
16
17  % Total Net Sales            24%        35%        41%      100%
18
19
20
```

Press: [↵]
Select: Legend
B
Type: Net Income [↵]
Select: Quit *(to leave the Options submenu)*
View

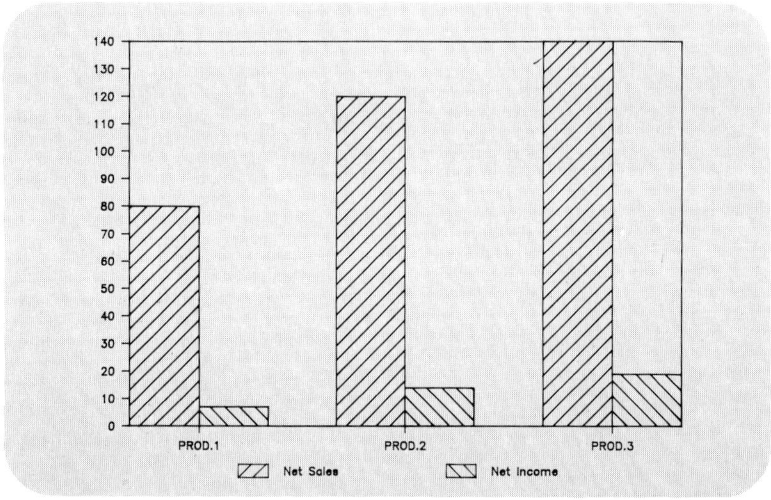

The legends appear at the bottom of the graph. Each legend represents a bar with a particular shading pattern. Notice that samples of the shading patterns appear next to each legend.

Note: There is another way to enter the text of a legend. Net Sales and Net Income are both row labels on the Income Statement. Instead of typing the legend, you can type the cell address of the matching label with a backslash (\ ) in front of it. Since Net Sales is in cell A8 of the Income Statement, you can type \A8 at the prompt. The notation \A8 appears on the control panel as the legend when you call up the Legend command, but the words Net Sales appear on the bar graph.

Titles

1-2-3 can print a two-line title at the top of a graph and one-line titles on the side and on the bottom. Each title can be up to 39 characters long. Selecting Titles from the Options submenu calls up a new menu used to specify the location of the title: above the graph (First, Second), on the bottom (X axis), or along the side (Y axis). You are going to add the title Income Statement and place it above the graph.

Press: ESC *(to remove the graph from the screen)*

Select: Options

Titles

First

Type: Income Statement

```
B14: (C0) 7                                                          EDIT
Enter graph title, top line: Income Statement

                 A                B          C          D          E
1                          Income Statement
2                          July-1-86  July-31-86
3
4   000's omitted             PROD.1     PROD.2     PROD.3      TOTAL
5   =================================================================
6   Gross Sales                 $100       $200       $200       $500
7     Sales Allowance            $20        $80        $60       $160
8   Net Sales                    $80       $120       $140       $340
9     Cost of Goods Sold         $30        $60        $70       $160
10  Gross Margin                 $50        $60        $70       $180
11    Marketing/G&A Expenses     $35        $30        $30        $95
12  EBIT                         $15        $30        $40        $85
13    Interest                    $1         $2         $2         $5
14    Taxes                       $7        $14        $19        $40
15  Net Income                    $7        $14        $19        $40
16
17  % Total Net Sales            24%        35%        41%       100%
18
19
20
```

Press: ↵

Select: Quit

View

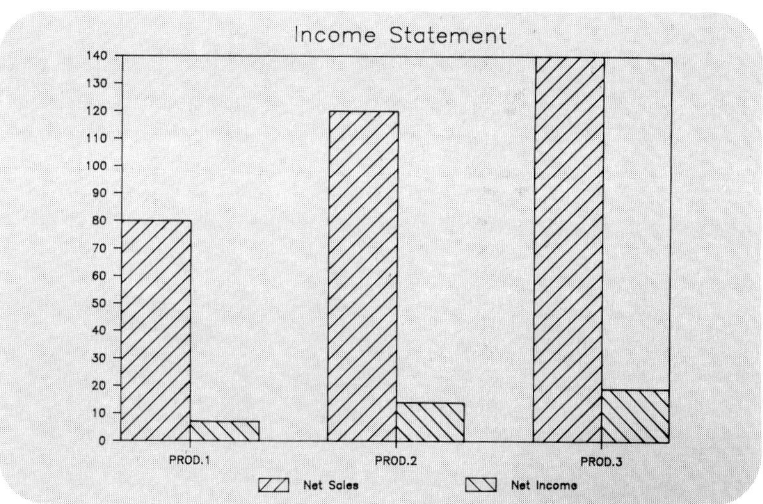

The title Income Statement now appears at the top and the bar graph is complete.

Graphing in Color

Hardware capable of a color-graphics display gives you the choice of displaying either shading patterns (in black and white) or colors on the screen. Since the 1-2-3 initial setting is shading patterns, you must change the setting to Color. This is done with the Color option on the Options submenu.

Note: If your hardware is not capable of color-graphics display, skip to the next section.

Press: ESC *(to remove the graph from the screen)*

Select: Options
Color
Quit
View

In order to change the display back to black and white, you can simply call up the Options menu again and select the B&W command.

Naming the Graph

The graph is now complete—the ranges and options are in place. However, in order to save this graph and its settings, you must give it a name. You can then retrieve the graph at any time. This facility allows you to create and work with several graphs in one worksheet file.

When naming a graph, use a name that appropriately describes it. You're going to name this one BARGRAPH.

Press: ESC *(to remove the graph from the screen)*
Select: Name
Create
Type: Bargraph

```
B14: (C0) 7                                                        EDIT
Enter graph name: Bargraph

            A                  B         C         D         E
1                          Income Statement
2                          July-1-86  July-31-86
3
4   000's omitted          PROD.1    PROD.2    PROD.3     TOTAL
5   ================================================================
6   Gross Sales               $100      $200      $200      $500
7     Sales Allowance          $20       $80       $60      $160
8   Net Sales                  $80      $120      $140      $340
9     Cost of Goods Sold       $30       $60       $70      $160
10  Gross Margin               $50       $60       $70      $180
11    Marketing/G&A Expenses   $35       $30       $30       $95
12  EBIT                       $15       $30       $40       $85
13    Interest                  $1        $2        $2        $5
14    Taxes                     $7       $14       $19       $40
15  Net Income                  $7       $14       $19       $40
16
17  % Total Net Sales          24%       35%       41%      100%
18
19
20
```

Press: ↵

You use the Name Use command to retrieve the graph. To delete it, use the Name Delete command. You can also modify any graph and rename it using the Name Create command again.

Saving a Graph for Printing

The graph is saved along with the worksheet in a WK1 file. However, you cannot use this file to print the graph. To print a graph (with the PrintGraph Program), you must save a "picture" of it in a 1-2-3 picture file. A picture file has a .PIC extension rather than the .WK1 extension used for worksheet files.

Save a picture of the bar graph. The process of saving is similar to that for saving a worksheet file. Type in a file name for the graph at the prompt. 1-2-3 automatically adds the .PIC extension.

Select: Save
Type: Bargraph [↵]
Select: Quit

Save the File

The graph named BARGRAPH is now part of the worksheet named INCOME. Save the file again so the graph will become part of the worksheet file on the disk.

Press: [/]
Select: File
Save
Press: [↵]
Select: Replace

Creating a Pie Chart

In this section you'll create a pie chart comparing Net Sales for the three products on the Income Statement. It will be drawn from the same worksheet data as the bar graph. You'll also add shading patterns and "explode" a slice of the pie.

Changing the Type of Graph

You have two options when creating a new graph. Whenever you name and create a graph, you are actually saving a series of specifications on the Graph menu. If the new graph needs some of the same ranges and titles as the previous graph, you can simply alter the old settings until the new graph is complete, and then name that series of settings. If the new graph needs all new settings, however, you can use the Reset command to delete the old settings and start with a clean slate. In this case you will use some of the settings from the bar graph.

The first step is to change the type of graph from Bar to Pie.

Press: [/]
Select: Graph
Type
Pie

Specifying Data

A pie chart uses only one range of data from a worksheet. Each slice of the pie represents one value in the data range. Leave the X range setting intact; it provides the labels for the slices of the pie. You'll use the same A range as in the bar graph. Delete the B range.

Select: Reset
B
Quit

Titling the Graph

Since the pie chart shows only one range of data, the bar graph title is not appropriate (Income Statement). Retitle the graph to describe the single data range (Net Sales). Then View the graph.

Select: Options
Titles
First

Press: [ESC] *(to erase the old title)*

Type: Net Sales [↵]

Select: Quit
View

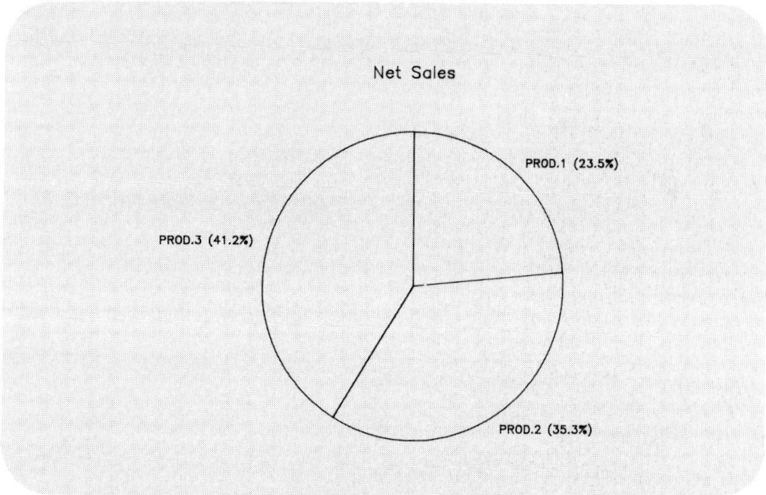

You now have a pie chart with three slices. Each slice represents a Net Sales value for one of the three products. 1-2-3 automatically calculates each slice's percentage of the whole and displays the percentage on the screen.

The X-range labels now serve to identify slices of the pie. Legends are unnecessary because only one numeric value can be associated with each label.

Pie Chart Shading Patterns

At this point the pie chart makes no distinction between the different slices of the pie. However, 1-2-3 offers a variety of shading patterns that you can assign to the slices. Shading patterns can improve the clarity and appearance of a graph.

There are seven different patterns; each corresponds to a number. See the illustration below for the assignment of the patterns. Notice that you can leave a slice of the pie blank by entering an 8 on the worksheet.

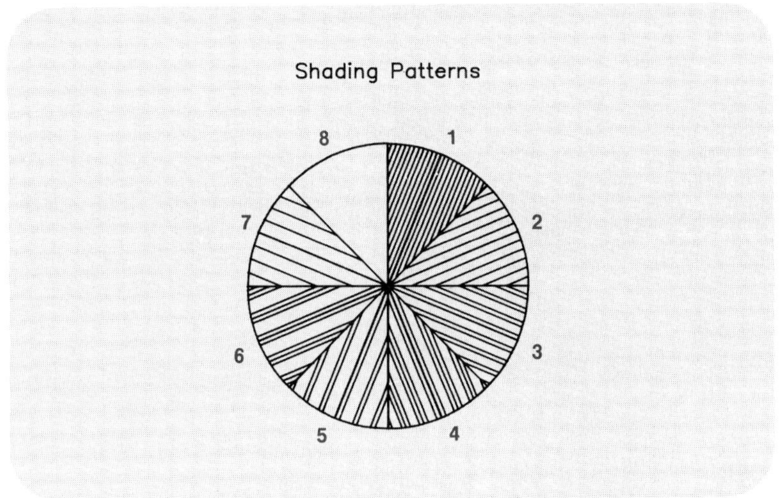

You have to create a new B range in order to add shading patterns to the slices. Since each slice represents one cell in a data range, you specify shading patterns for individual cells. Leave the Graph menu and return to the worksheet. Add values to create the B range.

Press: ESC

Select: Quit

Move to: cell G6

Type: 1 ▼
2 ▼
3 ↵

```
G8: [W20] 3                                                              READY

        B          C          D          E          F            G
 1  Income Statement                                        GROSS-MARGIN
 2  July-1-86  July-31-86                                   NET-SALES
 3                                                          PRODUCTS
 4    PROD.1     PROD.2     PROD.3      TOTAL
 5  ===========================================
 6       $100       $200       $200       $500                          1
 7        $20        $80        $60       $160                          2
 8        $80       $120       $140       $340                          3
 9        $30        $60        $70       $160
10        $50        $60        $70       $180
11        $35        $30        $30        $95
12        $15        $30        $40        $85
13         $1         $2         $2         $5
14         $7        $14        $19        $40
15         $7        $14        $19        $40
16
17        24%        35%        41%       100%
18
19
20
```

Press: [/]

Select: Graph

B

Move to: cell G6

Press: [.]

[▼] *(two times)*

[↵]

Select: View

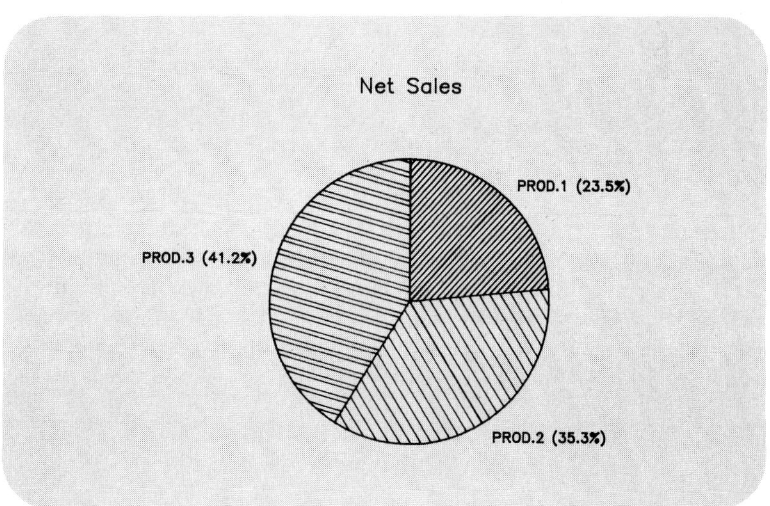

Now change the values on the worksheet and view the new patterns on the pie chart.

Press: [ESC]
Select: Quit
Move to: cell G6
Type: 4 [▼]
5 [▼]
6 [↵]
Press: [/]
Select: Graph
View

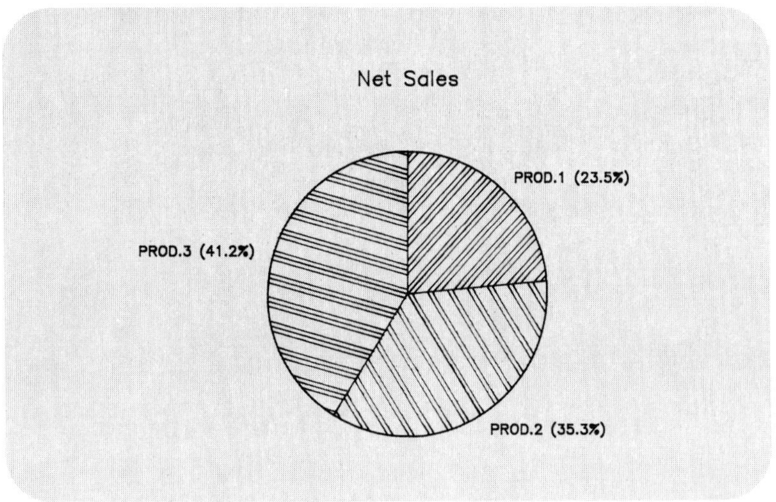

Exploding a Slice of the Pie

You can make one or more slices of a pie chart "explode," or break away, from the pie in order to emphasize a particular value or values. This is done by adding 100 to the shading pattern number entered on the worksheet. For example, to explode the slice defined by the shading pattern number 6, enter 106 on the worksheet. (Adding a value greater than 100 will not cause the slice to move farther away from the chart.)

Explode the pie slice representing Product 1. Then view the chart and return to the menu.

Press: ESC
Select: Quit
Move to: cell G6
Type: 104 ↵

```
G6: [W20] 104                                                        READY

         B          C          D          E          F            G
 1   Income Statement                                         GROSS-MARGIN
 2   July-1-86  July-31-86                                    NET-SALES
 3                                                            PRODUCTS
 4     PROD.1     PROD.2     PROD.3      TOTAL
 5   ==========================================
 6         $100       $200       $200       $500                        104
 7          $20        $80        $60       $160                          5
 8          $80       $120       $140       $340                          6
 9          $30        $60        $70       $160
10          $50        $60        $70       $180
11          $35        $30        $30        $95
12          $15        $30        $40        $85
13           $1         $2         $2         $5
14           $7        $14        $19        $40
15           $7        $14        $19        $40
16
17          24%        35%        41%       100%
18
19
20
```

Press: /
Select: Graph
View

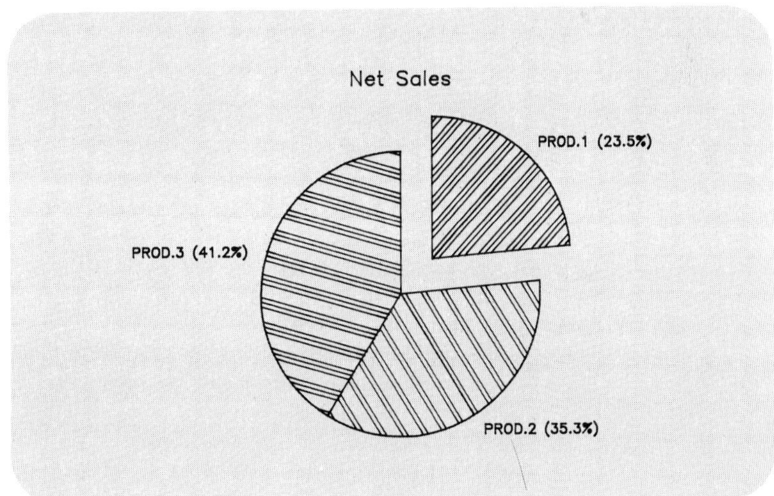

Name and Save the Graph

Again, to save the pie chart you must name it. Use the Name Create command to name the graph PIECHART.

Press: [ESC]
Select: Name
Create
Type: Piechart [↵]

Now save the pie chart in a picture file for later printing. Remember that 1-2-3 adds the extension .PIC automatically.

Select: Save
Type: Piechart [↵]
Select: Quit

Save the File

Now that the pie chart has been created and named, save the INCOME file again.

Press: [/]
Select: File
Save
Press: [↵]
Select: Replace

What-If Graphics

1-2-3 is an integrated program, and its automatic recalculation feature extends to graphs. Change a value on the worksheet, and a graph based on that value reflects the change the next time it is drawn. This feature means that you can create and test what-if scenarios with graphs just as you can with worksheets. You can even save and print what-if graphics (by naming different versions of a graph) and incorporate them in a report or presentation.

To see how changing values on the worksheet affects graphs that have already been created, you are going to change a value on the Income Statement and display the two graphs. Change the Gross Sales for Product 1 from 100 to 80.

Move to: cell B6
Type: 80 [↵]

```
B6: (C0) 80                                                          READY

              A                B          C          D          E
1                              Income Statement
2                              July-1-86  July-31-86
3
4   000's omitted              PROD.1     PROD.2     PROD.3     TOTAL
5   ==================================================================
6   Gross Sales                    $80       $200       $200       $480
7     Sales Allowance              $20        $80        $60       $160
8   Net Sales                      $60       $120       $140       $320
9     Cost of Goods Sold           $30        $60        $70       $160
10  Gross Margin                   $30        $60        $70       $160
11    Marketing/G&A Expenses       $35        $30        $30        $95
12  EBIT                          ($5)        $30        $40        $65
13    Interest                      $1         $2         $2         $5
14    Taxes                         $7        $14        $19        $40
15  Net Income                   ($13)        $14        $19        $20
16
17  % Total Net Sales              19%        38%        44%       100%
18
19
20
```

Notice that other values in the column for Product 1 change. Net Sales changes from 80 to 60 and Gross Margin from 50 to 30. Notice too that Net Income is now in parentheses: ($13). This means that it is a negative value.

When you display the pie chart, notice that the slice representing Net Sales for Product 1 is smaller than before and that the others are proportionately larger.

Press: /

Select: Graph
View

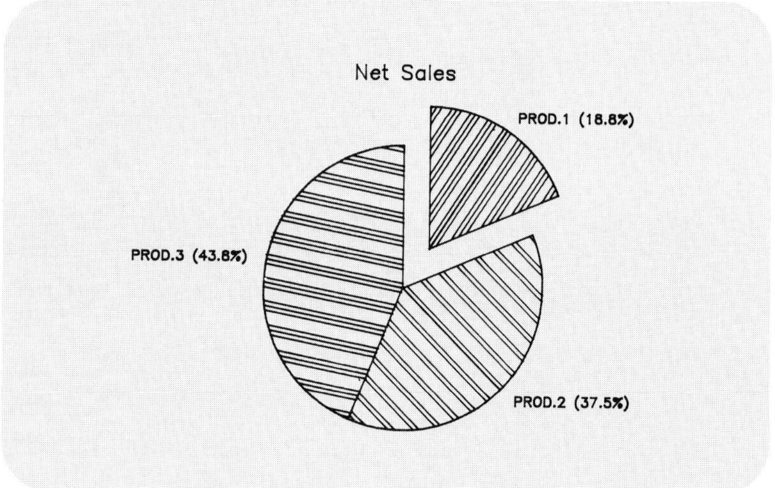

Note: There is another way to display the current graph. Pressing the Graph key calls up the graph most recently viewed—in this case it would be the pie chart. (To see the bar graph you would have to call up the Graph menu and use the Name Use command to select and view it.)

Now display the bar graph to see how the changes made to the worksheet were reflected.

Press: ESC

Select: Name
Use
BARGRAPH

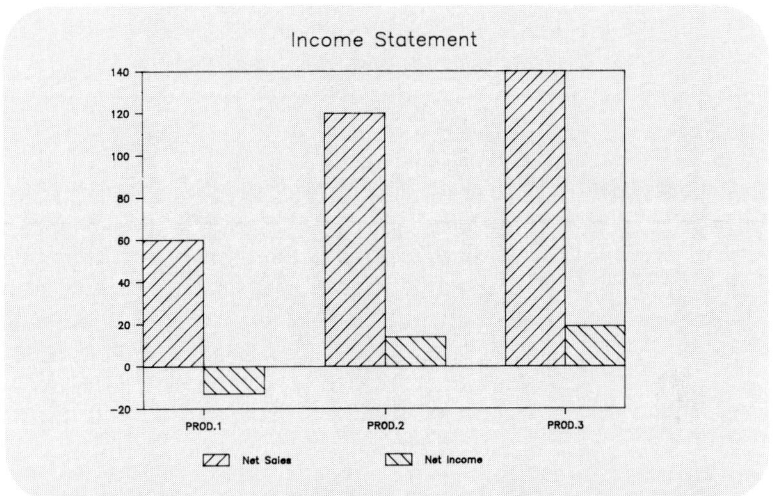

The bar graph shows both Net Sales and Net Income for each product. Both values for Product 1 have been affected by the change in Gross Sales because the formulas on the worksheet for Net Sales and Net Income depend on that value.

Net Income is a negative value; that is, when Gross Sales dips below a certain value, the company loses money on this product. Notice that the bar representing Net Income for Product 1 is below the X axis. 1-2-3 represents negative values on a bar graph in this way. The Y axis also expands to include the value -20, and the increments change from 10 to 20.

Press: ESC

Select: Quit

Printing a Graph

The following section discusses the basic steps for printing the bar graph created in this chapter. Before you start, be sure that your printer supports graphics and that you have run the 1-2-3 Install program for the printer. Finally, check to see that the printer is properly connected to the computer and turned on.

The PrintGraph Program

The 1-2-3 PrintGraph Program, stored on a separate disk, prints graphs created in 1-2-3. Several options in the PrintGraph Program let you enhance the printed version of the graph. For example, the Font setting offers eleven different type styles for titles and labels; the Range Colors setting lets you print the graph in color (if you have the right kind of printer); and the Size setting lets you alter the size and proportion of the graph. You can also define and save hardware settings so that you can print the graph on a variety of printers.

The first step is to exit 1-2-3 (make sure you have saved the final version of the worksheet and picture files first). You start the PrintGraph Program from the 1-2-3 Access menu.

Press: [/]
Select: Quit
Yes

The 1-2-3 Access menu should be on the monitor.

Starting the PrintGraph Program

If you have a computer with two disk drives, remove the 1-2-3 System Disk from drive A and insert the PrintGraph Program Disk. The data disk with the .PIC files should be in drive B. If you have a hard-disk computer, you can leave the disks in place.

Select: PrintGraph *(from the Access menu)*

Note: If you started 1-2-3 by typing *123* and skipping the Access menu, then exit 1-2-3 and type *pgraph* at the DOS prompt. With a hard-disk computer, you must be in the subdirectory in which all the 1-2-3 disks are copied.

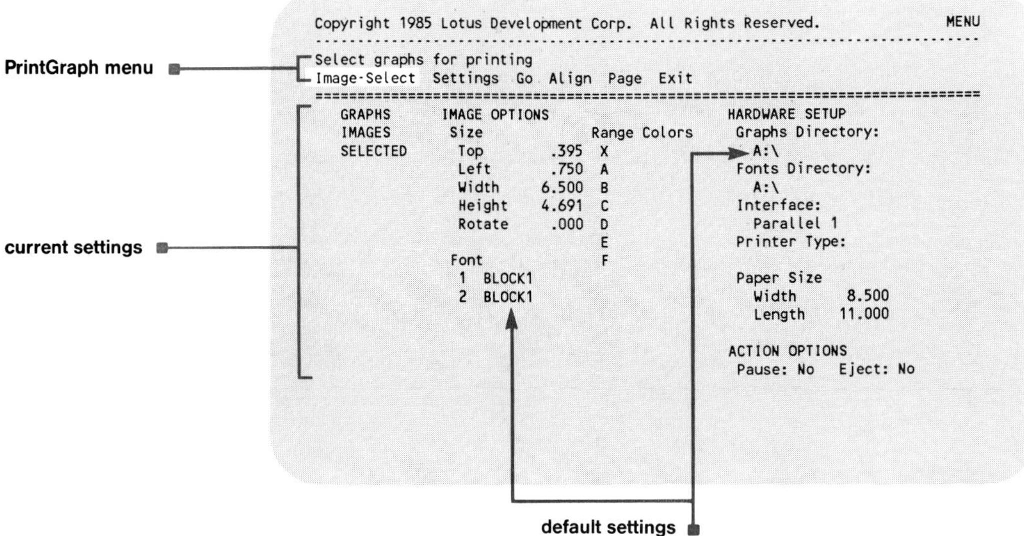

The PrintGraph screen appears. The top line of the screen contains copyright information; the next two lines contain the PrintGraph menu. The main part of the screen contains the current settings of the program.

Notice that some items have default settings. You are going to change the settings to those required to print the bar graph. Begin by calling up the Settings menu.

Select: Settings

```
Copyright 1985 Lotus Development Corp.  All Rights Reserved.                MENU
--------------------------------------------------------------------------------
Specify colors, fonts and size
Image  Hardware  Action  Save  Reset  Quit
================================================================================
   GRAPHS      IMAGE OPTIONS                          HARDWARE SETUP
   IMAGES       Size             Range Colors          Graphs Directory:
   SELECTED      Top        .395  X                      A:\
                 Left       .750  A                     Fonts Directory:
                 Width     6.500  B                      A:\
                 Height    4.691  C                     Interface:
                 Rotate     .000  D                      Parallel 1
                                  E                     Printer Type:
                Font              F
                 1  BLOCK1                              Paper Size
                 2  BLOCK1                               Width      8.500
                                                         Length    11.000

                                                       ACTION OPTIONS
                                                        Pause: No   Eject: No
```

The Settings menu contains the commands which specify hardware requirements, colors, and print style fonts for the graph. First you will enter the hardware specifications.

Hardware Setup

Disk Drive

You have to tell the PrintGraph Program which drive contains the disk where the .PIC files are stored. Use the Hardware Graphs-Directory command to indicate the drive containing the disk. The initial setting is drive A.

Select: Hardware
Graphs-Directory

Press: ESC

Type: B: *(for a computer with two disk drives)*
or
C:\ 123 *(for a hard-disk computer)*

Press: ↵

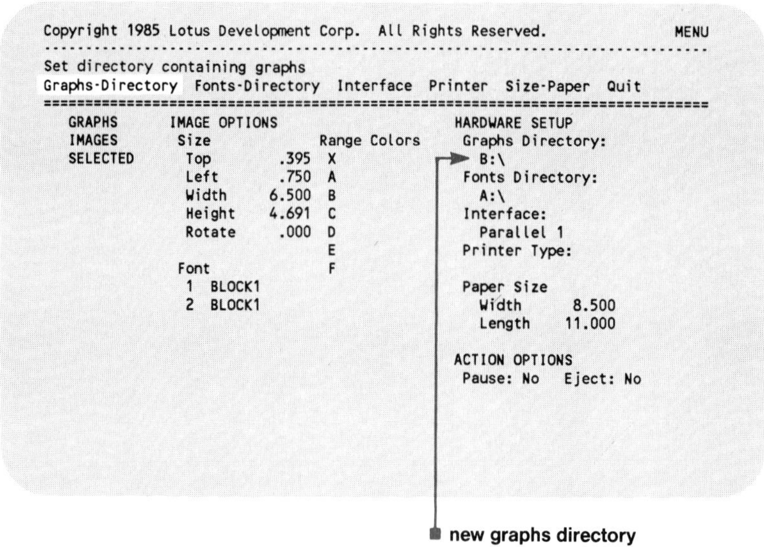

Notice that the new drive setting (Graphs Directory) appears on the right side of the screen under HARDWARE SETUP.

Printer

Use the Printer command to specify the printer you're using. The name of the graphics printer defined in the driver set is entered on the screen. If you defined a number of printers and plotters during the Install procedure, they are also listed.

Along with the list of printers defined in the driver set, you are also given the choice of densities. The density determines how many times the graph, titles, and legends are actually printed over. You should experiment with densities until you are satisfied with the result. Remember that the higher the density, the longer the graph will take to print—but the graph will be darker and easier to read. Use the commands described on the right side of the screen to select the appropriate printer and density.

Select: Printer
The appropriate printer and density

Press: [↵]

Select: Quit *(to return to the Settings menu)*

Font Directory

The Hardware Fonts-Directory command tells the PrintGraph Program where to look for the different font styles available for the titles and labels printed on the graph.

The initial setting is drive A. This is fine for a computer with two disk drives, since the PrintGraph Program Disk is in drive A. However, if you have a hard-disk computer in which the 1-2-3 disks have been copied onto the hard disk, you will have to change the initial setting.

For a hard-disk computer only:

Select: Hardware
Fonts-Directory

Press: [ESC]

Type: c:\subdirectory name *(in which 1-2-3 is copied)*

Press: [↵]

Select: Quit *(to return to the Settings menu)*

Saving Hardware Specifications

Now that you have specified your hardware settings, save them for future use.

Select: Save

Graph Specifications

Selecting the Fonts

The PrintGraph Program offers a variety of fonts for the labels and legends on the graph. The fonts differ in weight, size, and style. The Image command selects the fonts. Font 1 specifies the style of the titles at the top of the graph. Font 2 specifies the style of the graph labels and legends.

Select: Settings
Image
Font
1

A list of font styles appears on the screen. To select one for the title of the graph, you use the special commands listed on the right of the screen.

Press: ▼ *(until the highlight rests on ROMAN1)*
SPACE BAR *(to make the selection)*

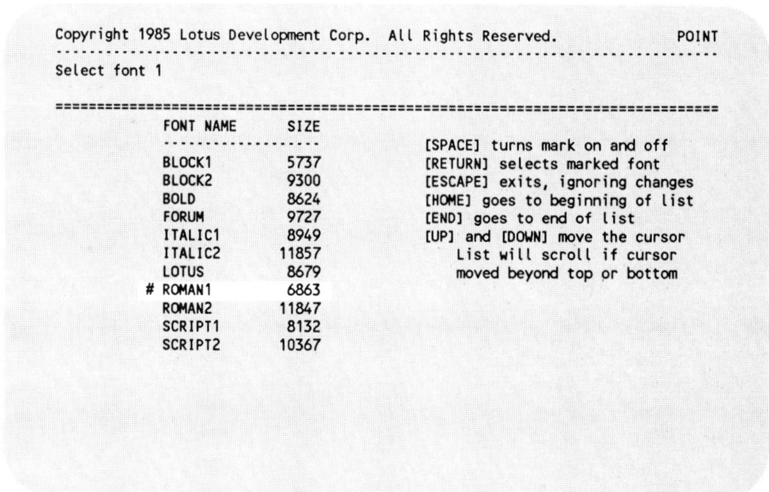

```
Copyright 1985 Lotus Development Corp.  All Rights Reserved.            POINT
-----------------------------------------------------------------------------
Select font 1

=============================================================================
             FONT NAME      SIZE
             ---------------------         [SPACE] turns mark on and off
             BLOCK1         5737           [RETURN] selects marked font
             BLOCK2         9300           [ESCAPE] exits, ignoring changes
             BOLD           8624           [HOME] goes to beginning of list
             FORUM          9727           [END] goes to end of list
             ITALIC1        8949           [UP] and [DOWN] move the cursor
             ITALIC2       11857               List will scroll if cursor
             LOTUS          8679               moved beyond top or bottom
           # ROMAN1         6863
             ROMAN2        11847
             SCRIPT1        8132
             SCRIPT2       10367
```

Notice that the number sign (#) has moved to the highlighted font. This indicates that the font has been selected.

Press: [↵]

Now select the print style for the labels on the graph.

Select: Font
2

Press: [▼] *(until the highlight rests on BLOCK2)*
[SPACE BAR]
[↵]

Select: Quit
Quit

Selecting the Graph

Now that the settings have been specified, you are ready to print the graph. The last step is to select the specific graph you want to print. Use the Image-Select command to select one or more graphs for printing.

Select: Image-Select

```
Copyright 1985 Lotus Development Corp.  All Rights Reserved.            POINT
-----------------------------------------------------------------------------
Select graphs for output

=============================================================================
   PICTURE     DATE     TIME      SIZE
   --------------------------------------     [SPACE] turns mark on and off
   BARGRAPH  12-26-86  11:25      1735        [RETURN] selects marked pictures
   PIECHART  12-26-86  12:30      2105        [ESCAPE] exits, ignoring changes
                                              [HOME] goes to beginning of list
                                              [END] goes to end of list
                                              [UP] and [DOWN] move the cursor
                                                 List will scroll if cursor
                                                 moved beyond top or bottom
                                              [GRAPH] displays selected picture
```

The files BARGRAPH and PIECHART are listed on the screen. The PrintGraph Program also notes the date and time the graphs were saved, as well as the size of each file.

Move to: BARGRAPH

Press: [SPACE BAR]

To get a preview of how the graph will look when printed, press the Graph key. The graph appears on the screen exactly as it will appear when printed—the increments on the Y axis will be the same, the titles will be in the correct proportion, and so on.

Press: ↵

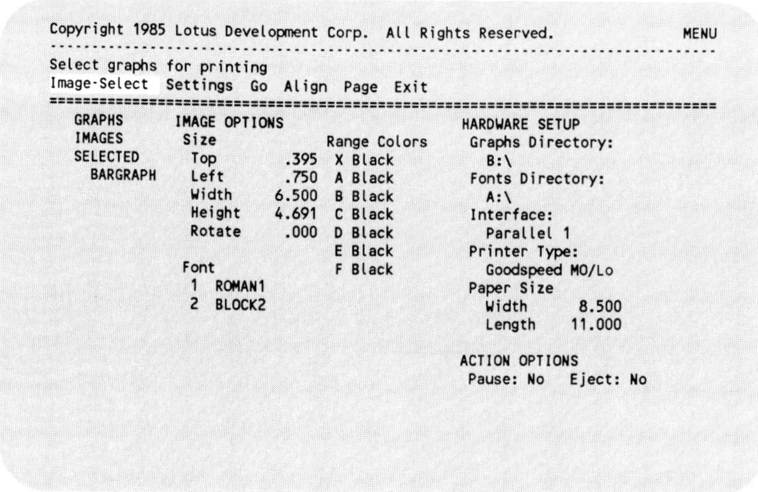

Printing the Graph

Now you can print the graph. Before you start, make sure the printer is turned on and the paper is aligned at the top of the page. Select Align before printing to tell 1-2-3 where the top edge of the paper starts.

Select: Align
Go

WAIT flashes in the mode indicator, and the following messages appear on the screen as 1-2-3 prepares the file for printing:

Loading Font: A: Roman 1
Loading Font: A: Block 2
Loading Picture: B: BARGRAPH
Generating Picture B: BARGRAPH

It takes a few moments for 1-2-3 to print the graph.

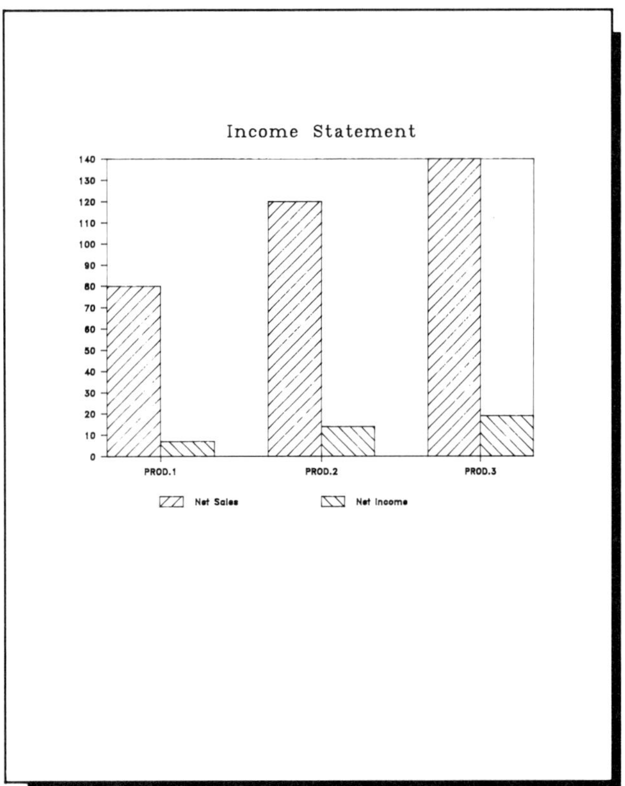
Income Statement
140
130
120
110
100
90
80
70
60
50
40
30
20
10
0
PROD.1
PROD.2
PROD.3
Net Sales
Net Income

Graph Menu Command Structure

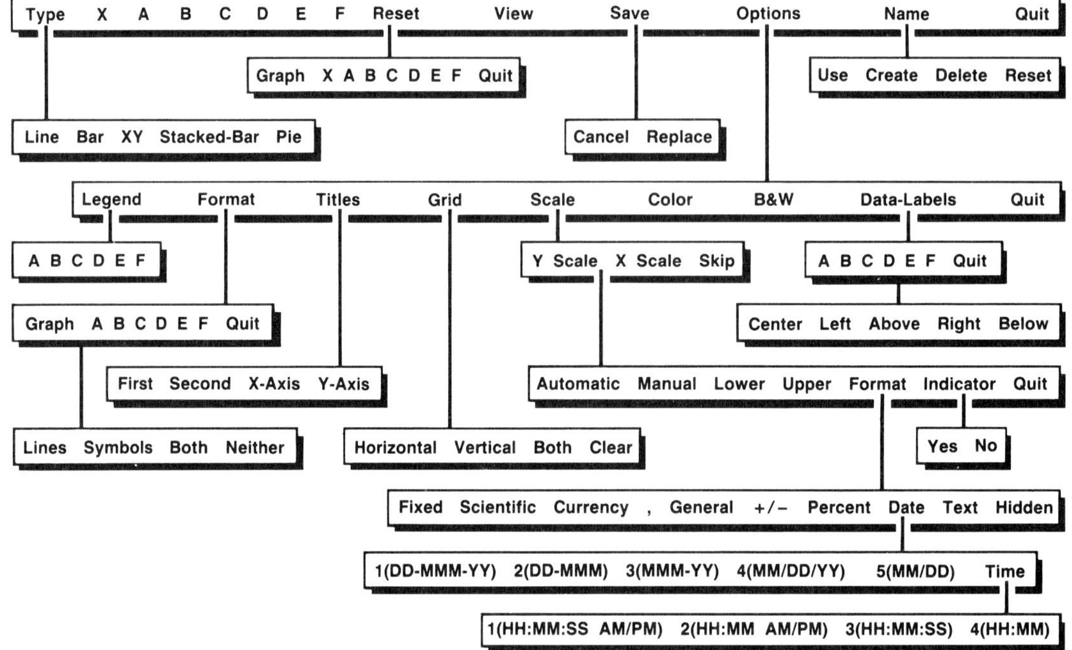

PrintGraph Menu Command Structure

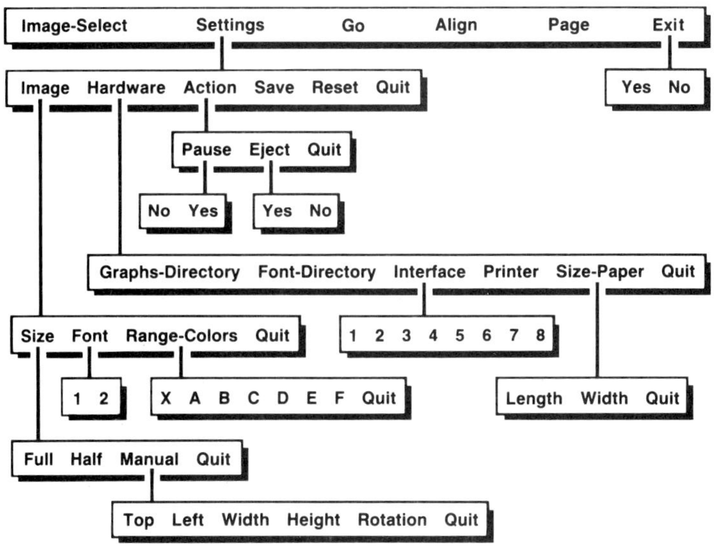

5

Cam
Bro
Bos
323-1231
221-2332
232-3121
123-1231
221-2312
Doe J
Doe Jane
Doe Joan
Doe John
Doe John
Doe John
Doe John
Doe John
Doe John
First St
Third Av

Database

A database is a collection of the same items of information about a group of people, places, or things. The information is divided into categories with the same format for each entry. A telephone book is an example of a simple database. It has separate categories for the same information for each person listed: name, address, and telephone number.

The most useful aspect of a database is its ability to hold and organize large amounts of information, or data, and to make any item of information immediately accessible. A database can expand or contract as necessary. The advantages of the electronic database for maintaining and manipulating data are immediately obvious. New entries can be added or old ones removed with instantaneous adjustment. The basic form itself can be adapted to add or remove specific categories of information.

The individual categories of information in the 1-2-3 database are called fields. The complete set of information contained in the fields for one entry constitute a record. In the phone book database, for example, the name, address, and number categories are the fields; each set for each person listed is a record.

The 1-2-3 Database

The 1-2-3 database is such a collection, or file, of records. However, since it is entered on the worksheet, it offers many advantages over the traditional database. You can perform mathematical calculations with data records and manipulate the records with the following operations:

Sort — Rearranges the order of records by any one of the fields, in alphabetical, numeric, or chronological order. This increases your ability to find a record. For example, if the phone book were a computerized database, you could sort the list according to name, address and/or phone number. This flexibility would allow you to find a record based on information from only one of those fields.

Query — Locates specific records in the database by matching criteria that you set up. This saves time and effort. You can ask 1-2-3 to find and extract all the records for those people who live on Hickory Lane, and 1-2-3 will instantly copy those records to a designated area on the worksheet.

The following illustration shows how a phone book looks in the 1-2-3 worksheet.

```
A1: [W13]                                                          READY

          A            B             C                    D           E
1                            Phone List
2
3     Last Name    First Name     Street Address         Town     Phone Number
4   Forbes        Barbara      35 Harvard Avenue      Brookline    566-2122
5   Forbes        Dana         245 Howe Avenue        Brighton     782-0113
6   Forbis        Livingston   1360 W Selam Road      Dorchester   265-7749
7   Forcelari     Bill         33 Washington Street   Boston       669-0643
8   Forcelledo    Michele H    19 Boman Street        Boston       266-6312
9   Forcelledo    Paul         2-1/2 Kensey Street    Brookline    277-1573
10  Forcier       Murray, Jr   1450 Westgate Street   Cambridge    492-6972
11  Forcina       Marie        82 Wendell Street      Boston       567-4173
12  Ford          M Sasha      132 E Lake Street      Somerville   623-5827
13  Ford          Norton       61 Thurston Street     Boston       826-3518
14  Ford          Sheila       3526 Lynnway Avenue    Brighton     276-6510
15  Ford          Walter       72 Hemingway Street    Boston       566-7699
16  Forde         Guy David    8190 Keno Street       Brookline    275-2571
17  Forelli       Lisa         94 Allston Street      Cambridge    943-1123
18  Foreman       Leroy        79 Walnut Street       Arlington    623-5270
19  Forester      Bruce        26 Granite Street      Somerville   726-2516
20  Fornar        Jim W        8 San Francisco Street Watertown    926-6574
```

Before You Start

For a computer with two disk drives:

- 1-2-3 should be set up to save files on a disk in drive B. (See Chapter 1, page 9.)
- The data disk should be in drive B.
- The Program Disk should be in drive A.

For a hard-disk computer:

- 1-2-3 should be set up to save files in the root directory or in a subdirectory. (See Chapter 1, page 11.)
- All the 1-2-3 disks should be copied in the root directory or in their own subdirectory on the hard disk.

Creating a Database

A 1-2-3 database is created in the 1-2-3 worksheet work environment. The database uses the column-row structure of the worksheet to store information. When creating a database, you use the basic worksheet keys to move around and enter data. Labels, or text entries, and values are treated the same way they are in the worksheet. (Refer to the Worksheet chapter for basic information on movement keys and cell entries.)

A 1-2-3 database contains one or more columns and at least two rows. The columns are called **fields**; they contain separate types of information for each entry. The first row contains **field names.** They identify the kind of information stored in each column. The subsequent rows are called **records** and contain the actual data. All the information in one row is included in a single record; the cells are linked and processed together as a unit.

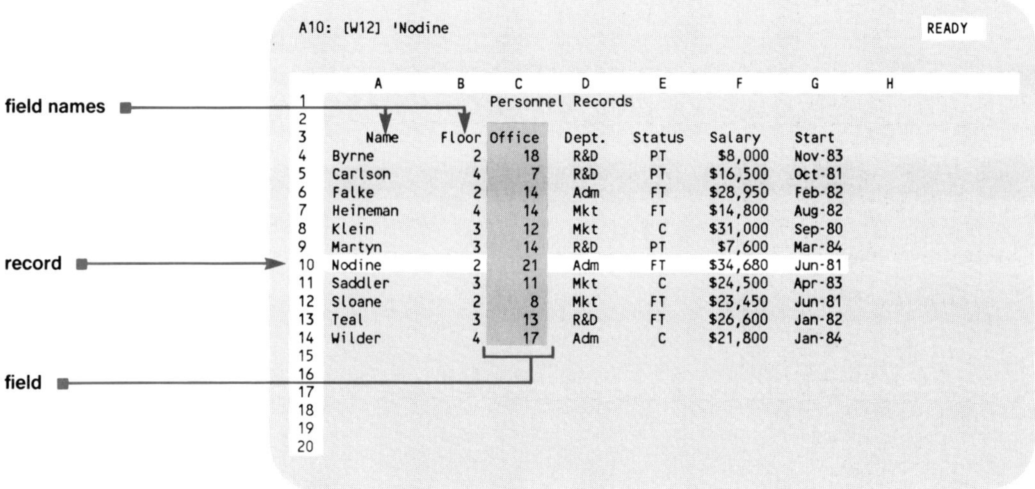

All database operations are carried out with the commands on the Data menu.

Data Menu

```
D4:                                                              MENU
Fill  Table  Sort  Query  Distribution  Matrix  Regression  Parse
Fill a range with numbers
         A         B      C      D       E        F       G       H
1
2
3
4
```

In this chapter you will build and refine a database. Then you will edit and sort the data records. Finally, you will find and extract data records.

Clear the Screen

Before you start, make sure the screen displays an empty worksheet. Take care to save any information on the screen that you might want later. When the blank worksheet displays, the mode indicator in the upper-right corner of the screen reads READY.

Press: [/]

Select: Worksheet
Erase
Yes

Entering Field Names

The first row of information in a 1-2-3 database always contains labels that serve as field names identifying the contents of each column. These field names are necessary for several of the database commands. There are two important guidelines concerning field names. First, no two fields can have the same name. Second, no blank spaces can be put at the beginning or end of a field name (1-2-3 reads the space as part of the name).

The first step is to enter the title of the database in the top row of the worksheet.

Move to: cell C1

Type: Personnel Records [↵]

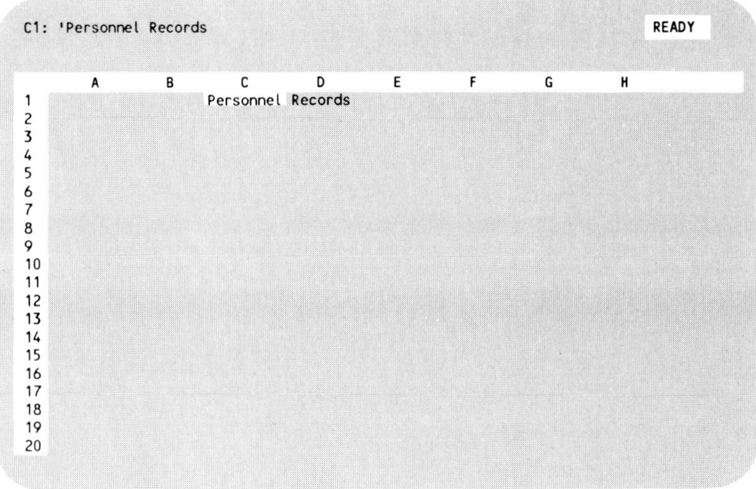

Next you will enter the field names. This example includes seven fields, each containing a different piece of information about the personnel.

Move to: cell A3

Type: Name ▶
Floor ▶
Office ▶
Dept. ▶
Status ▶
Salary ▶
Start ↵

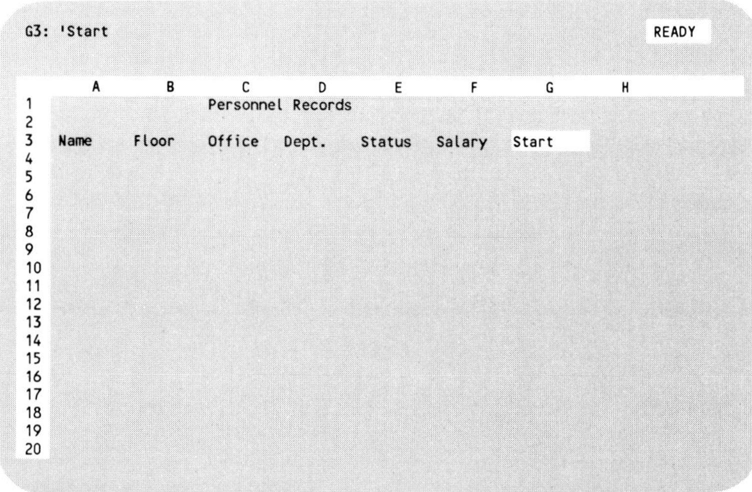

Entering Data Records

The first row of data in a database is always entered directly below the row containing the field names. Do not leave a blank line between the two rows because it can throw off certain operations. The 1-2-3 worksheet contains 256 columns, and all of them can be used in a database. Several of the database commands, however, can only address a maximum of 32 fields.

All the entries across a data row are included as part of the record. 1-2-3 treats all the cells as part of the same unit: they are moved and manipulated as a single record. A field can contain any kind of information that can be entered on a worksheet (labels, values, and formulas). The fields include all three types of entries in this example.

Enter the first data record.

Move to: cell A4

Type: Sloane [▶]
2 [▶]
8 [▶]
Mkt [▶]
FT [▶]
23450 [↵]

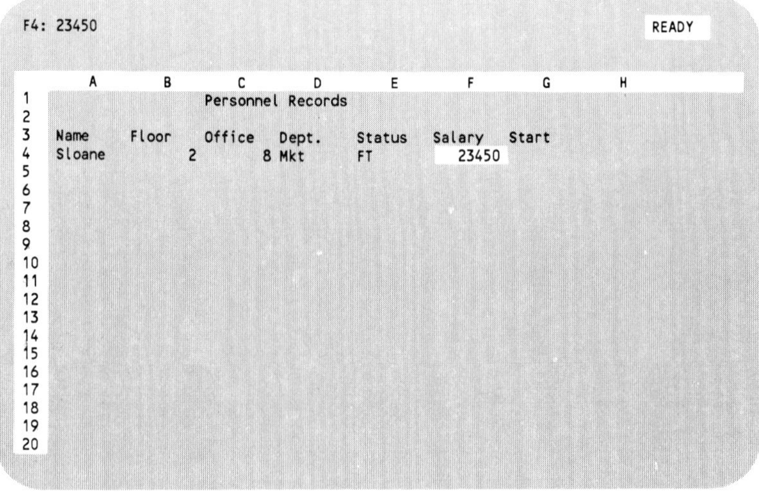

The last figure you entered is a salary. Notice that it appears on the screen exactly as you type it. This is because the cell is unformatted and not in currency format. You are going to format the cell to display its contents as currency. 1-2-3 adds both a dollar sign and a comma between the thousands. Follow the prompts to specify no decimal places and to format only one cell.

Move to: cell F4
Press: [/]
Select: Range
Format
Currency
Type: 0 [↵] *(to specify no decimal places)*
Press: [↵] *(to format only this cell)*

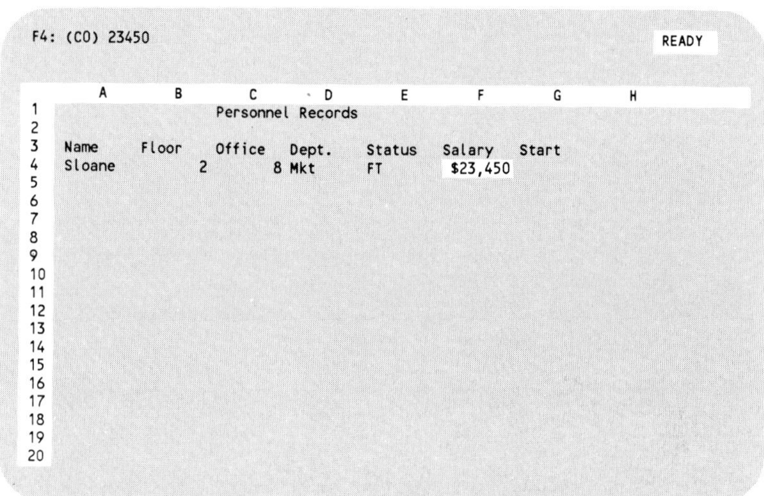

Entering Dates

The final field in the data record contains a date. A date is entered using the @DATE function. 1-2-3 actually stores dates as values (based on the number of days since the beginning of the century). The date formats translate the value into any of five standard forms that can include the day, the month, and/or the year.

After specifying the @DATE function, you enter the date using numbers to refer to the year, month, and day. 1-2-3 translates the date into a value; you then format the value to display as a date with one of 1-2-3's date formats.

Enter the @DATE function for June 4, 1981.

Move to: cell G4

Type: @date(81,6,4) [↵]

```
G4: @DATE(81,6,4)                                                   READY

         A         B         C         D         E         F         G         H
1                            Personnel Records
2
3    Name      Floor     Office    Dept.     Status    Salary    Start
4    Sloane            2         8 Mkt       FT          $23,450     29741
5
6
7
8
9
10
11
12
13
14
15
16
17
18
19
20
```

The cell displays the value 29741. Next use the Range Format Date command to display the cell contents as a date.

Press: [/]

Select: Range
Format
Date

The five options for date formats appear on the second line of the control panel. You should choose a format based on what kind of information you want to include (year, month, and/or day). Some date formats are longer than others and will require you to adjust the column width. You are going to use the third format. The second line of the control panel reads 3 (MMM-YY); this means three letters for the month, a hyphen, and two numbers for the year (Jun-81).

Select: 3 (MMM-YY)

Press: ↵

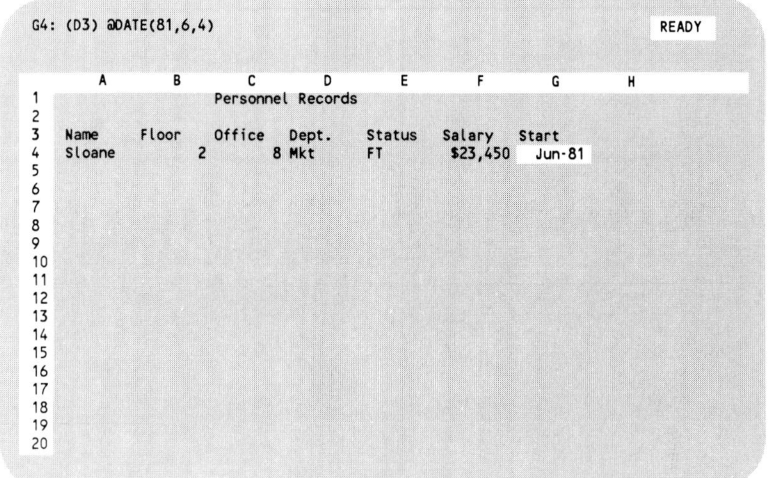

Refining the Appearance of the Database

The physical appearance of the database is important. It must be easy to read for you or anyone else who might work with it. Now that you've built the basic structure and entered one record, refine the database so that it is easier to read.

Centering Field Names

The 1-2-3 default setting aligns labels entered in the worksheet on the left side of the cell and values on the right. See how the appearance is improved by centering the field names.

Move to: cell A3

Press: [/]

Select: Range
Label
Center

Press: [▶] *(six times to highlight the range A3..G3)*
[↵]

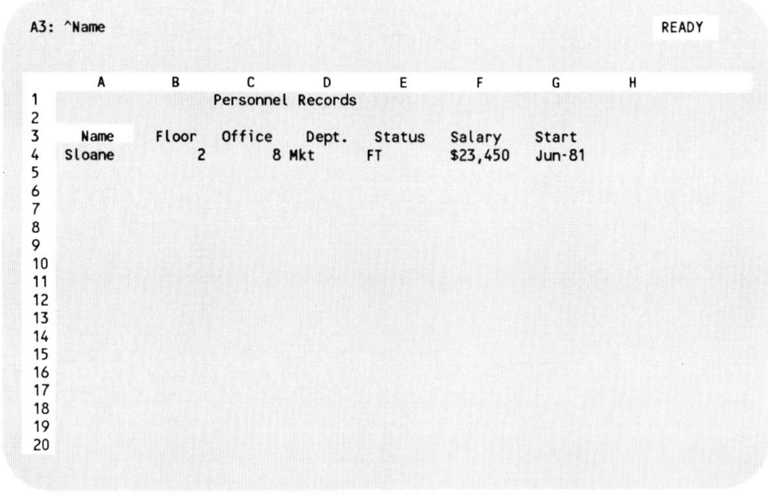

The field names are centered in the cells. If you place the pointer on a cell in the row and look in the first line of the control panel, you'll see that the labels are now preceded by a caret (^) — the centered label prefix.

Changing Column Widths

The worksheet initial setting for column width is nine characters. While this has been sufficient to accommodate the data entered so far, it makes sense to alter some of the columns to fit the data better. The first step is to widen column A to accommodate the names.

Move to: cell A4
Press: [/]
Select: Worksheet
Column
Set-Width
Press: [▶] *(three times to specify a width of 12)*

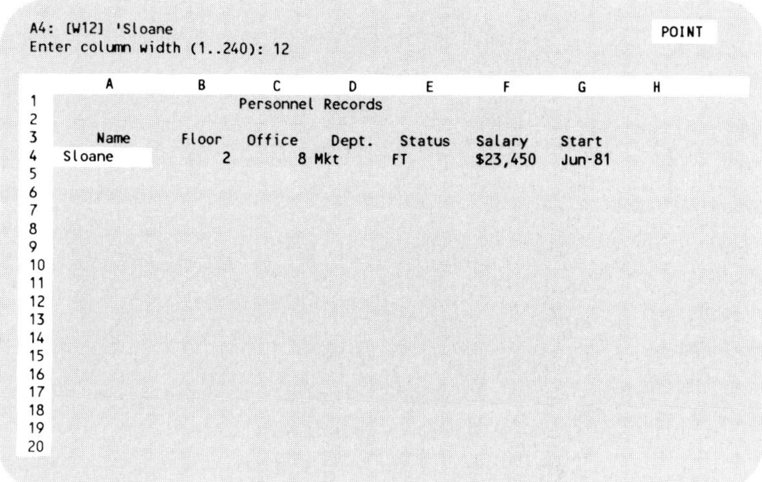
A4: [W12] 'Sloane
Enter column width (1..240): 12

POINT

	A	B	C	D	E	F	G	H
1			Personnel Records					
2								
3	Name	Floor	Office	Dept.	Status	Salary	Start	
4	Sloane	2	8	Mkt	FT	$23,450	Jun-81	
5								
6								
7								
8								
9								
10								
11								
12								
13								
14								
15								
16								
17								
18								
19								
20								

Press: [↵]

Now decrease the width of columns B and C to seven.

Move to: cell B4
Press: [/]
Select: Worksheet
Column
Set-Width
Press: [◀] *(two times)*
[↵]

Move to cell C4 and repeat this procedure, making the column seven characters wide.

```
C4: [W7] 8                                                   READY

        A          B      C       D         E          F          G          H
1                        Personnel Records
2
3       Name       Floor Office  Dept.     Status     Salary     Start
4   Sloane             2       8 Mkt       FT         $23,450    Jun-81
5
6
7
8
9
10
11
12
13
14
15
16
17
18
19
20
```

Formatting Columns

You've entered and formatted data in columns F and G to display entries in currency and date format respectively. You can format both columns so that future entries will be formatted in the same way.

Move to: cell F4

Press: [/]

Select: Range
Format
Currency

Type: 0 [↵]

Press: [▼] *(ten times to highlight the range F4..F14)*

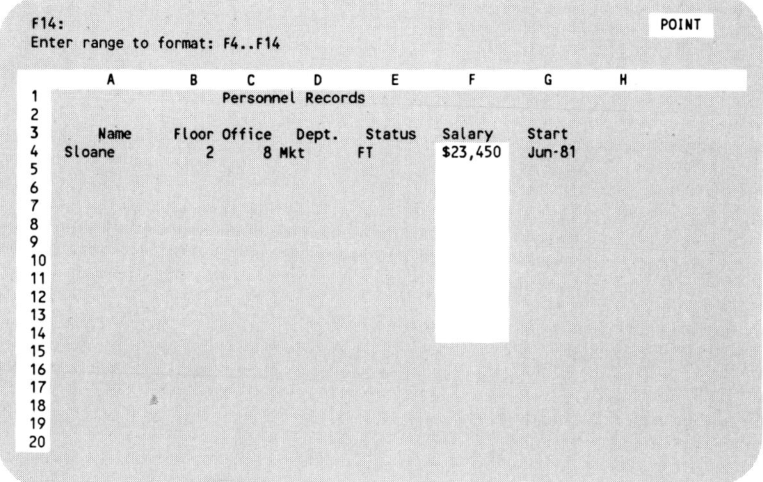

Press: [↵]

Now format column G to display dates.

Move to: cell G4

Press: [/]

Select: Range
Format
Date
3 (MMM-YY)

Press: [▼] *(ten times to highlight the range G4..G14)*
[↵]

Columns F and G are now formatted to display their contents as currency and dates, respectively. Now all entries made in either of those columns will appear in the appropriate form.

Entering Remaining Data Records

Now that the database has been set up, refined, and formatted, you can enter the remaining data records. Enter the data as shown in the screen illustrated below. Be careful to enter the dates in column G using the @DATE function: @DATE(YY,MM,DD). Notice that you must include a day of the month in the function even though it will not display with the format you're using.

```
G13: (D3) @DATE(81,6,4)                                          READY

        A          B     C       D        E         F        G        H
1                        Personnel Records
2
3         Name     Floor Office   Dept.   Status    Salary    Start
4    Sloane            2      8 Mkt       FT       $23,450   Jun-81
5    Byrne             2     18 R&D       PT        $8,000   Nov-83
6    Falke             2     14 Adm       FT       $28,950   Feb-82
7    Teal              3     13 R&D       FT       $26,600   Jan-82
8    Martyn            3     14 R&D       PT        $7,600   Mar-84
9    Heineman          4     14 Mkt       FT       $14,800   Aug-82
10   Carlson           4      7 R&D       PT       $16,500   Oct-81
11   Wilder            4     17 Adm       C        $21,800   Jan-84
12   Klein             3     12 Mkt       C        $31,000   Sep-80
13   Nodine            2     21 Adm       FT       $34,680   Jun-81
14
15
16
17
18
19
20
```

Centering Labels

As a final step in refining the appearance of the database, center the labels in columns D and E. (You cannot format a range to center the labels until all the labels have actually been entered.)

Move to: cell D4

Press: [/]

Select: Range
Label
Center

Press: [▶]
[▼] *(nine times to highlight the range D4..E13)*
[↵]

D4: ^Mkt READY

	A	B	C	D	E	F	G	H
1			Personnel Records					
2								
3	Name	Floor	Office	Dept.	Status	Salary	Start	
4	Sloane	2	8	Mkt	FT	$23,450	Jun-81	
5	Byrne	2	18	R&D	PT	$8,000	Nov-83	
6	Falke	2	14	Adm	FT	$28,950	Feb-82	
7	Teal	3	13	R&D	FT	$26,600	Jan-82	
8	Martyn	3	14	R&D	PT	$7,600	Mar-84	
9	Heineman	4	14	Mkt	FT	$14,800	Aug-82	
10	Carlson	4	7	R&D	PT	$16,500	Oct-81	
11	Wilder	4	17	Adm	C	$21,800	Jan-84	
12	Klein	3	12	Mkt	C	$31,000	Sep-80	
13	Nodine	2	21	Adm	FT	$34,680	Jun-81	
14								
15								
16								
17								
18								
19								
20								

Save the File

Now that the database is complete, save the file. Since this is the first time you have saved the file, you will have to give it a name: name it DATABASE.

Press: [/]

Select: File
Save

Type: Database [↵]

Sorting Database Records

When you first set up a database, records are listed in the order in which you enter them. The 1-2-3 sorting facility enables you to change the order. There are three types of sorting processes, or sorts: alphabetical, numeric, and chronological. Each sort is according to one or two of the fields in the database. And each sort can be done in either ascending or descending order.

You could, for example, sort the database in ascending order according to the Name field. Since this is a label field, the sort will be alphabetical—from the first record in the alphabet (Byrne) to the last (Wilder). Or you could do a descending sort by the Salary field. Since this is a value field, the first record would be for the person with the highest salary and the last record for the person with the lowest.

The commands used for sorting are found on the Data menu. Sorting is a two-step process: (1) specify the range that contains the data records you want sorted, and (2) choose the field(s) on which you want the sort based. In the next few steps you will sort the database you just created.

Identifying the Data Range

The range of cells containing the data records to be sorted is called the **data range.** There are two things to remember when specifying the data range. First, be sure to include only cells that contain data records. Be especially careful not to include the field name row. Second, you do not have to include the entire database in a sort. You can sort portions if you prefer.

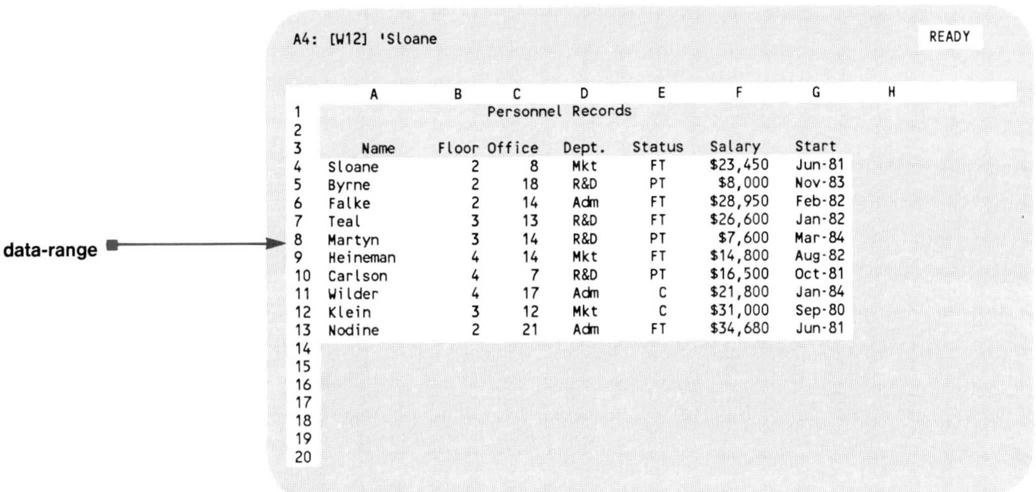

A4: [W12] 'Sloane READY

	A	B	C	D	E	F	G	H
1			Personnel Records					
2								
3	Name	Floor	Office	Dept.	Status	Salary	Start	
4	Sloane	2	8	Mkt	FT	$23,450	Jun-81	
5	Byrne	2	18	R&D	PT	$8,000	Nov-83	
6	Falke	2	14	Adm	FT	$28,950	Feb-82	
7	Teal	3	13	R&D	FT	$26,600	Jan-82	
8	Martyn	3	14	R&D	PT	$7,600	Mar-84	
9	Heineman	4	14	Mkt	FT	$14,800	Aug-82	
10	Carlson	4	7	R&D	PT	$16,500	Oct-81	
11	Wilder	4	17	Adm	C	$21,800	Jan-84	
12	Klein	3	12	Mkt	C	$31,000	Sep-80	
13	Nodine	2	21	Adm	FT	$34,680	Jun-81	
14								
15								
16								
17								
18								
19								
20								

All the database commands are on the Data menu. Call it up and identify the data range. You are going to include all the data records in rows 4 through 13.

Move to: cell A4

Press: [/]

Select: Data

Sort

Data-Range

Press: [.]

[▼] *(nine times to expand the highlight to row 13)*

[▶] *(six times to highlight the range A4..G13)*

G13: (D3) @DATE(81,6,4) POINT

Enter Data-Range: A4..G13

	A	B	C	D	E	F	G	H
1			Personnel Records					
2								
3	Name	Floor	Office	Dept.	Status	Salary	Start	
4	Sloane	2	8	Mkt	FT	$23,450	Jun-81	
5	Byrne	2	18	R&D	PT	$8,000	Nov-83	
6	Falke	2	14	Adm	FT	$28,950	Feb-82	
7	Teal	3	13	R&D	FT	$26,600	Jan-82	
8	Martyn	3	14	R&D	PT	$7,600	Mar-84	
9	Heineman	4	14	Mkt	FT	$14,800	Aug-82	
10	Carlson	4	7	R&D	PT	$16,500	Oct-81	
11	Wilder	4	17	Adm	C	$21,800	Jan-84	
12	Klein	3	12	Mkt	C	$31,000	Sep-80	
13	Nodine	2	21	Adm	FT	$34,680	Jun-81	
14								
15								
16								
17								
18								
19								
20								

The Data menu will not disappear after a command has been completed. (You have to select Quit to exit the menu.)

Press: ↵

Sort Keys

When 1-2-3 sorts a database, it needs to know which field or fields to base the sort on. The sort keys specify this. Use the Primary-Key command for the main sort; it sorts the entire database. For a secondary sort, use the Secondary-Key; it sorts records too closely matched for Primary-Key to distinguish.

For example, sorting the personnel records by Status groups them according to employment status. Those people who have the same status (such as those who work full-time and have FT in the Status field) require further differentiation. The Secondary-Key command can be used to sort them alphabetically.

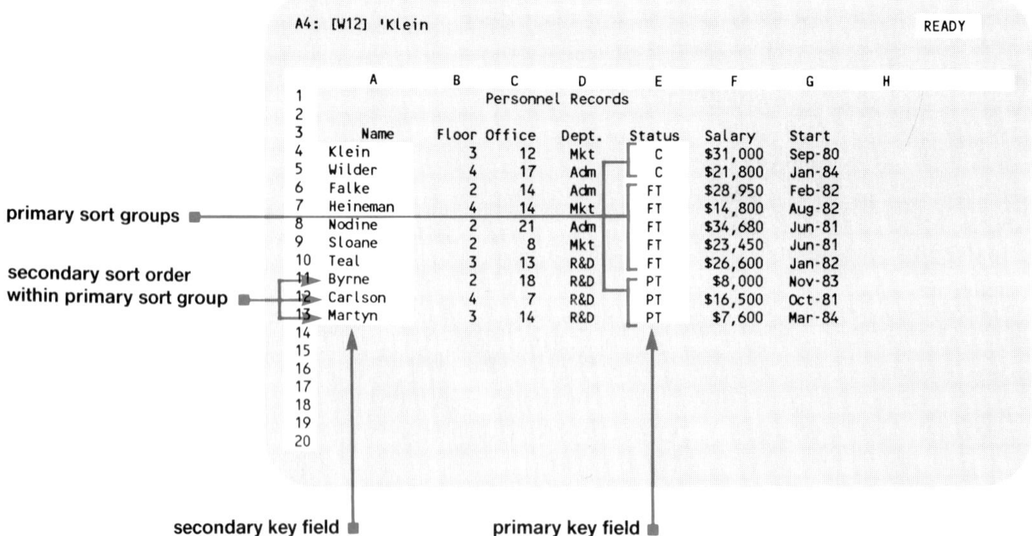

The database in this example is small enough to require only one sort key for most sorts. You are going to sort by the Name field in ascending alphabetical order.

When you select Primary-Key, a prompt on the control panel will read `Primary sort key: A4`. Locating the pointer in this cell tells 1-2-3 to sort by the Name field. A second prompt then asks you to specify ascending or descending order. Finally, you select Go to activate the sort.

Select: Primary-Key

Press: ↵ *(to accept A4)*

Type: A

```
A4: [W12] 'Sloane                                                    EDIT
Primary sort key : A4                    Sort order (A or D): A

          A         B     C      D      E       F         G        H
1                     Personnel Records
2
3        Name      Floor Office  Dept.  Status  Salary    Start
4    Sloane            2      8   Mkt     FT    $23,450   Jun-81
5    Byrne             2     18   R&D     PT     $8,000   Nov-83
6    Falke             2     14   Adm     FT    $28,950   Feb-82
7    Teal              3     13   R&D     FT    $26,600   Jan-82
8    Martyn            3     14   R&D     PT     $7,600   Mar-84
9    Heineman          4     14   Mkt     FT    $14,800   Aug-82
10   Carlson           4      7   R&D     PT    $16,500   Oct-81
11   Wilder            4     17   Adm      C    $21,800   Jan-84
12   Klein             3     12   Mkt      C    $31,000   Sep-80
13   Nodine            2     21   Adm     FT    $34,680   Jun-81
14
15
16
17
18
19
20
```

Press: ↵

Select: Go

The database is now in alphabetical order and the Data menu is gone from the screen.

```
A4: [W12] 'Byrne                                                     READY

          A         B     C      D      E       F         G        H
1                     Personnel Records
2
3        Name      Floor Office  Dept.  Status  Salary    Start
4    Byrne             2     18   R&D     PT     $8,000   Nov-83
5    Carlson           4      7   R&D     PT    $16,500   Oct-81
6    Falke             2     14   Adm     FT    $28,950   Feb-82
7    Heineman          4     14   Mkt     FT    $14,800   Aug-82
8    Klein             3     12   Mkt      C    $31,000   Sep-80
9    Martyn            3     14   R&D     PT     $7,600   Mar-84
10   Nodine            2     21   Adm     FT    $34,680   Jun-81
11   Sloane            2      8   Mkt     FT    $23,450   Jun-81
12   Teal              3     13   R&D     FT    $26,600   Jan-82
13   Wilder            4     17   Adm      C    $21,800   Jan-84
14
15
16
17
18
19
20
```

Try sorting the database again, this time using Salary as the sort key. Notice that you do not need to specify the data range again; 1-2-3 remembers and offers the last range you specified. Put the list in descending order.

Press: [/]
Select: Data
Sort
Primary-Key
Move to: cell F4
Press: [↵]
Type: D [↵]
Select: Go

A4: [W12] 'Nodine READY

	A	B	C	D	E	F	G	H
1			Personnel	Records				
2								
3	Name	Floor	Office	Dept.	Status	Salary	Start	
4	Nodine	2	21	Adm	FT	$34,680	Jun-81	
5	Klein	3	12	Mkt	C	$31,000	Sep-80	
6	Falke	2	14	Adm	FT	$28,950	Feb-82	
7	Teal	3	13	R&D	FT	$26,600	Jan-82	
8	Sloane	2	8	Mkt	FT	$23,450	Jun-81	
9	Wilder	4	17	Adm	C	$21,800	Jan-84	
10	Carlson	4	7	R&D	PT	$16,500	Oct-81	
11	Heineman	4	14	Mkt	FT	$14,800	Aug-82	
12	Byrne	2	18	R&D	PT	$8,000	Nov-83	
13	Martyn	3	14	R&D	PT	$7,600	Mar-84	
14								
15								
16								
17								
18								
19								
20								

Adding a Record

The entire database is now sorted according to the salary field, in descending order. From now on, however, any new data record you add needs to be incorporated into the database in the proper location. You can do this easily with the 1-2-3 database. Simply enter the record at the end of the database, redefine the data range to include that row, and sort the list.

First, enter a new record in row 14.

Move to: cell A14

Type: Saddler [→]

3 [→]

11 [→]

Mkt [→]

C [→]

24500 [→]

@date(83,4,4) [↵]

Center the labels in columns D and E.

```
D14: ^Mkt                                                          READY

        A         B      C       D        E         F         G         H
 1                    Personnel Records
 2
 3      Name      Floor Office  Dept.   Status    Salary    Start
 4   Nodine           2     21   Adm      FT     $34,680   Jun-81
 5   Klein            3     12   Mkt       C     $31,000   Sep-80
 6   Falke            2     14   Adm      FT     $28,950   Feb-82
 7   Teal             3     13   R&D      FT     $26,600   Jan-82
 8   Sloane           2      8   Mkt      FT     $23,450   Jun-81
 9   Wilder           4     17   Adm       C     $21,800   Jan-84
10   Carlson          4      7   R&D      PT     $16,500   Oct-81
11   Heineman         4     14   Mkt      FT     $14,800   Aug-82
12   Byrne            2     18   R&D      PT      $8,000   Nov-83
13   Martyn           3     14   R&D      PT      $7,600   Mar-84
14   Saddler          3     11   Mkt       C     $24,500   Apr-83
15
16
17
18
19
20
```

Redefine the data range to include the new record. Again you'll notice that 1-2-3 offers the data range that you specified in the last sort. This time you'll amend it to extend the range down one row.

Press: [/]

Select: Data
Sort
Data-Range

Press: [▼]

```
G14: (D3) @DATE(83,4,4)                                              POINT
Enter Data-Range: A4..G14

         A           B     C       D        E        F         G        H
1                          Personnel Records
2
3        Name        Floor Office  Dept.   Status   Salary    Start
4   Nodine              2     21    Adm      FT    $34,680   Jun-81
5   Klein               3     12    Mkt      C     $31,000   Sep-80
6   Falke               2     14    Adm      FT    $28,950   Feb-82
7   Teal                3     13    R&D      FT    $26,600   Jan-82
8   Sloane              2      8    Mkt      FT    $23,450   Jun-81
9   Wilder              4     17    Adm      C     $21,800   Jan-84
10  Carlson             4      7    R&D      PT    $16,500   Oct-81
11  Heineman            4     14    Mkt      FT    $14,800   Aug-82
12  Byrne               2     18    R&D      PT     $8,000   Nov-83
13  Martyn              3     14    R&D      PT     $7,600   Mar-84
14  Saddler             3     11    Mkt      C     $24,500   Apr-83
15
16
17
18
19
20
```

Press: [↵]

The Sort menu remains on the screen. Notice that 1-2-3 also remembers the most recent specification entered for the primary key. Since you are simply resorting according to the same criterion, you do not need to specify a new primary key.

Select: Go

```
A4: [W12] 'Nodine                                                    READY

       A          B     C       D        E         F          G         H
1                   Personnel Records
2
3        Name      Floor Office  Dept.   Status    Salary     Start
4   Nodine            2     21    Adm      FT     $34,680    Jun-81
5   Klein             3     12    Mkt       C     $31,000    Sep-80
6   Falke             2     14    Adm      FT     $28,950    Feb-82
7   Teal              3     13    R&D      FT     $26,600    Jan-82
8   Saddler           3     11    Mkt       C     $24,500    Apr-83
9   Sloane            2      8    Mkt      FT     $23,450    Jun-81
10  Wilder            4     17    Adm       C     $21,800    Jan-84
11  Carlson           4      7    R&D      PT     $16,500    Oct-81
12  Heineman          4     14    Mkt      FT     $14,800    Aug-82
13  Byrne             2     18    R&D      PT      $8,000    Nov-83
14  Martyn            3     14    R&D      PT      $7,600    Mar-84
15
16
17
18
19
20
```

The new record is positioned correctly in the database (row 8, between Teal and Sloane). New records can be added to the database up to the maximum of 8192 rows in the 1-2-3 worksheet. You will always be able to resort the list and put new records in their proper places.

Querying the Database

One of the major advantages of an electronic database is the ease and speed with which you can find and select specific data records. You use the Query commands for this, specifying the criterion for the records you want to find. 1-2-3 queries the database and finds those records that match.

Assume, for example, that you want to know who works in the marketing department. The Dept. field contains the relevant information for each record. Simply specify the word Mkt in the Dept. field as the criterion.

You can set up a number of criteria. For example, you can query who works in marketing on a full-time basis and earns over $20,000 a year. 1-2-3 can search the database and select only those records that contain that specific information.

Query Submenu

```
D17: 'Mkt                                                                    MENU
Input  Criterion  Output  Find  Extract  Unique  Delete  Reset  Quit
Set the range containing data records
          A          B       C          D          E          F          G          H
1
2
3
4
```

The Query menu includes a number of options, including four different query operations.

Find	As you move the pointer down the rows in the database, 1-2-3 moves to and highlights the selected records.
Extract	1-2-3 finds the records that match the criteria and copies them to a designated place on the worksheet.
Unique	1-2-3 performs the Extract operation but also makes sure that none of the records is the same. Only unique records are included.
Delete	1-2-3 finds and deletes the selected records. The other records shift to fill in the blank rows.

In order to use these Query commands, a number of ranges must be set up first.

Input Range

You must specify the area to be searched. This is called the input range. (It is similar to the data range that must be specified for the Sort command.) The input range must include the row of field names. This is an important reference for 1-2-3 when it attempts to match the criteria. The input range does not necessarily have to include the entire database; there may be a case when you want to search only part of it.

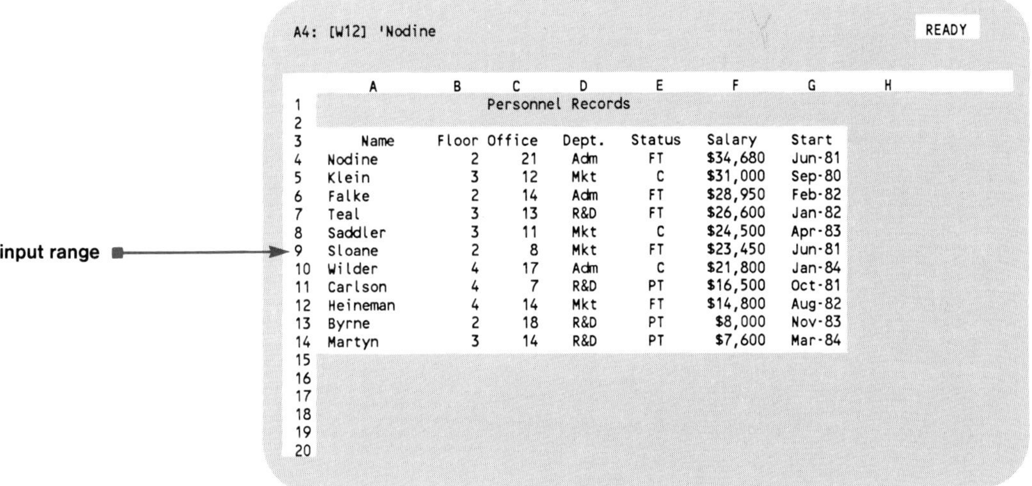

	A	B	C	D	E	F	G	H
1			Personnel Records					
2								
3	Name	Floor	Office	Dept.	Status	Salary	Start	
4	Nodine	2	21	Adm	FT	$34,680	Jun-81	
5	Klein	3	12	Mkt	C	$31,000	Sep-80	
6	Falke	2	14	Adm	FT	$28,950	Feb-82	
7	Teal	3	13	R&D	FT	$26,600	Jan-82	
8	Saddler	3	11	Mkt	C	$24,500	Apr-83	
9	Sloane	2	8	Mkt	FT	$23,450	Jun-81	
10	Wilder	4	17	Adm	C	$21,800	Jan-84	
11	Carlson	4	7	R&D	PT	$16,500	Oct-81	
12	Heineman	4	14	Mkt	FT	$14,800	Aug-82	
13	Byrne	2	18	R&D	PT	$8,000	Nov-83	
14	Martyn	3	14	R&D	PT	$7,600	Mar-84	
15								
16								
17								
18								
19								
20								

Setting Up the Input Range

The first step in any Query command is setting up the input range. 1-2-3 has to know what area of the database to search. By this point the process of specifying a database range should be familiar.

Move to: cell A3

Press: [/]

Select: Data

Query

Input

Press: [.]

[▼] *(eleven times to expand the highlight to row 14)*

[▶] *(six times to specify the range A3..G14)*

```
G14: (D3) @DATE(84,3,4)                                              POINT
Enter Input range: A3..G14

        A          B     C       D       E        F         G         H
1                      Personnel Records
2
3       Name       Floor Office  Dept.   Status   Salary    Start
4   Nodine             2     21  Adm     FT       $34,680   Jun-81
5   Klein              3     12  Mkt     C        $31,000   Sep-80
6   Falke              2     14  Adm     FT       $28,950   Feb-82
7   Teal               3     13  R&D     FT       $26,600   Jan-82
8   Saddler            3     11  Mkt     C        $24,500   Apr-83
9   Sloane             2      8  Mkt     FT       $23,450   Jun-81
10  Wilder             4     17  Adm     C        $21,800   Jan-84
11  Carlson            4      7  R&D     PT       $16,500   Oct-81
12  Heineman           4     14  Mkt     FT       $14,800   Aug-82
13  Byrne              2     18  R&D     PT        $8,000   Nov-83
14  Martyn             3     14  R&D     PT        $7,600   Mar-84
15
16
17
18
19
20
```

Press: [↵]

Select: Quit *(to leave the Data Query menu)*

Criterion Range

The criterion range establishes the criteria that 1-2-3 uses in the search for matching records. The criterion range consists of two or more rows. The first row contains the field names from the input range. The field names in the criterion range must match those in the input range exactly since 1-2-3 uses both sets of field names as cross-references. The second row and any additional rows contain the actual criteria.

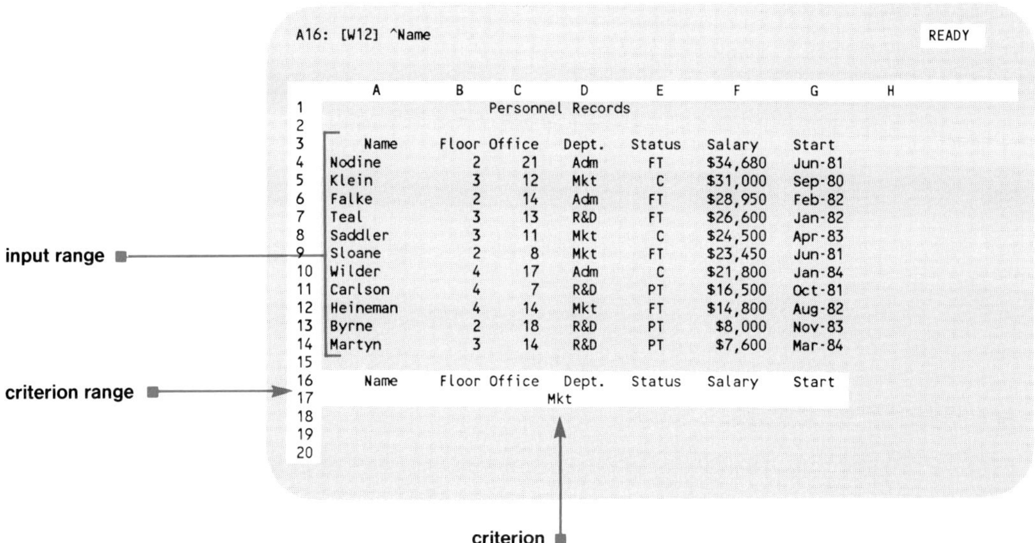

A16: [W12] ^Name READY

	A	B	C	D	E	F	G	H
1			Personnel Records					
2								
3	Name	Floor	Office	Dept.	Status	Salary	Start	
4	Nodine	2	21	Adm	FT	$34,680	Jun-81	
5	Klein	3	12	Mkt	C	$31,000	Sep-80	
6	Falke	2	14	Adm	FT	$28,950	Feb-82	
7	Teal	3	13	R&D	FT	$26,600	Jan-82	
8	Saddler	3	11	Mkt	C	$24,500	Apr-83	
9	Sloane	2	8	Mkt	FT	$23,450	Jun-81	
10	Wilder	4	17	Adm	C	$21,800	Jan-84	
11	Carlson	4	7	R&D	PT	$16,500	Oct-81	
12	Heineman	4	14	Mkt	FT	$14,800	Aug-82	
13	Byrne	2	18	R&D	PT	$8,000	Nov-83	
14	Martyn	3	14	R&D	PT	$7,600	Mar-84	
15								
16	Name	Floor	Office	Dept.	Status	Salary	Start	
17				Mkt				
18								
19								
20								

For example, if you want to find the personnel in the marketing department, you set up a criterion range with two rows. The first contains all the field names from the database, including the word Dept. for that field. The second contains the word Mkt, to correspond to the way that information is listed in the database. When 1-2-3 searches the database, it looks for records that contain the information listed in the criterion range; in this case, it looks for those that list the word Mkt in the Dept. range.

Setting Up the Criterion Range

To set up the criterion range, you have to leave the Data Query menu and return to the worksheet. Here you copy the row of field names to another location on the worksheet. This copy ensures that this row will be an exact duplicate of the original. (You do not have to use all the fields when you set up your criteria.)

Move to: cell A3

Press: [/]

Select: Copy

Press: [▶] *(six times to highlight the range A3..G3)*

[↵]

Move to: cell A16 *(where the names are to be copied to)*

Press: [↵]

The row of field names appears in row 16, directly beneath the database.

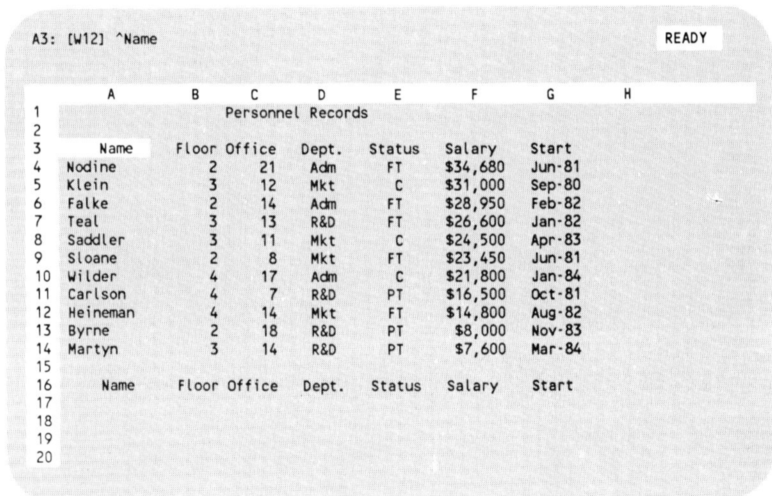

A3: [W12] ^Name   READY

	A	B	C	D	E	F	G	H
1			Personnel	Records				
2								
3	Name	Floor	Office	Dept.	Status	Salary	Start	
4	Nodine	2	21	Adm	FT	$34,680	Jun-81	
5	Klein	3	12	Mkt	C	$31,000	Sep-80	
6	Falke	2	14	Adm	FT	$28,950	Feb-82	
7	Teal	3	13	R&D	FT	$26,600	Jan-82	
8	Saddler	3	11	Mkt	C	$24,500	Apr-83	
9	Sloane	2	8	Mkt	FT	$23,450	Jun-81	
10	Wilder	4	17	Adm	C	$21,800	Jan-84	
11	Carlson	4	7	R&D	PT	$16,500	Oct-81	
12	Heineman	4	14	Mkt	FT	$14,800	Aug-82	
13	Byrne	2	18	R&D	PT	$8,000	Nov-83	
14	Martyn	3	14	R&D	PT	$7,600	Mar-84	
15								
16	Name	Floor	Office	Dept.	Status	Salary	Start	
17								
18								
19								
20								

Now you are going to call up the Data Query menu again to establish the criterion range. The range includes the row directly below the row of field names. This is where you will enter the actual criteria.

Move to: cell A16

Press: [/]

Select: Data
Query
Criterion

Press: [.]
[▼]
[▶] *(six times to highlight the range A16..G17)*

```
G17:                                                          POINT
Enter Criterion range: A16..G17

        A          B     C       D       E        F         G        H
1                    Personnel Records
2
3       Name       Floor Office  Dept.   Status   Salary    Start
4   Nodine             2     21  Adm     FT       $34,680   Jun-81
5   Klein              3     12  Mkt     C        $31,000   Sep-80
6   Falke              2     14  Adm     FT       $28,950   Feb-82
7   Teal               3     13  R&D     FT       $26,600   Jan-82
8   Saddler            3     11  Mkt     C        $24,500   Apr-83
9   Sloane             2      8  Mkt     FT       $23,450   Jun-81
10  Wilder             4     17  Adm     C        $21,800   Jan-84
11  Carlson            4      7  R&D     PT       $16,500   Oct-81
12  Heineman           4     14  Mkt     FT       $14,800   Aug-82
13  Byrne              2     18  R&D     PT        $8,000   Nov-83
14  Martyn             3     14  R&D     PT        $7,600   Mar-84
15
16      Name       Floor Office  Dept.   Status   Salary    Start
17
18
19
20
```

Press: [↵]

Select: Quit

Finding Data Records

The Find command points out selected records. You'll notice that when you select Find, the pointer moves to and highlights the first record that satisfies the selection criteria. You can then use the Up and Down keys to move the pointer among the selected records.

Finding Records

Now that you have established the input range and the criterion range, the final step before using the Find command is to enter the actual criteria. In this example, you want to locate the records of those personnel who work in the marketing department. Specify this as the criterion by entering the word Mkt in the Dept. field of the criterion range.

Move to: cell D17

Type: Mkt [↵]

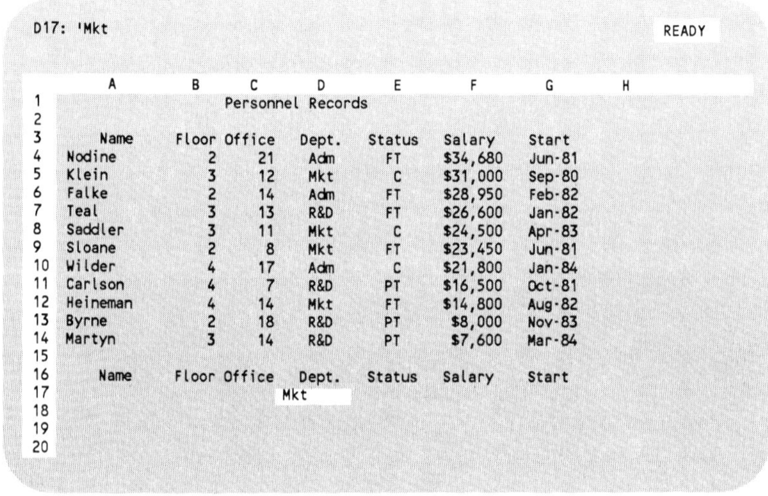

D17: 'Mkt READY

	A	B	C	D	E	F	G	H
1			Personnel Records					
2								
3	Name	Floor	Office	Dept.	Status	Salary	Start	
4	Nodine	2	21	Adm	FT	$34,680	Jun-81	
5	Klein	3	12	Mkt	C	$31,000	Sep-80	
6	Falke	2	14	Adm	FT	$28,950	Feb-82	
7	Teal	3	13	R&D	FT	$26,600	Jan-82	
8	Saddler	3	11	Mkt	C	$24,500	Apr-83	
9	Sloane	2	8	Mkt	FT	$23,450	Jun-81	
10	Wilder	4	17	Adm	C	$21,800	Jan-84	
11	Carlson	4	7	R&D	PT	$16,500	Oct-81	
12	Heineman	4	14	Mkt	FT	$14,800	Aug-82	
13	Byrne	2	18	R&D	PT	$8,000	Nov-83	
14	Martyn	3	14	R&D	PT	$7,600	Mar-84	
15								
16	Name	Floor	Office	Dept.	Status	Salary	Start	
17				Mkt				
18								
19								
20								

You are now ready to return to the Data Query menu and select the Find command. As 1-2-3 starts the process, you'll see that the menu disappears, and that the mode indicator reads FIND. 1-2-3 stops when it finds the first record that matches the criterion (Klein). The entire record will be highlighted (from column A to column G).

Press: [/]

Select: Data
Query
Find

```
A5: [W12] 'Klein                                                    FIND

           A          B     C       D       E        F         G        H
 1                         Personnel Records
 2
 3        Name      Floor Office   Dept.  Status   Salary     Start
 4   Nodine             2     21    Adm     FT    $34,680    Jun-81
 5   Klein              3     12    Mkt      C    $31,000    Sep-80
 6   Falke              2     14    Adm     FT    $28,950    Feb-82
 7   Teal               3     13    R&D     FT    $26,600    Jan-82
 8   Saddler            3     11    Mkt      C    $24,500    Apr-83
 9   Sloane             2      8    Mkt     FT    $23,450    Jun-81
10   Wilder             4     17    Adm      C    $21,800    Jan-84
11   Carlson            4      7    R&D     PT    $16,500    Oct-81
12   Heineman           4     14    Mkt     FT    $14,800    Aug-82
13   Byrne              2     18    R&D     PT     $8,000    Nov-83
14   Martyn             3     14    R&D     PT     $7,600    Mar-84
15
16        Name      Floor Office   Dept.  Status   Salary     Start
17                                 Mkt
18
19
20
```

Now press the Down key to move to the next matching record.

Press: [▼]

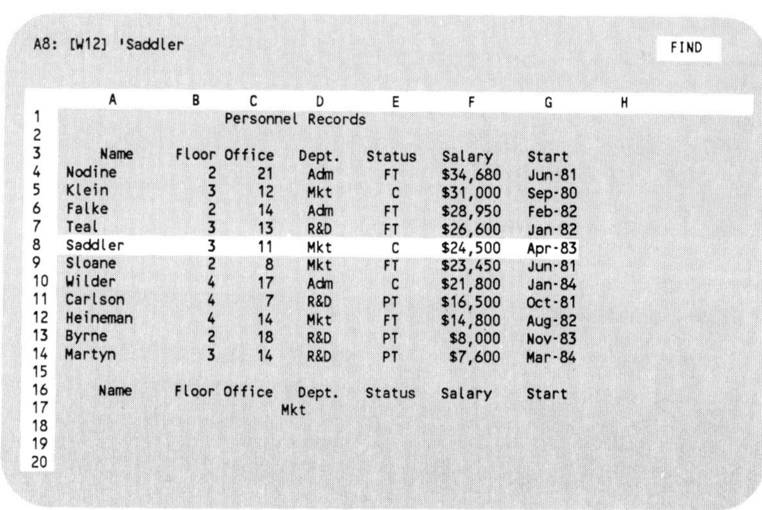

```
A8: [W12] 'Saddler                                                  FIND

           A          B     C       D       E        F         G        H
 1                         Personnel Records
 2
 3        Name      Floor Office   Dept.  Status   Salary     Start
 4   Nodine             2     21    Adm     FT    $34,680    Jun-81
 5   Klein              3     12    Mkt      C    $31,000    Sep-80
 6   Falke              2     14    Adm     FT    $28,950    Feb-82
 7   Teal               3     13    R&D     FT    $26,600    Jan-82
 8   Saddler            3     11    Mkt      C    $24,500    Apr-83
 9   Sloane             2      8    Mkt     FT    $23,450    Jun-81
10   Wilder             4     17    Adm      C    $21,800    Jan-84
11   Carlson            4      7    R&D     PT    $16,500    Oct-81
12   Heineman           4     14    Mkt     FT    $14,800    Aug-82
13   Byrne              2     18    R&D     PT     $8,000    Nov-83
14   Martyn             3     14    R&D     PT     $7,600    Mar-84
15
16        Name      Floor Office   Dept.  Status   Salary     Start
17                                 Mkt
18
19
20
```

The highlight moves down to the next record that lists Mkt (Saddler).

Press: [▼] *(two times to reach the last matching record)*

At this point, pressing the Down key again causes the computer to beep. Press the Up key to move the pointer up the list.

Press: [ESC] *(to return to the Data Query menu)*

Select: Quit

Try another query. You are going to search the database for those personnel who work full-time. The ranges can remain the same, but the criterion must be changed. The first step is to erase the old criterion, and then enter the word FT into the Status field.

Move to: cell D17

Press: [/]

Select: Range

Erase

Press: [↵] *(to accept the range D17..D17)*

Move to: cell E17

Type: FT [↵]

```
E17: 'FT                                                          READY

        A          B     C       D        E        F         G        H
1                      Personnel Records
2
3       Name       Floor Office  Dept.   Status   Salary    Start
4   Nodine           2     21    Adm       FT    $34,680   Jun-81
5   Klein            3     12    Mkt        C    $31,000   Sep-80
6   Falke            2     14    Adm       FT    $28,950   Feb-82
7   Teal             3     13    R&D       FT    $26,600   Jan-82
8   Saddler          3     11    Mkt        C    $24,500   Apr-83
9   Sloane           2      8    Mkt       FT    $23,450   Jun-81
10  Wilder           4     17    Adm        C    $21,800   Jan-84
11  Carlson          4      7    R&D       PT    $16,500   Oct-81
12  Heineman         4     14    Mkt       FT    $14,800   Aug-82
13  Byrne            2     18    R&D       PT     $8,000   Nov-83
14  Martyn           3     14    R&D       PT     $7,600   Mar-84
15
16      Name       Floor Office  Dept.   Status   Salary    Start
17                                       FT
18
19
20
```

Finally, select the Find command.

Press: [/]

Select: Data
Query
Find

A4: [W12] 'Nodine FIND

	A	B	C	D	E	F	G	H
1			Personnel Records					
2								
3	Name	Floor	Office	Dept.	Status	Salary	Start	
4	Nodine	2	21	Adm	FT	$34,680	Jun-81	
5	Klein	3	12	Mkt	C	$31,000	Sep-80	
6	Falke	2	14	Adm	FT	$28,950	Feb-82	
7	Teal	3	13	R&D	FT	$26,600	Jan-82	
8	Saddler	3	11	Mkt	C	$24,500	Apr-83	
9	Sloane	2	8	Mkt	FT	$23,450	Jun-81	
10	Wilder	4	17	Adm	C	$21,800	Jan-84	
11	Carlson	4	7	R&D	PT	$16,500	Oct-81	
12	Heineman	4	14	Mkt	FT	$14,800	Aug-82	
13	Byrne	2	18	R&D	PT	$8,000	Nov-83	
14	Martyn	3	14	R&D	PT	$7,600	Mar-84	
15								
16	Name	Floor	Office	Dept.	Status	Salary	Start	
17					FT			
18								
19								
20								

Use the Down and Up keys to move among the records that contain FT in the Status field.

Press: [ESC]

Select: Quit

Extracting Records

Often you will want to collect the queried data records in one place. The Extract command finds the data records that match the criteria and copies them to a designated area on the worksheet.

Output Range

An output range is necessary to use either the Extract or Unique commands. These commands locate selected records and copy them to a designated place on the worksheet. That designated place is called the output range. The first row of the output range must contain the field names from the database.

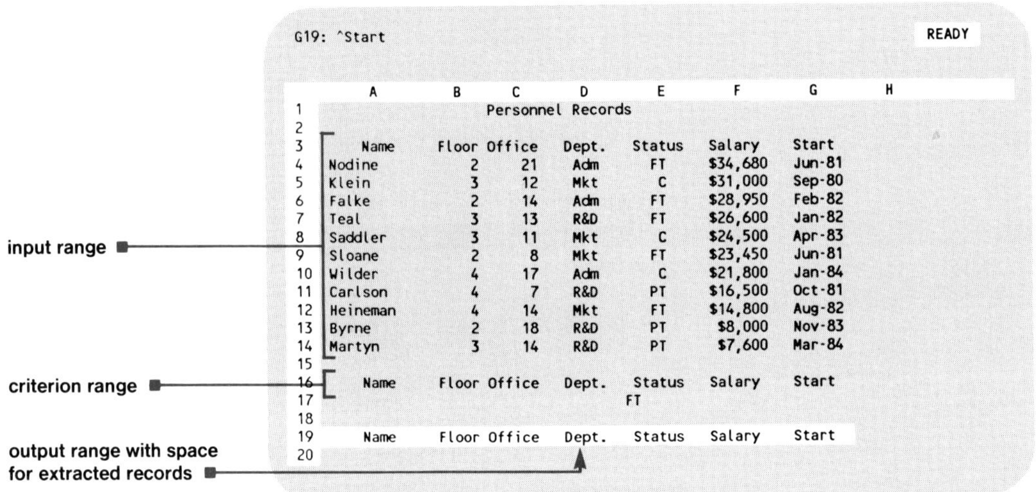

G19: ^Start READY

	A	B	C	D	E	F	G	H
1			Personnel	Records				
2								
3	Name	Floor	Office	Dept.	Status	Salary	Start	
4	Nodine	2	21	Adm	FT	$34,680	Jun-81	
5	Klein	3	12	Mkt	C	$31,000	Sep-80	
6	Falke	2	14	Adm	FT	$28,950	Feb-82	
7	Teal	3	13	R&D	FT	$26,600	Jan-82	
8	Saddler	3	11	Mkt	C	$24,500	Apr-83	
9	Sloane	2	8	Mkt	FT	$23,450	Jun-81	
10	Wilder	4	17	Adm	C	$21,800	Jan-84	
11	Carlson	4	7	R&D	PT	$16,500	Oct-81	
12	Heineman	4	14	Mkt	FT	$14,800	Aug-82	
13	Byrne	2	18	R&D	PT	$8,000	Nov-83	
14	Martyn	3	14	R&D	PT	$7,600	Mar-84	
15								
16	Name	Floor	Office	Dept.	Status	Salary	Start	
17					FT			
18								
19	Name	Floor	Office	Dept.	Status	Salary	Start	
20								

When specifying the output range, you may choose to designate a range that is just one row deep (the row of field names). 1-2-3 then uses the area below that row for the output range. (Remember that when 1-2-3 copies information to the output range, it erases the area first; make sure there is no data you want in the area.)

Setting Up the Output Range

You are going to set up the output range directly below the criterion range. In this example you will be able to see all the ranges on the same screen. The output range need be no more than the row of field names. 1-2-3 knows to copy the selected records to the area below that row.

The first step is to copy the row of field names to that area.

Move to: cell A3

Press: [/]

Select: Copy

Press: [▶] *(six times to highlight the range A3..G3)*

[↵]

Move to: cell A19

Press: [↵]

The row of field names appears directly below the criterion range. Next you designate this row as the output range.

Move to: cell A19

Press: [/]

Select: Data

Query

Output

Press: [.]

[▶] *(six times to highlight the range A19..G19)*

```
G19: ^Start                                                     POINT
Enter Output range: A19..G19

          A          B     C      D       E        F        G        H
 1                      Personnel Records
 2
 3        Name      Floor Office  Dept.   Status   Salary   Start
 4   Nodine            2     21   Adm       FT     $34,680  Jun-81
 5   Klein             3     12   Mkt        C     $31,000  Sep-80
 6   Falke             2     14   Adm       FT     $28,950  Feb-82
 7   Teal              3     13   R&D       FT     $26,600  Jan-82
 8   Saddler           3     11   Mkt        C     $24,500  Apr-83
 9   Sloane            2      8   Mkt       FT     $23,450  Jun-81
10   Wilder            4     17   Adm        C     $21,800  Jan-84
11   Carlson           4      7   R&D       PT     $16,500  Oct-81
12   Heineman          4     14   Mkt       FT     $14,800  Aug-82
13   Byrne             2     18   R&D       PT      $8,000  Nov-83
14   Martyn            3     14   R&D       PT      $7,600  Mar-84
15
16        Name      Floor Office  Dept.   Status   Salary   Start
17                                        FT
18
19        Name      Floor Office  Dept.   Status   Salary   Start
20
```

Press: [↵]

Extracting Records

Now that you have set up the input range, the criterion range, and the output range, you can use the Extract command. First you have to establish the criteria. The last criterion you specified was full-time personnel. Use that criterion again.

In the Find operation in the last section, 1-2-3 moved to and highlighted the data records of personnel working full-time. In the Extract operation, 1-2-3 finds those records and then copies them to the output range.

Select: Extract
Quit

After you select Extract, a number of records appear directly below the output range. They all contain the word FT in the Status field. Use the Down key to scroll the worksheet down and look at all the extracted records.

A24: [W12] 'Heineman READY

	A	B	C	D	E	F	G	H
5	Klein	3	12	Mkt	C	$31,000	Sep-80	
6	Falke	2	14	Adm	FT	$28,950	Feb-82	
7	Teal	3	13	R&D	FT	$26,600	Jan-82	
8	Saddler	3	11	Mkt	C	$24,500	Apr-83	
9	Sloane	2	8	Mkt	FT	$23,450	Jun-81	
10	Wilder	4	17	Adm	C	$21,800	Jan-84	
11	Carlson	4	7	R&D	PT	$16,500	Oct-81	
12	Heineman	4	14	Mkt	FT	$14,800	Aug-82	
13	Byrne	2	18	R&D	PT	$8,000	Nov-83	
14	Martyn	3	14	R&D	PT	$7,600	Mar-84	
15								
16	Name	Floor	Office	Dept.	Status	Salary	Start	
17					FT			
18								
19	Name	Floor	Office	Dept.	Status	Salary	Start	
20	Nodine	2	21	Adm	FT	$34,680	Jun-81	
21	Falke	2	14	Adm	FT	$28,950	Feb-82	
22	Teal	3	13	R&D	FT	$26,600	Jan-82	
23	Sloane	2	8	Mkt	FT	$23,450	Jun-81	
24	Heineman	4	14	Mkt	FT	$14,800	Aug-82	

Using a Formula as Criterion

Now try extracting the data records of those personnel who work full-time and earn over $20,000. This selection requires two criteria. The first, the word FT in the Status field, is already set up. The second, specifying a salary over $20,000, must be in the form of a formula.

When creating a formula criterion, keep the following in mind: (1) write the formula as a test of the first record (second row) of the database; and (2) when specifying a cell address that refers to a database field, use a relative cell address; when specifying a cell address that refers to a value outside the database, use an absolute cell address.

You are going to enter a formula in the salary field of the criterion range (cell F17). The formula refers to cell F4 (the salary entry in the first record) and uses a relative reference: +F4>20000. This means if the value in cell F4 is greater than 20,000, include it.

Move to: cell F17

Type: +F4>20000 [↵] *(don't forget the + sign to indicate a formula)*

F17: +F4>20000 READY

	A	B	C	D	E	F	G	H
5	Klein	3	12	Mkt	C	$31,000	Sep-80	
6	Falke	2	14	Adm	FT	$28,950	Feb-82	
7	Teal	3	13	R&D	FT	$26,600	Jan-82	
8	Saddler	3	11	Mkt	C	$24,500	Apr-83	
9	Sloane	2	8	Mkt	FT	$23,450	Jun-81	
10	Wilder	4	17	Adm	C	$21,800	Jan-84	
11	Carlson	4	7	R&D	PT	$16,500	Oct-81	
12	Heineman	4	14	Mkt	FT	$14,800	Aug-82	
13	Byrne	2	18	R&D	PT	$8,000	Nov-83	
14	Martyn	3	14	R&D	PT	$7,600	Mar-84	
15								
16	Name	Floor	Office	Dept.	Status	Salary	Start	
17					FT	1		
18								
19	Name	Floor	Office	Dept.	Status	Salary	Start	
20	Nodine	2	21	Adm	FT	$34,680	Jun-81	
21	Falke	2	14	Adm	FT	$28,950	Feb-82	
22	Teal	3	13	R&D	FT	$26,600	Jan-82	
23	Sloane	2	8	Mkt	FT	$23,450	Jun-81	
24	Heineman	4	14	Mkt	FT	$14,800	Aug-82	

The value 1 appears in the cell in the criterion range. This means that the value in the cell in the formula fulfills the condition. If it did not, the cell in the criterion range would display 0. Now use these criteria for the Extract operation.

Press: [/]

Select: Data
Query
Extract
Quit

```
F17: +F4>20000                                                 READY

        A          B      C      D       E        F         G        H
5   Klein          3     12     Mkt      C     $31,000   Sep-80
6   Falke          2     14     Adm     FT     $28,950   Feb-82
7   Teal           3     13     R&D     FT     $26,600   Jan-82
8   Saddler        3     11     Mkt      C     $24,500   Apr-83
9   Sloane         2      8     Mkt     FT     $23,450   Jun-81
10  Wilder         4     17     Adm      C     $21,800   Jan-84
11  Carlson        4      7     R&D     PT     $16,500   Oct-81
12  Heineman       4     14     Mkt     FT     $14,800   Aug-82
13  Byrne          2     18     R&D     PT      $8,000   Nov-83
14  Martyn         3     14     R&D     PT      $7,600   Mar-84
15
16      Name     Floor Office   Dept.  Status  Salary     Start
17                                     FT             1
18
19      Name     Floor Office   Dept.  Status  Salary     Start
20  Nodine         2     21     Adm     FT     $34,680   Jun-81
21  Falke          2     14     Adm     FT     $28,950   Feb-82
22  Teal           3     13     R&D     FT     $26,600   Jan-82
23  Sloane         2      8     Mkt     FT     $23,450   Jun-81
24
```

Notice that one of the records extracted in the previous query disappears. The records in the output range now match two criteria: They contain the word FT in the Status field and a value over $20,000 in the Salary field.

Save the File

Now that you have set up the various ranges, save the database again.

Press: [/]

Select: File
Save

Press: [↵]

Select: Replace

Data Menu Command Structure

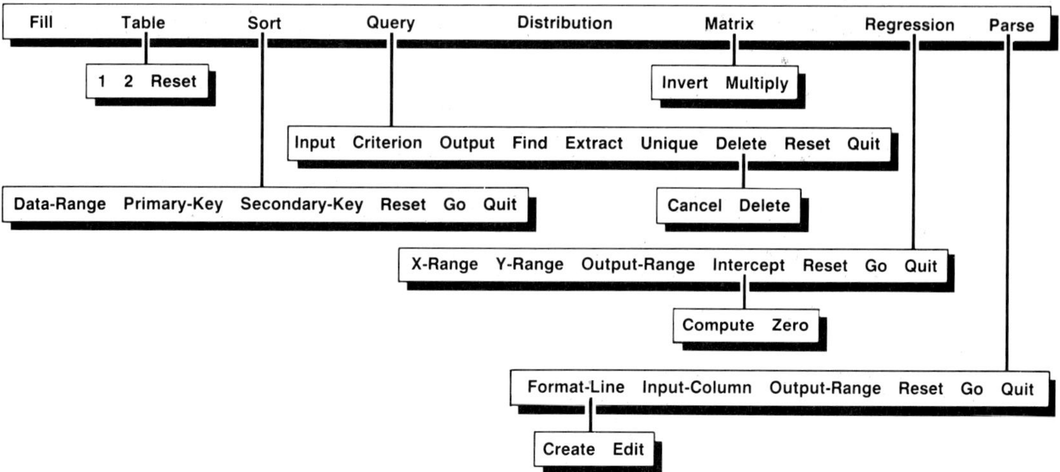

6

Macros

Any task that 1-2-3 can perform, from the simplest to the most complex, can be automated with the 1-2-3 macro facility. A macro is made up of a series of steps, each of which represents an instruction to 1-2-3. Regardless of how many steps a macro includes, it can be invoked with only two activating keystrokes.

You can use macros to:

- Simplify repetitive tasks and cut down on keystrokes by grouping many related keystrokes
- Save time by combining and executing several instructions at once rather than keystroking each one individually
- Simplify a user's interaction with the system by creating and displaying customized menus and prompts
- Increase accuracy and ensure consistency by consolidating a set of keystrokes into one macro.

In this chapter you will explore the uses and construction of macros. You will be introduced to macro keystroke sequences, keywords, and 1-2-3's advanced macro capability. You will create several simple macros, and you will build a more complex macro to add information to the database that you created in the Database chapter. Finally, you will be provided with a selection of macros that you can use to start your own macro library.

Basic Information about Macros

Macros are composed of keystroke sequences and special commands needed for 1-2-3 to perform a certain task. For example, suppose you frequently instruct 1-2-3 to move to a certain location on the worksheet so you can refer to information there, and then you move the pointer back to the previous location. Instead of typing the Goto command and the cell address twice—in order to move and then return—you can accomplish the same movement with a macro that is activated by only two keystrokes. This macro would include the very keystrokes and commands that you use to perform the task manually.

Macros can include any of the following components, individually or in combination:

Key names. Commands that represent the keys on the keyboard. Such keys include the pointer movement keys, the Return key, and the function keys. For example, a macro that contains the key name {right} will move the pointer one cell to the right. Key names within a macro are always enclosed in braces ({}).

Keystrokes that select menu items. A series of keystrokes always begins with the slash key. The menu commands themselves are abbreviated to the first letter of the command.

Keystrokes that represent labels or values. These keystrokes will cause the macro to enter a label or a value in a particular location on the worksheet.

Formulas and @functions. The formula +b5+b6 in a macro will add the contents of those two cells as part of the execution of the macro.

1-2-3 advanced macro commands. Pre-programmed commands perform certain operations specific to macros. For example, the advanced macro command Get followed by a cell address suspends execution of the macro until you type a single keystroke and then stores that information in the worksheet location you have specified.

There are a number of important rules and guidelines to follow when entering and invoking macros.

All macro commands—keystroke sequences, key names, and advanced macro commands—must be entered as labels. If the macro begins with a character that 1-2-3 interprets as a value, you must type a label prefix before entering the macro. Macros that begin with the slash (/), the plus sign (+), the at sign (@), or any other non-alphabetic character, must be preceded by an apostrophe or another label prefix. Advanced macro commands and key names entered in braces (for example, {right}) are interpreted as labels, so 1-2-3 adds the label prefix automatically.

Macros are stored in ranges on the worksheet. A range containing a macro is given a range name consisting of a backslash (\) and a single letter. The macro is invoked by a command composed of the Macro key and the letter that names the range. Thus, a macro in a range named \A will be invoked by the command Macro-A. If you were to enter that command, 1-2-3 would move to that range on the worksheet and begin executing the commands that it finds there. When 1-2-3 is executing a macro, the status indicator in the lower-right portion of the screen reads CMD.

Examples of Macros

The following examples illustrate some simple macros.

The first macro retrieves a file named Budget. This macro could be invoked by pressing the Macro key and typing B (for "budget"); the range in which the macro is stored would be named \B.

```
'/frBUDGET~
```

Each instruction in the macro represents the keystrokes you would use to perform the task manually. This macro is equivalent to the following keystrokes:

Press: [/]
Select: File
Retrieve
Type: BUDGET
Press: [↵]

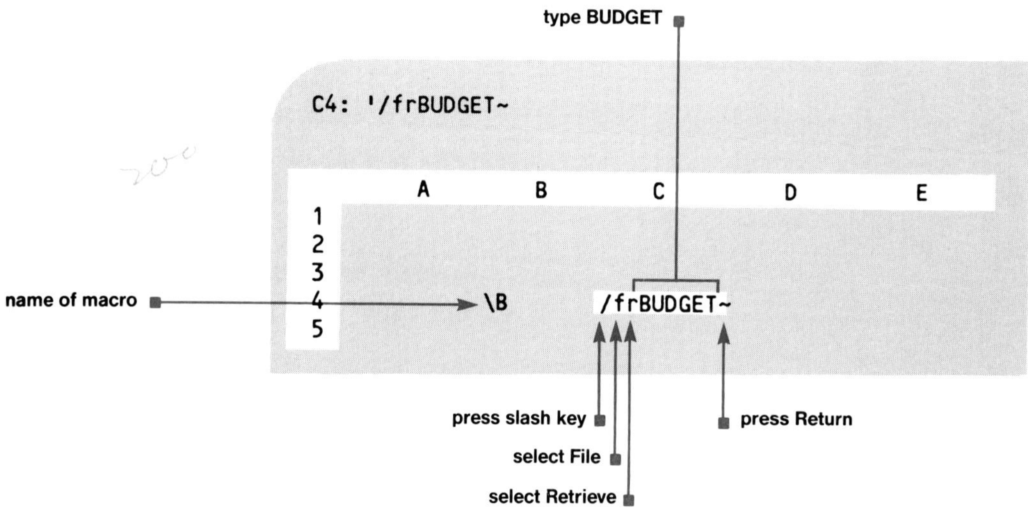

The following macro occupies three cells to make it easier to read; however, it could be entered into only one cell.

```
{goto}c5~
Budget Worksheet
{down}{down}
```

The macro moves the pointer to cell C5, enters the words "Budget Worksheet," and moves the pointer down two rows.

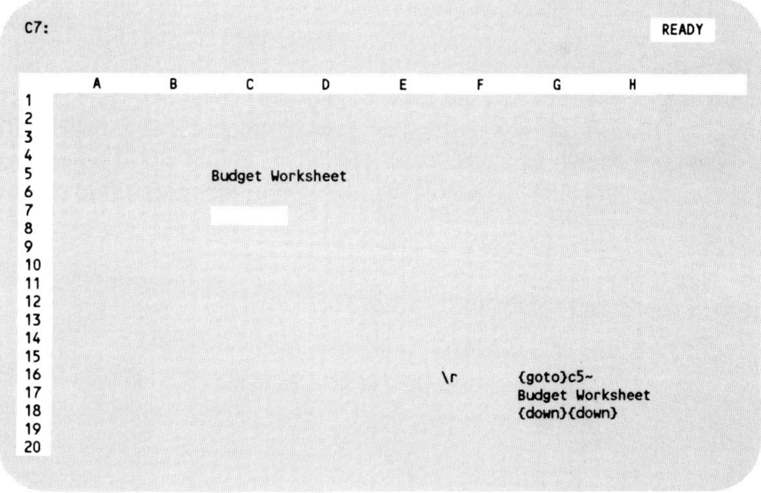

The third example selects commands from the menu—in this case, the File Save command.

'/fs~r

This is equivalent to pressing the slash key to call up the main menu, selecting File and Save, pressing Return to accept the file name, and selecting Replace.

Finally, these two macros will add the contents of three cells.

'+a1+a2+a3~ or '@sum(a1.a3)~

The first option is equivalent to typing a formula adding cells A1, A2, and A3, and then pressing the Return key. The second option uses an @function, @SUM, to enter the same formula.

Build a Macro

Now you will build a simple macro that moves the pointer down three rows. When you build any macro, you must perform three steps to ensure that it will function properly for you. First, name the range the macro will occupy. Second, document the macro: type into an adjacent cell the command that invokes the macro (i.e. the range name), to serve as a reminder of that command. Third, enter the macro into the named range on the worksheet. These steps can be performed in any order, though the above order is recommended.

First, name the range that will contain the macro. The range name for the macro is the command which subsequently will be used to invoke it. Name the range \M, representing the Macro key and "move."

Move to: cell D1
Press: [/]
Select: Range
Name
Create
Type: \m [↵]
Press: [↵] *(to select the range)*

Next, document the macro. In the cell to the left of the macro, enter the range name that will invoke the macro. By documenting the macro in this way, you will be able to refer to the command in case you need to change or recall it.

Move to: cell C1

Type: '\m [↵] *(don't forget the apostrophe)*

Finally, enter the macro into cell D1.

Move to: cell D1

Type: {down}{down}{down} [↵]

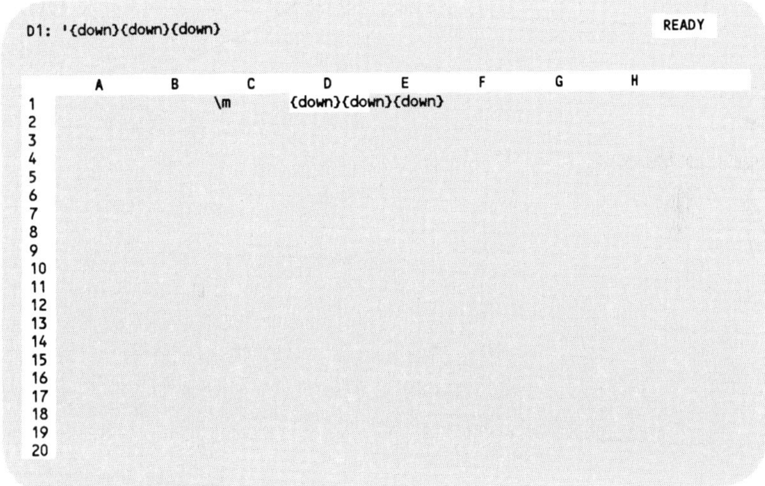

This macro consists of a key name, {down}, repeated three times. This represents pressing the Down arrow three times.

Test the macro. To invoke it, hold down the Macro key and then type the letter representing the macro.

Press: [MACRO] -m

When you invoke the macro the pointer moves down three rows. Move to another location on the worksheet and test the macro again. The macro works anywhere on the worksheet.

1-2-3 Function Keys and Special Keys in Macros

1-2-3 function keys, the pointer movement keys, and the Return key are represented in macros by key names. When entered into a macro, these key names are spelled out and enclosed in braces ({}). Some keys are represented by the actual names assigned to them in 1-2-3, while others are not.

The following list shows how these keys are represented in a macro. When entering any of the following key names in a macro, you can type in either uppercase or lowercase letters (for example, {home} or {HOME}). Lowercase letters are used in this book.

Key Names in Macros	Key Names
~	Return key
{edit}	Edit function key
{name}	Name function key
{abs}	Absolute function key
{goto}	Goto function key
{window}	Window function key
{query}	Query function key
{table}	Table function key
{calc}	Calc function key
{graph}	Graph function key
{escape} or {esc}	Escape key
{backspace} or {bs}	Backspace key
{delete}	Delete key
{insert}	Insert key
{down}	▼
{up}	▲
{left}	◄
{right}	►
{home}	Home key
{end}	End key
{tab}	Tab key
{pgdn}	Page Down key
{pgup}	Page Up key

Note: When using the same pointer movement key more than once in a macro, you can abbreviate the command sequence by entering the appropriate key name and the number of times you want that action performed. For example, to move the pointer to the right seven times, type {right 7} in your macro.

A Procedure for Developing a Macro

When developing a macro it is wise to plan carefully and to make certain decisions before actually entering the macro. As when you are building a worksheet, there is sure to be some trial and error involved in developing a macro. Often, a bit of forethought can minimize potential problems. The following steps are recommended to help the process.

1. Plan the macro.

   Determine each instruction in the macro. Figure out what you want to accomplish and actually keystroke the entire task on the keyboard once to make sure your instructions are accurate.

2. Position the macro.

   Always place a macro in a remote area of the worksheet—an area that you do not anticipate using for anything else. Usually this involves moving far to the right of the active area of the worksheet. Determine which cells you want to use for the macro.

3. Name the range, and document and enter the macro.

   You can accomplish these steps in any order, but you should perform all three.

   - Assign a range name to the macro. The range name is always a backslash followed by a letter. The range name is subsequently used to invoke the macro. You only need to give a range name to the first cell of a macro.
   - Document the macro by entering its range name in a cell to the left of the range it occupies. This reminds you and others who may use the macro of the keystrokes needed to invoke it. If your worksheet contains a number of macros, documenting them means that you don't have to struggle to remember all the names.
   - Enter the macro as you have planned it.

4. Invoke the macro.

   Invoke the macro by holding down the Macro key and typing the letter assigned to the macro. 1-2-3 will execute the instructions in the macro.

5. Debug the macro.

   You may find it necessary to debug the macro if it did not achieve the desired results, or if an incorrect instruction resulted in an error message.

Using Macros in a Worksheet

You are going to use a macro to build the simple worksheet illustrated below. Then, you will enter another macro which will accomplish some calculations and demonstrate the functionality of macros.

This small worksheet is designed to track the inventory of various parts on a month-by-month basis. Notice that the labels in the range B1..F1 all begin with "PART NO."; the only difference between the headings is the specific part number itself. You will write a macro to enter these headings.

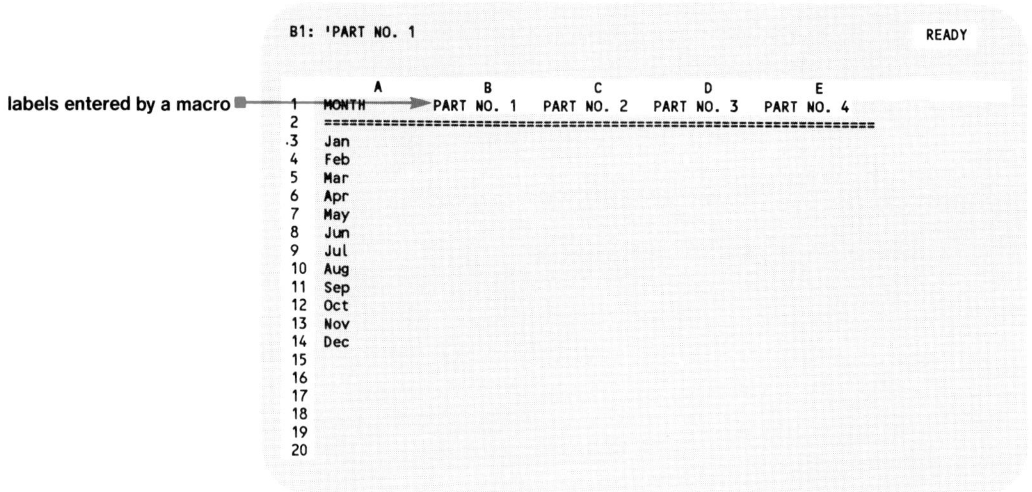

Begin with a new worksheet, and follow the directions to widen the columns, draw the double line, and enter the labels in the column.

Move to: cell A1
Press: [/]
Select: Worksheet
Global
Column-Width
Type: 13 [↵]
MONTH [▼]
\= [↵]
Press: [/]
Select: Copy
Press: [↵] *(to specify the FROM range)*
[▶] *(to move to cell B2)*
[.] *(to anchor the range)*
[▶] *(four times to specify the range B2..F2)*
[↵]
Move to: cell A3
Type: Jan [▼]

Now enter the remaining months in column A as illustrated above. When you've finished entering the months, save the worksheet in a file named Macro1.

Press: [/]
Select: File
Save
Type: MACRO1 [↵]

You're now ready to write the first macro. Remember, always enter a macro in a remote place on the worksheet. Be sure that the area does not contain data, and that it is an area that you will not want to use later to enter data.

In this example you will first create a range name for the cell which will contain the macro. This macro only occupies one cell, but many macros use a larger range of cells. Regardless of how many cells the macro occupies, you only need to name the top cell of the range.

Name the range of the macro.

Move to: cell J1
Press: [/]
Select: Range
Name
Create
Type: \p [↵]
Press: [↵] *(to select the range)*

Now document the macro. Enter the command you will use to invoke the macro in cell I1, which is directly to the left of the cell that will contain the macro. Use the command \P, signifying "Part." Start the entry with an apostrophe to indicate to 1-2-3 that the entry is a label.

Move to: cell I1
Type: '\p [↵]

Type in the keystrokes that comprise the macro. The macro will tell 1-2-3 to type PART NO., and then stop and wait for you to type the number of the part. As soon as you enter the part number and press Return, the macro will enter the entire phrase into the cell and move the pointer one cell to the right. You can then invoke the macro for a new label if necessary.

Type the macro exactly as indicated below, including spaces.

Move to: cell J1
Type: PART NO. {?}{right} ↵

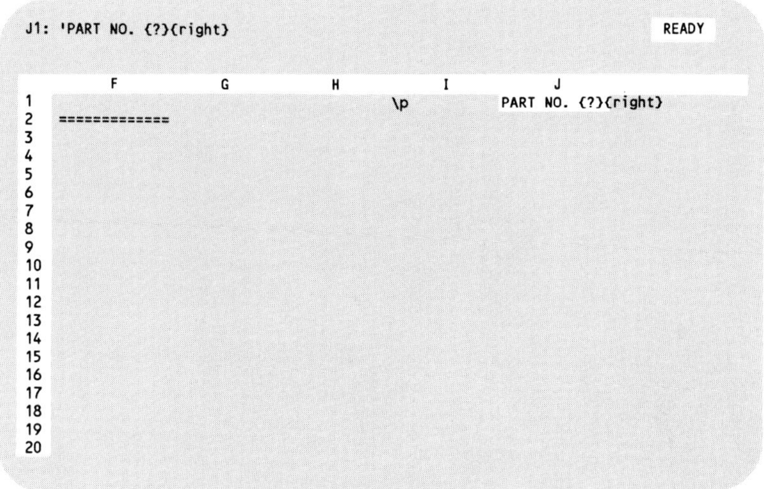

In this macro, the space following NO. indicates to 1-2-3 that it should leave a space after the PART NO. prompt and before your entry of the part number. The question mark in braces tells 1-2-3 to halt macro execution until you type an entry and press Return. Finally, the macro will move the pointer one cell to the right after the entry is made.

Now try the macro. Move the pointer to cell B1, the cell that will contain the first PART NO. label.

Move to: cell B1
Press: MACRO -p
Type: 1 ↵

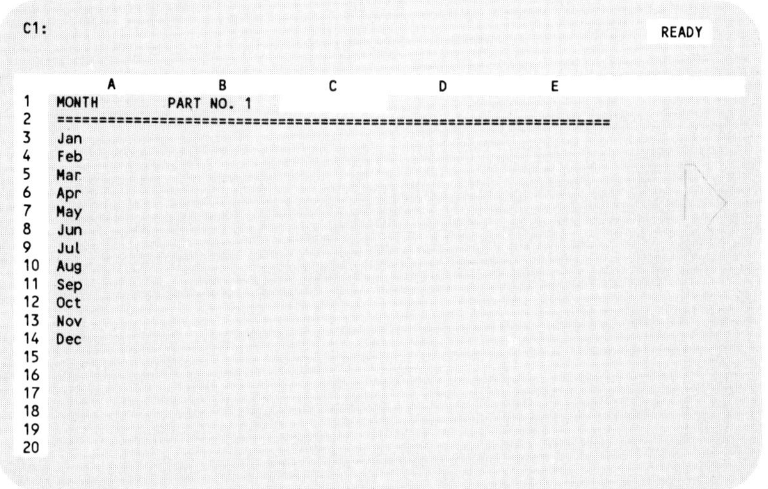
```
C1:                                                        READY

        A          B          C          D          E
 1  MONTH       PART NO. 1
 2  ===============================================================
 3  Jan
 4  Feb
 5  Mar
 6  Apr
 7  May
 8  Jun
 9  Jul
10  Aug
11  Sep
12  Oct
13  Nov
14  Dec
15
16
17
18
19
20
```

The label is entered in cell B1 and the pointer moves to C1. Now invoke the macro four more times, entering the numbers 2, 3, 4, and 5 in cells C1, D1, E1, and F1 respectively.

Now that the first macro and the worksheet structure are complete, you should save the file. Because a macro consists of one or more cell entries, it is saved on the worksheet along with the rest of the data in the file.

Instead of saving the file the usual way, you can write a macro to save a file. This new macro will call up 1-2-3's main menu, select menu items, respond to prompted entries, and enter Return.

Again, the recommended steps are to move to the worksheet area containing the macro, name the range for the macro, document the macro, and enter it. You'll name this macro \S, for save.

Move to: cell J4
Press: [/]
Select: Range
Name
Create
Type: \s [↵]
Press: [↵]
[◄]
Type: '\s [↵]

Now enter the macro.

Move to: cell J4
Type: '/fs~r [↵]

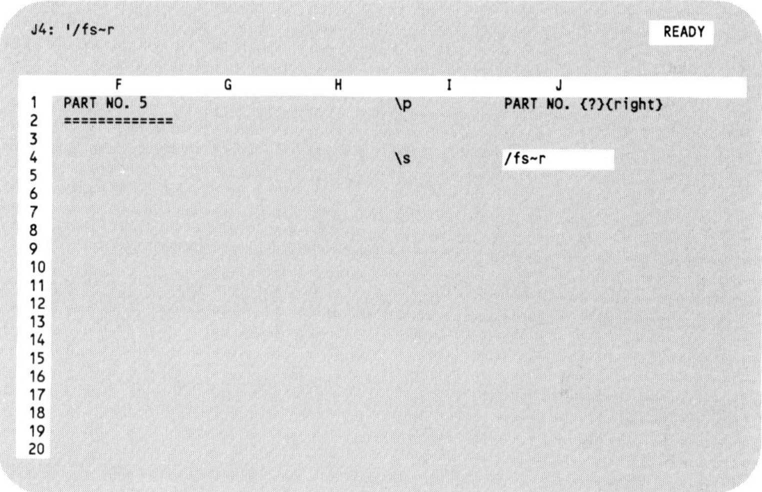

The macro itself contains five instructions. The slash calls up the menu; "f" selects the File command; "s" selects the Save item from the submenu; the tilde represents pressing the Return key to accept the file name MACRO1; and the "r" selects the Replace item, writing over the existing macro file.

Now try the macro. Since the macro does not perform an operation in a specific cell or range, it does not matter where the pointer is resting when you invoke the macro.

Type: MACRO - s

The disk drive light flashes briefly as 1-2-3 writes the file to disk.

How Macros Work

One cell can hold a macro up to 240 characters in length. However, it is often better to split up a macro into two or more cells. This can make a macro easier to enter, to read, and, if necessary, to debug.

1-2-3 executes a macro by reading down a column of cells. That is, 1-2-3 reads the instructions in the first cell and then proceeds to the cell directly below for further instructions. Macro execution stops when 1-2-3 encounters an empty cell, a cell containing a value (a nonlabel cell), or the advanced macro command Quit. This book generally uses a blank cell to terminate a macro.

The number of cells a macro occupies has no effect on the execution of the macro itself. The first macro you wrote has ten separate instructions. If you were to enter each instruction in its own cell, the macro would still work the same way. For example, you could enter the macro in any of the following ways:

PART NO. {?}	PART NO.	PAR
{right}	{?}	T NO. {?}
	{right}	{right}

Notice, however, that you cannot break up individual key names or advanced macro commands into two or more cells. Any commands enclosed in a set of braces—including additional keystrokes or arguments within the braces—must be entered in one cell.

Advanced Macro Commands

Advanced macro commands add tremendous power and sophistication to the 1-2-3 macro capability. Like @functions, advanced macro commands accomplish specific pre-programmed tasks. These advanced macro commands together work like a powerful programming language to perform nearly any task that can be done with a programming language such as BASIC. You can use 1-2-3's advanced macro commands to perform an individual task or a complex series of tasks. You can even create interactive operations initiated by customized menus.

Like key names, the 1-2-3 advanced macro commands must appear within braces in the macro. However, macro commands differ from key names in one significant respect: they are followed, in most cases, by an argument which the command uses to perform its function. An argument specifies the information the advanced macro command will act upon. For example, think of an advanced macro command as a verb in a sentence, and the argument as an object. The keyword (or verb) gives the action; the argument (or object) is what is acted upon or used by the advanced macro command. Only a few advanced macro commands do not take any arguments.

Advanced Macro Command Formats

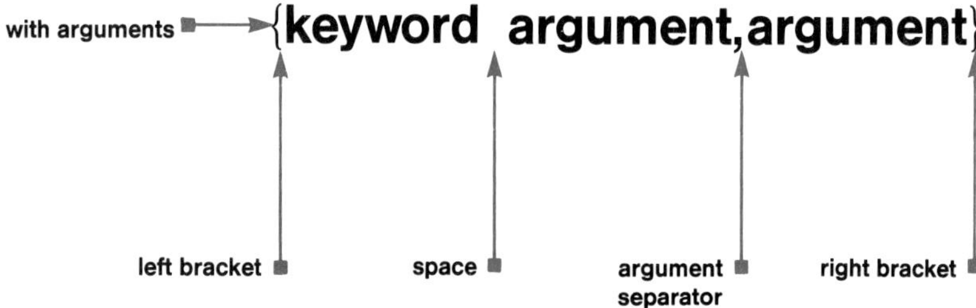

For example, the advanced macro command Getlabel needs two arguments. The first argument serves as a prompt. The argument is typed into the macro exactly as 1-2-3 will display it when the macro is invoked. (Getlabel causes the macro to halt execution while the prompt is displayed.) The second argument, naming a cell address or range on the worksheet, gives the macro the location in which it should store the data entered after the prompt.

The arguments appear in the braces along with the advanced macro command. Above, the first argument specifies the prompt "Enter Last Name." The second argument specifies the range LAST-NAME, the location where the last name entry should be stored.

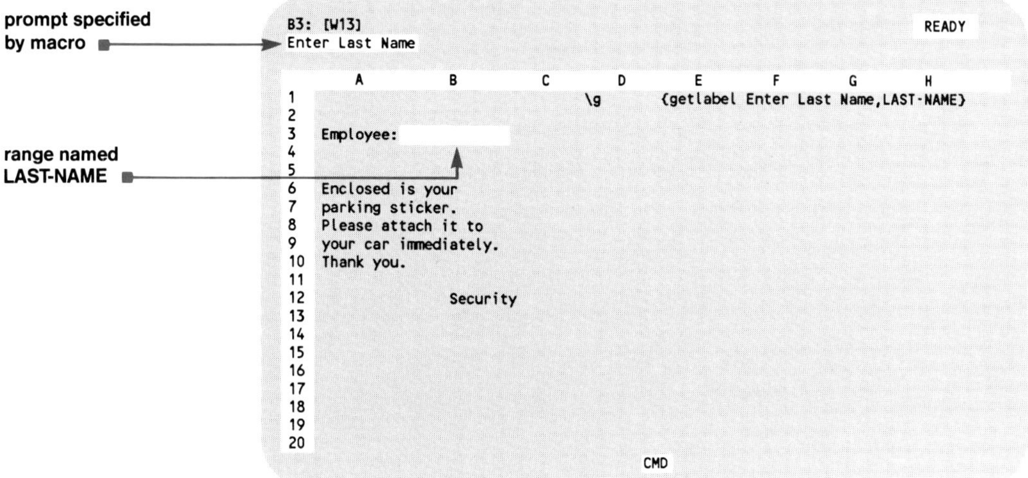

The following example shows the Branch command, another advanced macro command. The Branch command tells 1-2-3 to go to (or branch to) another location on the worksheet. The Branch command would appear within a larger macro, and is followed by one argument, a location.

{branch TOTALS}

Here, the Branch command tells 1-2-3 to go to the range named TOTALS for another instruction.

Create a Macro Using Advanced Macro Commands

In this section you will build a macro that first prompts you to enter two numbers and then totals them. This macro combines an advanced macro command, Getnumber, with a keystroke sequence. The Getnumber command presents a prompt and then enters the value typed by the user into a specific location on the worksheet.

Start with a clean worksheet. If the Macro1 file is still on the screen, save it with the File Save macro (invoked by \S) and then erase the worksheet.

First name and document the macro. Name this macro \A (for "add").

Move to: cell E1
Press: [/]
Select: Range
Name
Create
Type: \a [↵]
Press: [↵] *(to specify the range)*
[◄]
Type: '\a
Press: [↵]

Enter the macro according to the following steps. You're going to use four cells to contain the macro.

Move to: cell E1
Type: {home}
Press: ▼
Type: {getnumber Enter Number ,a1}{down}
Press: ▼
Type: {getnumber Enter Number ,a2}{down}
Press: ▼
Type: '@sum(a1.a2)~ ↵

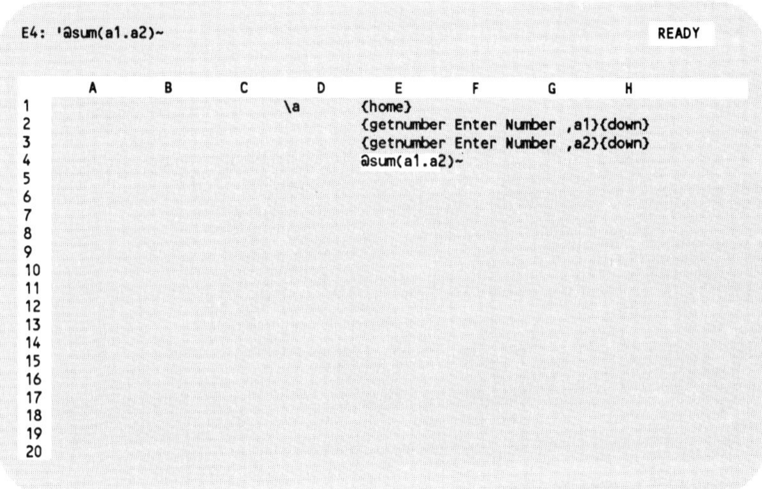

The Getnumber command will display the prompt "Enter Number," and await a typed response. It will then store the response in cell A1 or A2 when the pointer moves down. Finally, the macro will calculate the sum of the two values entered.

Always enter a space between the advanced macro command and the first argument (for example, {getnumber Enter number...}). There should never be a space between the arguments themselves; arguments should be separated by commas. If you would like a space to appear after the prompt (so your response will not run into the prompt), you can enter a space *before* the comma; this is a purely cosmetic measure that has been taken in this example.

Invoke the macro to see how it works.

Press: MACRO - a

Type: 100 ↵

200 ↵

```
A3: @SUM(A1..A2)                                                    READY

        A         B         C         D         E         F         G         H
1      100                           \a        {home}
2      200                                     {getnumber Enter Number ,a1}{down}
3      300                                     {getnumber Enter Number ,a2}{down}
4                                              @sum(a1.a2)~
5
6
7
8
9
10
11
12
13
14
15
16
17
18
19
20
```

The macro enters the numbers that you type in response to the prompts and then adds the two numbers together and displays the result in cell A3.

Create a Looping Macro

You are going to create a new macro that is designed to repeat itself until the user instructs it to quit. This type of macro, called a looping macro, is useful for a series of repetitive tasks. A looping macro removes the need to invoke the macro over and over again.

The macro below automates the Range Justify command so that you can more easily enter text in the 1-2-3 worksheet. When you invoke this macro, it puts you into 1-2-3's Edit mode and waits for you to enter text. When you finish entering a section of text and press Return, the macro enters the text and breaks it into several shorter lines to fit the column. Finally, the last instruction returns the macro to the beginning (the Edit mode), where it starts over. This loop enables you to continue entering data without stopping to re-invoke the macro.

Start with a blank worksheet. Name, document, and enter the macro in separate cells as indicated in the keystrokes. Name the macro \T, for "text."

Move to: cell F1
Press: [/]
Select: Range
Name
Create
Type: \t
Press: [↵] *(twice)*
[◄]
Type: '\t [►]
{edit}{?}~ [▼]
'/rj~ [▼]
{end}{down} [▼]
{branch \t} [↵]

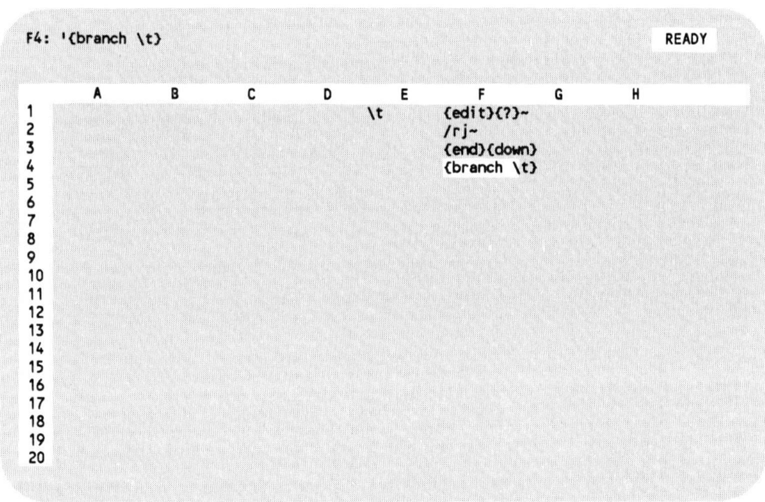

The first key name, {edit}, puts you in 1-2-3's Edit mode. The question mark within braces instructs the macro to wait for input from the keyboard; you enter the text and press Return. The tilde in the first line serves as a Return key, which inserts the text into the cell and turns off the Edit mode.

The slash key then calls up the main menu, and the macro selects the Range and Justify commands. The tilde accepts the range where you just entered text as the range to justify. The text in that range is automatically realigned in the column.

The third line of the macro selects End and Down to move the cell pointer to the last cell in the column containing data. The text you typed fills the column to this point.

The last line of the macro contains an advanced macro command. This command, {branch \t}, instructs 1-2-3 to look to another location (in this case the range named \T) for further instructions. The range \T is the first cell of this macro. When 1-2-3 branches to that location, it executes the macro's instructions once again. You can add another section of text and press Return and that text will also be justified.

The advanced macro command Branch creates a looping macro. This command takes one argument: a location, which can be identified either by a cell address or by a range name.

Test the macro.

Move to: cell A1

Select: [/]

Worksheet

Column

Set-Width

Type: 22 [↵] *(to widen the column)*

Press: [MACRO] -t *(to invoke the macro)*

Type: The 1-2-3 program was designed to process numbers rather than words. With a macro that uses the Range Justify command to align the text automatically, processing text in 1-2-3 is as easy as processing numbers.

Notice that the mode indicator reads EDIT.

Press: ↵

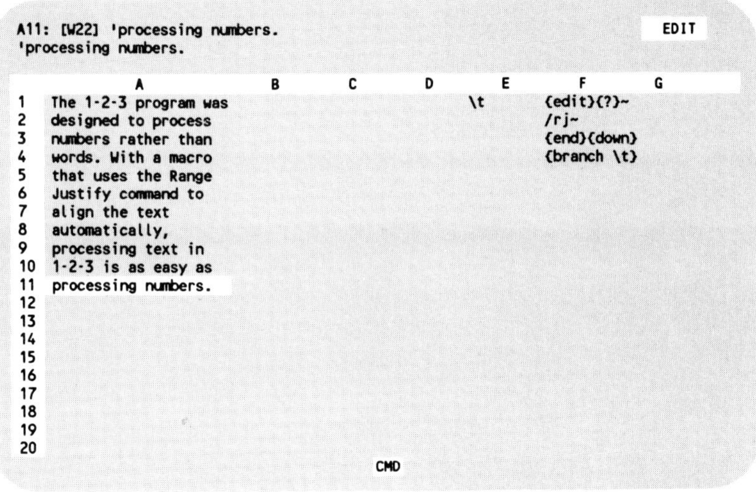

The text is now formatted into 11 cells in column A and the pointer is resting in the cell containing the last line of text. The macro is still active, as shown by CMD in the status indicator and EDIT in the mode indicator. At this point you can add another section of text. Add a space before you begin typing.

Type: A second entry is entered starting in the last line of the first entry. ↵

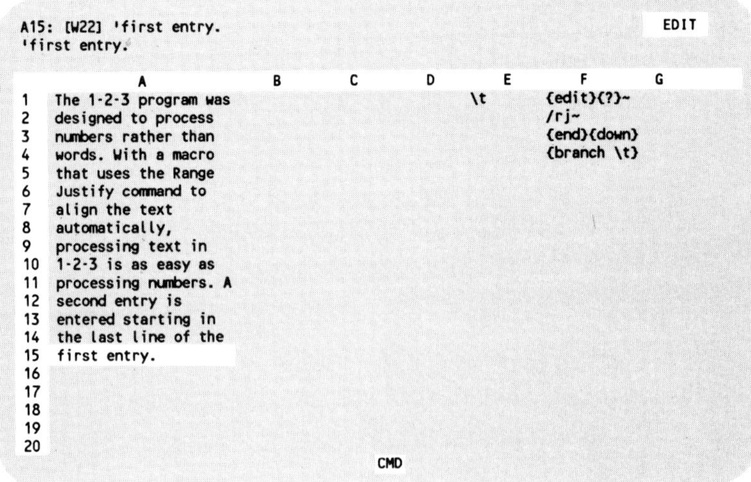

Again, the text you just entered is formatted into the column.

In order to exit a looping macro, you must hold down the Control key and press the Break key. This action will result in an Error message, which you can eliminate by pressing Escape.

Press: CTRL - BREAK
ESC

Debugging a Macro

Occasionally you will forget to enter a specific instruction in a macro that 1-2-3 needs in order to complete the requested operation. This simple omission may produce an entirely different, and possibly confusing, result. Unless you are thoroughly familiar with how 1-2-3 functions, you could spend a great deal of time in the effort to debug the macro.

You can debug a short macro by analyzing the few instructions within it and running it again to observe precisely where the macro stops working. However, to debug longer macros you will want to use a 1-2-3 macro feature called the single-step mode. This facility allows you to observe the macro in execution, one step at a time, and thereby discern at what point it stops.

To practice debugging a macro, enter a mistake in the text justifying macro you just wrote. Then run the macro again to see the effects of the error.

First, remove a tilde from the second line of the looping macro.

Move to: cell F2

Press: EDIT *(to display the second line of the macro in the control panel)*

BACKSPACE *(to delete the tilde at the end of the line)*

↵

Now invoke the altered macro.

Move to: cell A17

Press: MACRO -t

Type: When a macro fails to work, the results can be very confusing. ↵

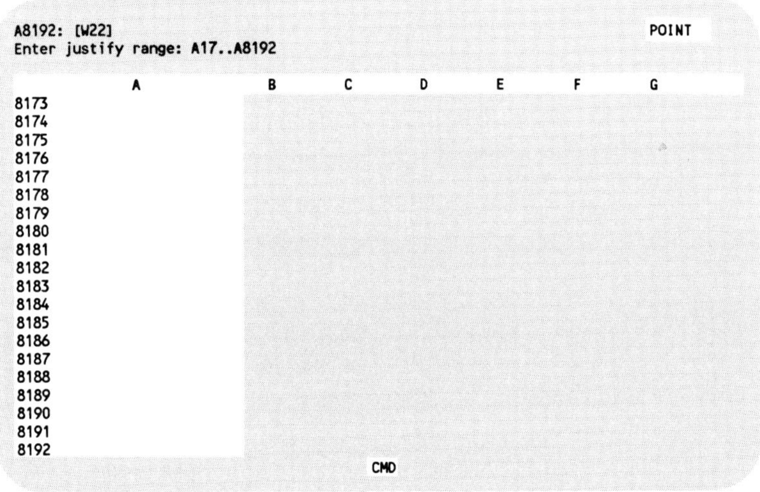

Column A is now highlighted from the cell where you made the entry to row 8192, the bottom of the worksheet, and the macro has stopped. The one small error in the macro has caused serious problems. Now use 1-2-3 to help determine what went wrong.

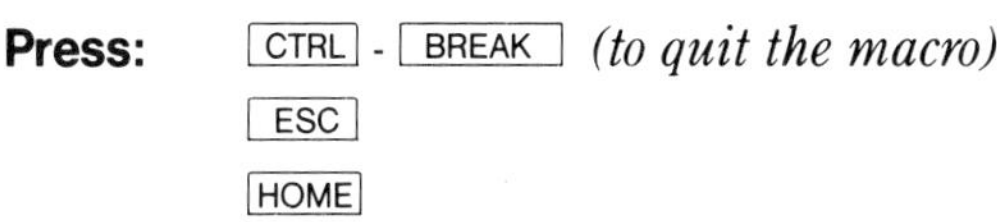


```
A1: [W22] 'The 1-2-3 program was                                          READY

              A               B         C         D         E         F         G
1   The 1-2-3 program was                                  \t        {edit}{?}~
2   designed to process                                              /rj
3   numbers rather than                                              {end}{down}
4   words. With a macro                                              {branch \t}
5   that uses the Range
6   Justify command to
7   align the text
8   automatically,
9   processing text in
10  1-2-3 is as easy as
11  processing numbers. A
12  second entry is
13  entered starting in
14  the last line of the
15  first entry.
16
17  When a macro fails to work, the results can be very confusing.
18
19
20
```

Notice that the text was entered in the cell, but it was not justified.

You are going to use the single-step mode to debug the macro. In the single-step mode, 1-2-3 executes the macro one step at a time. After executing each particular step, 1-2-3 waits for you to press any key before it goes on to the next step of the macro.

In the effort to debug the macro, you will turn on single-step mode and invoke the macro in the usual way. Then you will press the spacebar to step through the macro. You activate single-step mode by holding down the Macro key and pressing the Edit key. The same key combination turns off single-step mode.

Move to: cell A19

Press: STEP *(to turn on single-step mode)*

MACRO -t *(to activate the macro)*

SPACE BAR

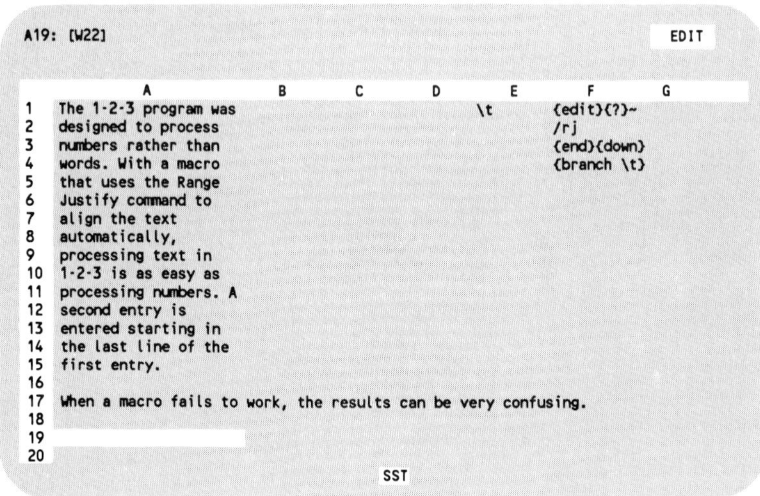

The mode indicator now reads EDIT, indicating that the first step of the macro, activating the Edit mode, has been executed. Move to the next step of the macro.

Press: SPACE BAR

The second step, represented in the macro by {?}, halts the macro and awaits text entry. Enter the text you tried to enter earlier.

Type: When a macro fails to work, the results can be very confusing. ↵

Press: SPACE BAR

Notice that when you pressed Return, the text was not entered into the worksheet. The single-step mode required you to press the spacebar before advancing the macro to the next step, that of executing the Return key to enter the words.

Now that the text has appeared on the worksheet, activate the next step. In the macro, the next element is the slash key, which calls up the main menu.

Press: SPACE BAR

The main menu appears. The macro will choose commands from the menu.

Press: SPACE BAR

The macro selected the Range command, and the Range submenu appears on the screen.

Press: SPACE BAR

The Justify item on the Range menu has been selected, and 1-2-3 prompts you for the range within which to justify the text. You want to accept the range that is displayed. Activate the next step.

Press: SPACE BAR

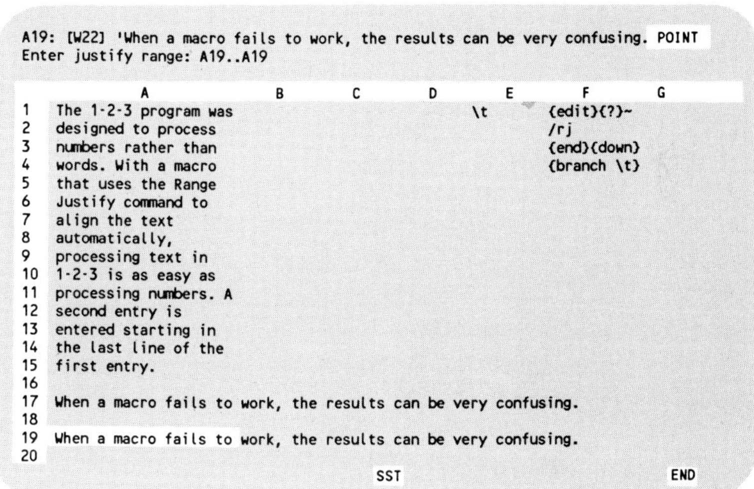

This is the point at which the macro should have accepted the range indicated in the control panel as the range to justify. If this had happened, the text would have been reformatted into the accepted range. However, the `Enter justify range` prompt remains on the screen. In addition, the END indicator appears, showing that the step the macro most recently performed was pressing the End key.

Press: SPACE BAR

After a moment, column A is highlighted to row 8192. Pressing the spacebar activated the next instruction in the macro: pressing the Down key. The combination of pressing the End key and the Down key together, while the justify range prompt was awaiting an entry, resulted in the highlight expanding to the end of the worksheet.

Now that you have isolated the error, leave the macro, turn off the single-step mode, and correct the macro.

Press: CTRL - BREAK

ESC

MACRO - EDIT *(to turn off the single-step mode)*

Move to: cell F2

Press: EDIT

Type: ~ ↵

Save the file in order to save the text macro you built.

Single-step mode is also useful for gaining an understanding of the function of complex macros. Turn on single-step mode and, while stepping through the macro, observe what happens on the screen.

Using Macros in a Database

Macros can play an extremely useful role in databases. Data records are usually remarkably similar, and they need to be entered and formatted in a standard manner. By fashioning a macro to facilitate data entry you can speed up and simplify the process, and eliminate the need to format the data with a separate set of commands. You can also use macros to aid others who will be entering data into the database but who may not be as familiar with the type of data to be entered or the formatting requirements.

You will create a macro to be used with the database you created in the Database chapter. First, retrieve the file Database.wk1.

Press: [/]
Select: File
Retrieve
DATABASE.WK1

```
A1: [W12]                                                        READY

        A          B     C       D        E         F          G         H
1                    Personnel Records
2
3       Name      Floor Office   Dept.   Status    Salary     Start
4   Nodine           2     21    Adm       FT     $34,680    Jun-81
5   Klein            3     12    Mkt        C     $31,000    Sep-80
6   Falke            2     14    Adm       FT     $28,950    Feb-82
7   Teal             3     13    R&D       FT     $26,600    Jan-82
8   Saddler          3     11    Mkt        C     $24,500    Apr-83
9   Sloane           2      8    Mkt       FT     $23,450    Jun-81
10  Wilder           4     17    Adm        C     $21,800    Jan-84
11  Carlson          4      7    R&D       PT     $16,500    Oct-81
12  Heineman         4     14    Mkt       FT     $14,800    Aug-82
13  Byrne            2     18    R&D       PT      $8,000    Nov-83
14  Martyn           3     14    R&D       PT      $7,600    Mar-84
15
16      Name      Floor Office   Dept.   Status    Salary     Start
17                                      FT              1
18
19      Name      Floor Office   Dept.   Status    Salary     Start
20  Nodine           2     21    Adm       FT     $34,680    Jun-81
```

You will be adding data records to the existing file. Begin by erasing the criterion and output ranges that occupy the bottom rows on the screen.

Move to: cell A16
Press: [/]
Select: Range
Erase
Press: [END]
[HOME]
[↵]

You will work with only part of the database. Hide the four middle columns with the field names Floor, Office, Dept., and Status, and the last column named Start.

Move to: cell B3
Press: [/]
Select: Worksheet
Column
Hide
Press: [.] *(to anchor the range)*
[▶] *(three times)*
[↵]

Hide the Start field as well.

Move to: cell G3
Press: [/]
Select: Worksheet
Column
Hide
Press: [↵]

```
H3:                                                          READY

         A         F         H         I         J         K         L         M
1
2
3      Name      Salary
4   Nodine       $34,680
5   Klein        $31,000
6   Falke        $28,950
7   Teal         $26,600
8   Saddler      $24,500
9   Sloane       $23,450
10  Wilder       $21,800
11  Carlson      $16,500
12  Heineman     $14,800
13  Byrne         $8,000
14  Martyn        $7,600
15
16
17
18
19
20
```

The macro you will write adds new records to the database into the fields Name and Salary. Since the macro will consist of several lines of instructions, select a remote area of the worksheet with several blank rows.

First, name the range that the macro will occupy. Name the range \D (for database).

Move to: cell K1

Press: [/]

Select: Range
Name
Create

Type: \d

Press: [↵] *(twice to enter the name and select the range)*

Now document the macro in an adjacent cell.

Move to: cell J1

Type: '\d [↵]

The instructions starting the macro cause it to position the pointer at the next available blank record in the database. Enter these instructions.

Move to: cell K1

Type: {home}{end}{down}{end}{down 2} [↵]

```
K1: '{home}{end}{down}{end}{down 2}                              READY

          F         H        I        J        K        L        M        N
1                                    \d       {home}{end}{down}{end}{down 2}
2
3     Salary
4     $34,680
5     $31,000
6     $28,950
7     $26,600
8     $24,500
9     $23,450
10    $21,800
11    $16,500
12    $14,800
13     $8,000
14     $7,600
15
16
17
18
19
20
```

Now try out the macro.

Press: MACRO -d

```
A15: [W12]                                                          READY

       A          F        H        I        J        K        L        M
1                                           \d       {home}{end}{down}{end}{down
2
3      Name       Salary
4   Nodine       $34,680
5   Klein        $31,000
6   Falke        $28,950
7   Teal         $26,600
8   Saddler      $24,500
9   Sloane       $23,450
10  Wilder       $21,800
11  Carlson      $16,500
12  Heineman     $14,800
13  Byrne         $8,000
14  Martyn        $7,600
15
16
17
18
19
20
```

The pointer moves to the first blank row of the database, and you can enter a new record at this location.

Return to the cell containing the macro. Enter an advanced macro command that accepts a new entry and places it in the Name field of the database. The advanced macro command is Getlabel, which needs two arguments. The first argument is a prompt which the macro will display. When you type a response to the prompt and press Return, the command takes what you have typed and, referring to the second argument, enters the data in a specified location on the worksheet.

In this example of the Getlabel command, you need to enter data for new records into different fields in the database. Therefore, the cell address for each entry will be different. Because of this variable, it is impossible to write into the macro the exact cell addresses for the entries.

The alternative is for the macro to store each entry, as it is made, in a temporary location on the worksheet, and then copy the data into the cell where the pointer is currently located. This temporary location will be a range named Temp. Create the temporary range.

Move to: cell I1
Press: [/]
Select: Range
Name
Create
Type: TEMP [↵]
Press: [↵]

Enter the second line of the macro. This line displays a prompt for a new name entry to the database, and places the entry in the current cell address.

Move to: cell K2
Type: {getlabel Enter Name ,TEMP}/cTEMP~ ~{right} [↵]

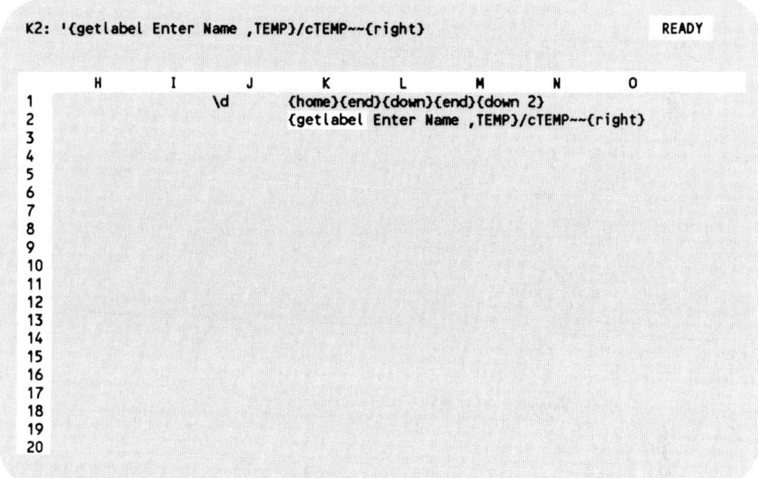

This advanced macro command presents a prompt, Enter Name , in the control panel. After you make the entry and press the Return key, the macro places the entry into the range named Temp. The macro then selects Copy from the main menu (represented in the macro by /c), and copies the contents of Temp into the current cell address. The pointer then moves to the next field, one column to the right, enabling you to make another entry.

The next line of instructions in the macro will enter data into the Salary field. For this, use the Getnumber advanced macro command. Getnumber is similar to Getlabel—it accepts an entry of a value in response to the prompt, and places the entry on the worksheet. This command will place the entry into the Temp range and then copy the contents of that range into the current cell. Also, the macro will format the value for currency with no decimal places, making it match the other entries in the Salary field.

Move to: cell K3

Type: {getnumber Enter Salary ,TEMP}/cTEMP~~/rfc0~~ ↵

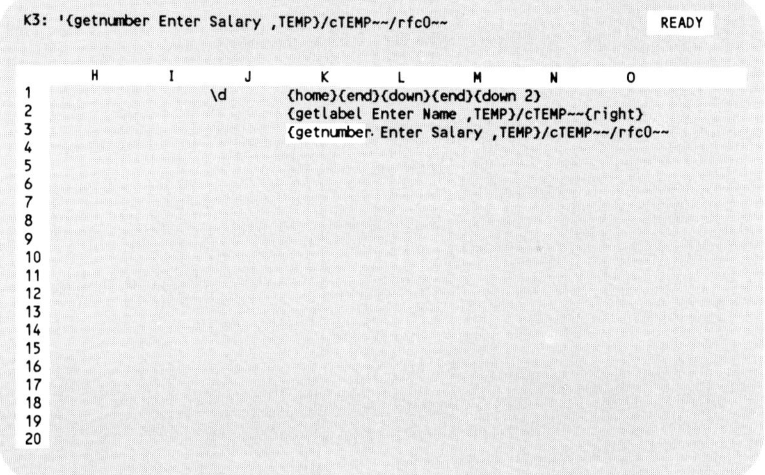

Test the macro and enter some new data.

Press: MACRO -d

Type: Smith ↵

12500 ↵

```
F15: (C0) 12500                                                    READY

        A           F          H        I          J       K          L        M
1                                       12500 \d           {home}{end}{down}{end}{down
2                                                          {getlabel Enter Name ,TEMP}/
3       Name        Salary                                 {getnumber Enter Salary ,TEM
4   Nodine          $34,680
5   Klein           $31,000
6   Falke           $28,950
7   Teal            $26,600
8   Saddler         $24,500
9   Sloane          $23,450
10  Wilder          $21,800
11  Carlson         $16,500
12  Heineman        $14,800
13  Byrne            $8,000
14  Martyn           $7,600
15  Smith           $12,500
16
17
18
19
20
```

The status indicator CMD appears at the bottom of the screen. The macro provides prompts for each field entry you must make. Your responses are temporarily stored in the Temp range, and then copied into the current cell.

You can continue to enter records by invoking the macro repeatedly. However, if you have a number of data records to enter, try converting this macro into a looping macro. To do this, add the Branch command to the end of the macro; this command causes the macro to return to the first instruction and start over.

Add the Branch command to the macro.

Move to: cell K4

Type: {branch \d} ↵

```
K4: '{branch \d}                                                READY

        A            F          H        I       J        K         L         M
 1                                     12500 \d          {home}{end}{down}{end}{down
 2                                                       {getlabel Enter Name ,TEMP}/
 3        Name       Salary                              {getnumber Enter Salary ,TEM
 4    Nodine        $34,680                              {branch \d}
 5    Klein         $31,000
 6    Falke         $28,950
 7    Teal          $26,600
 8    Saddler       $24,500
 9    Sloane        $23,450
10    Wilder        $21,800
11    Carlson       $16,500
12    Heineman      $14,800
13    Byrne          $8,000
14    Martyn         $7,600
15    Smith         $12,500
16
17
18
19
20
```

This moves the cell pointer to the named range \D, the first cell of the macro. The macro will continue indefinitely, until you exit it by pressing Ctrl-Break.

Create a Menu Macro

Many tasks, such as updating a database, involve several specific activities that could easily be presented as items in a menu. Using 1-2-3's macro capability, you can create your own menus that include specific tasks. When you select an item from such a menu, the menu macro automatically branches to another macro that performs that operation.

For example, a menu for the Personnel Records database could list a few standard tasks, such as ENTER, for entering a new record, SORT, for rearranging records after new ones have been entered, and QUIT, for discontinuing data entry and exiting the macro. The menu macro, when invoked, would call up this menu. If you selected SORT, another macro would perform the appropriate sort operation and then return you to the menu, from which you could make another selection.

Menu macros are invoked using the advanced macro commands Menubranch or Menucall. Menus invoked with either of these commands are identical in appearance to 1-2-3's built-in command menus, and they can be used in exactly the same manner. The menus appear in the usual place, on the second line of the control panel. The third line of the control panel displays your own one-line descriptions of the menu items. You select a menu item by typing the first letter of the word or by highlighting the word and pressing Return.

Locate the menu macro in a remote area of the worksheet. The macro instructions for each menu item should be entered in the cell directly below the menu item. When you make a selection from the menu, 1-2-3 executes the instructions that occupy the cells directly below the menu choice.

In this example, you will create a menu macro that displays a menu with the items Enter (to enter a new record) or Quit (to stop entering records). The Enter item in this menu macro utilizes the data entry macro you just created.

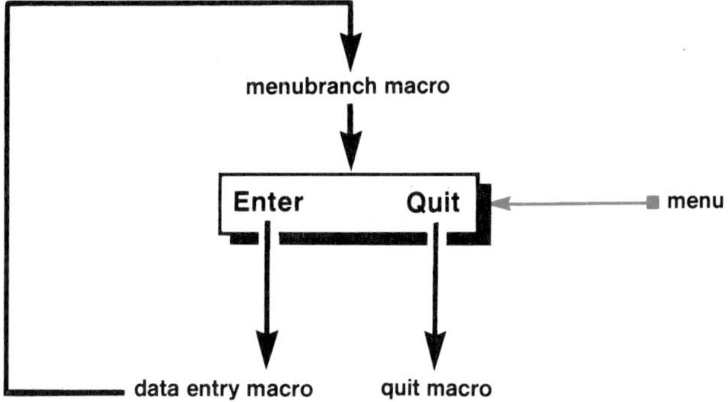

First, assign the name Menu to a blank range. This range will hold the menu items, their descriptions, and the macro routines that tell 1-2-3 what to do when that menu item is selected. Document this range in the cell to the left.

Move to: cell K6
Press: [/]
Select: Range
Name
Create
Type: MENU [↵] *(to enter the name)*
Press: [↵] *(to select the current range)*
Move to: cell J6
Type: MENU [↵]

In the Menu range, enter the items you want available on the menu. Be sure to type the menu items into adjacent columns. All menu items, their descriptions, and the related macro routines must be contained in the Menu range. Below each menu item, type a description of the item. Begin by widening the column so all the text you enter will be visible.

Move to: cell K6
Press: [/]
Select: Worksheet
Column
Set-Width
Type: 18 [↵]
Enter [▼]
Enter New Record [↵]
Move to: cell L6
Type: Quit [▼]
Quit Entering Records [↵]

Now enter the macro routines that will be associated with each of the two menu items. The macro for the Enter item will tell 1-2-3 to use the data entry macro you just completed (named \D), when that item is selected. Type a Branch command into the cell below the description of the Enter item.

Move to: cell K8

Type: {branch \d} ↵

The Quit menu item will invoke a macro that uses the advanced macro command Quit. This command stops the macro. Enter this macro below the description of the Quit item.

Move to: cell L8

Type: {quit} ↵

```
L8: '{quit}                                                        READY

          F       H       I        J          K                  L         M
 1                        12500 \d       {home}{end}{down}{end}{down 2}
 2                                       {getlabel Enter Name ,TEMP}/cTEMP~~{righ
 3   Salary                              {getnumber Enter Salary ,TEMP}/cTEMP~~/r
 4   $34,680                             {branch \d}
 5   $31,000
 6   $28,950                     MENU    Enter             Quit
 7   $26,600                             Enter New Record  Quit Entering Records
 8   $24,500                             {branch \d}       {quit}
 9   $23,450
10   $21,800
11   $16,500
12   $14,800
13    $8,000
14    $7,600
15   $12,500
16
17
18
19
20
```

Now that the menu items and their related macros are complete, you can enter the macro containing the command Menubranch. This advanced macro command takes one argument: a location telling 1-2-3 where to find the menu items and their related macros. Name the range, and document and enter the macro.

Move to: cell K10
Press: [/]
Select: Range
Name
Create
Type: \m [↵]
Press: [↵] *(to select the range)*
Move to: cell J10
Type: '\m [↵]
Move to: cell K10
Type: {menubranch MENU} [↵]

```
K10: [W18] '{menubranch MENU}                                    READY

      F        H         I      J          K               L          M
1                      12500  \d      {home}{end}{down}{end}{down 2}
2                                     {getlabel Enter Name ,TEMP}/cTEMP~~{righ
3    Salary                           {getnumber Enter Salary ,TEMP}/cTEMP~~/r
4    $34,680                          {branch \d}
5    $31,000
6    $28,950                  MENU    Enter           Quit
7    $26,600                          Enter New Record Quit Entering Records
8    $24,500                          {branch \d}     {quit}
9    $23,450
10   $21,800                  \m      {menubranch MENU}
11   $16,500
12   $14,800
13    $8,000
14    $7,600
15   $12,500
16
17
18
19
20
```

Before testing the macro, recall that the data entry macro, now to be used by 1-2-3 to execute the Enter menu item, is itself a looping macro. It includes a Branch command of its own which causes the macro to return to the beginning, allowing uninterrupted entry of database records. Because the new menu macro automatically provides the Enter or Quit items, the looping capability of the database macro is no longer needed. So, change it to branch to the menu macro instead of to itself.

Move to: cell K4

Press: [EDIT]

[BACKSPACE] *(three times to delete \d})*

Type: \m} [↵]

Now you are ready to test the menu.

Press: [MACRO] -m

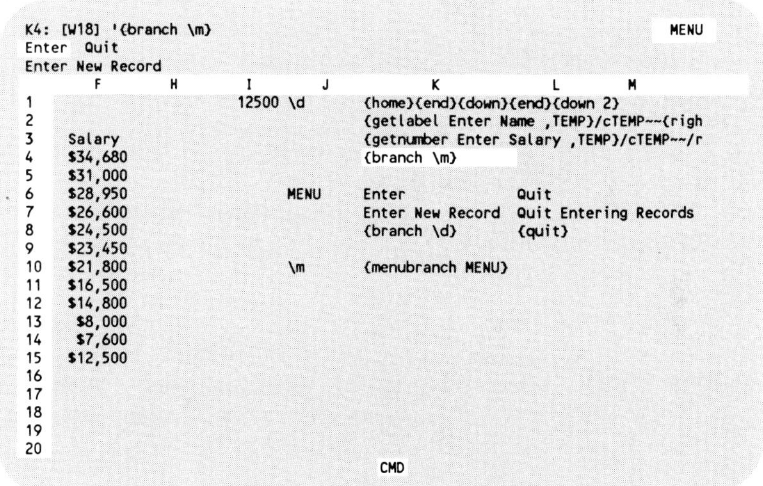

The menu appears in the control panel.

Select: Enter

Type: Avinger [↵]

16700 [↵]

When you type Macro-M, the menu appears in the control panel; you can select Enter or Quit. When you select Enter and type in a record, that record is added to the database and the menu is redisplayed. Selecting Quit leaves the macro and returns you to the database.

Select: Quit

A Macro Library

The macros in the first part of this section—Macros for Any 1-2-3 Worksheet—are generic. You can build them on any worksheet at any time. Use them to start your own library of macros. Once you have built and tested those macros you want to keep in your library, you may want to create a special worksheet file that contains just the macro library; you can then copy that file into new worksheet files you create.

To import the library file into another worksheet file, use the File Combine command. This command enables you to choose whether to import the entire source file or only a portion, and to select the area on the target worksheet to be occupied. After you have combined the two files, you will have to rename the ranges containing the macros. You can use the Range Name Labels command to name the macros ranges in the new file. Then you will be able to use those macros when building and using the worksheet.

More often, macros grow out of specific needs of individual worksheets. These macros automate operations that are performed over and over. The second part of this section—Macros with Special Uses—offers examples of macros that apply to the database file built in the Database chapter of this book. Although these macros are particular to that file, you can see how the same principles apply to other worksheets. You should take your cue from these and other macros, and learn to fashion macros that meet your demands.

Keep in mind these guidelines when reviewing the macros in the library and creating your own macros.

1. Remember that the contents of a macro often represent actual keystrokes in 1-2-3. When testing these macros and developing some of your own, try to imagine running through the keystrokes, and attempt to visualize what happens on the screen.
2. Macro names always consist of a backslash and a letter.
3. Values can appear in a macro only when prefaced with an apostrophe, transforming them into label entries.
4. Always place a blank cell at the end of a macro to signal 1-2-3 to stop.
5. Be careful not to include any unnecessary spaces in the macro.

Macros for Any 1-2-3 Worksheet

1. Range Name Create Macro

a. The Basic Macro

When you're creating macros, you always invoke the Range Name Create command. While naming a range is not very time-consuming, it does involve a number of keystrokes. This macro simply automates that process, saving you most of the keystrokes.

Be aware that this macro assumes that the pointer is resting in the cell you wish to name—it includes a keystroke to accept the range offered by the prompt. Also notice that it accepts only one cell as the range. This macro is not appropriate for naming larger ranges.

Suggested name: \N

Macro: /rnc{?}~ ~

When you invoke this macro, you will be prompted for the name; enter it and press Return, and the range will automatically be accepted and named.

b. Using the Name Key

A variation on this macro enables you to see a screen listing the names already assigned to ranges before you enter a name for the current range. This prevents you from assigning the same name to two ranges—resulting in a loss of the more recently-assigned range.

Suggested name: \K

Macro: /rnc{name}{?}~ ~

This macro includes the equivalent of pressing the Name key after selecting Range Name Create. The Name key calls up a screen that displays all the range names currently saved; move the pointer among them by using the Arrow keys, and the second line of the control panel displays the range assigned to each.

2. Pointer Movement Macros

The pointer movement area of the IBM-PC keyboard doubles as a numeric keypad when the Number Lock key is pressed. This type of keypad is convenient for users accustomed to calculators or adding machines. When the Number Lock feature is on, however, the pointer movement keys are inactivated; they can only be used to move the pointer when the Number Lock key is turned off.

You can write pointer movement macros which make it possible to use the Number Lock feature and move the pointer at the same time. Create four separate macros, one each for up, down, right, and left. Choose the direction in which you want to enter the figures, and invoke that macro. When you enter a number and press Return, 1-2-3 accepts the entry, and the pointer then automatically jumps in the direction you have chosen.

These are looping macros. They include the Branch command, which causes the macro to loop back on itself and repeat the sequence. You stay in the command mode, and the pointer moves indefinitely in the direction you specify. To break the loop and leave the macro, press Ctrl-Break and Escape.

Down macro:

Suggested name: \D

Macro:

```
{?}
{down}
{branch \ d}
```

Up macro:

Suggested name: \U

Macro:

```
{?}
{up}
{branch \u}
```

Right macro:

Suggested name: \R

Macro:

```
{?}
{right}
{branch \r}
```

Left macro:

Suggested name: \L

Macro:

```
{?}
{left}
{branch \ l}
```

To invoke one of the macros, simply press the Macro key and the letter. To break the loop, press Ctrl-Break.

3. Column Width Macro

Setting column widths is a common operation. This macro can help you accomplish it more efficiently.

Suggested name: \W
Macro: /wcs{?}~

When you invoke the macro, you will be prompted for the desired width of the column. Enter it (either by typing it in or by pressing the Arrow keys) and press Return; the column in which the pointer is resting will be set to the specified width.

4. Macros for Printing

a. Printing the Entire Worksheet

Printing the worksheet is a common activity, and one that you may want to repeat again and again to reflect different what-if scenarios, for example, on the same worksheet. This printing macro can lessen the time you take to accomplish the task.

This macro calls up the Print menu, clears previous settings, specifies the entire active worksheet as the range to be printed, and activates the print process. Once the worksheet has printed, the macro moves the paper to the end of the page and quits the Print menu.

Suggested name: \P
Macro:
```
/ppca
r{home}.{end}{home}~
agpq
```

The meaning of each portion of the macro:

/ppca: Calls up the Print menu, clears the previous settings.

r{home}.{end}{home}~: Selects the range to be printed by moving the pointer to cell A1, anchoring the range, moving to the end of the active worksheet, and accepting the highlighted range.

agpq: Chooses Align and Go from the menu; then, after the worksheet has printed, moves the paper down and quits the Print menu.

b. Printing Cell Contents

As explained in the Tips section of this book, 1-2-3 offers the facility to print the contents of each cell. To automate the keystrokes involved, create a slightly revised version of the macro that prints the entire worksheet.

Suggested name: \C

Macro:

```
/ppca
r{home}.{end}{home}~
oocqagp
ooaqq
```

The third line calls up the Options submenu and chooses Cell-Formulas before printing; the last line returns to the Options submenu after printing and eliminates that setting so it is not in effect the next time you print.

c. Printing Borders

Rather than remembering all the keystrokes involved in printing row and column borders, consolidate the steps into a macro. This macro prompts you for the print range and then for the column and the row to use as borders on the printout.

Note that this macro does not automatically specify the entire active area of the worksheet as the range to be printed: you must specify the range to be printed, making sure it doesn't include the borders.

This macro also uses an unusual addition in the form of the Beep command.

Suggested name: \B

Macro:

```
/ppr{beep 3}{?}~
obc{beep 4}{?}~
br{beep 5}{?}~
qagpq
```

This macro includes beeps to alert you when 1-2-3 is awaiting information. Notice that specifying different numbers results in beeps of different pitches. The beeps are especially useful in a macro that takes a long time to execute; they can notify you when the program reaches a prompt.

5. Word Wrap Macro

1-2-3 offers some text editing capabilities, centered around the Range Justify command. This command acts on a label that extends into adjacent cells, breaking it up and fitting it into the columns specified. You can create a macro that automates the justifying process, making it much easier to enter text uninterrupted by the periodic need to format it into a column. The macro described earlier in the section of the macro chapter called Create a Looping Macro demonstrates this type of macro.

Suggested name: \T
Macro:
```
{edit}{?}~
/rj~
{end}{down}
{branch \t}
```

6. Cell Formatting Macros

1-2-3 offers various options for formatting the worksheet. You can format the entire worksheet with the Global menu commands, or a range of cells with the Range menu commands. For those times when you want to format only individual cells, these formatting macros might help. They allow you to format a single cell with any of the format options; they save time and keystrokes.

Listed below are macros covering four of the most common format choices.

Currency, 0 decimal places: **/rfc0~~**
Percent, 0 decimal places: **/rfp0~~**
Punctuated, 0 decimal places: **/rf,0~~**
Date, 2nd choice (DD-MMM): **/rfd2~**

Each macro calls up the main menu, selects Range and Format, and then chooses the type of format. It then specifies the number of decimal places, or, in the case of the date, the style of date. Finally, it presses Return twice (once, for the date format) to enter the number and accept the range.

You can adapt these macros or create new ones for any of the other format options and for any number of decimal places. You can also create a macro that uses {?} instead of the final tilde so you can manually specify the range to be formatted.

7. Ruled Line Macros

For those times when you want to add ruled lines to the worksheet to divide it into more legible sections, these two macros automate the process.

Macro for a double ruled line:

\=~
/c~{?}~

Macro for a single ruled line:

\-~
/c~{?}~

These macros enter the ruled line in the cell where the pointer is located, and then copy the line into the range you specify. At the {?}, when the program awaits the designated range, you must enter a period to anchor the range. This period may be added to the macro if you wish for the range to be anchored automatically.

Note that the backslash, usually signifying the macro key, is used in these macros as a repeating character key.

8. File Save Macro

For all the times you must save the file, write a macro to make the task as speedy as possible. The macro below can be used only after you have saved the file once, thereby giving it a name. The macro simply accepts the name already assigned to the file.

Suggested name: \S
Macro: /fs~r

9. Macro Giving Today's Date

This macro simplifies the process of entering today's date, a task which usually includes entering the @DATE function and formatting the results.

Suggested name: \A
Macro: @now~
/rfd2~

The "2" in the macro indicates that the second date format is used. Adapt the macro so it uses your preferred format.

Macros with Special Uses

A Menu Macro for a Database

This section presents a menu macro, consisting of seven separate macros, all built in the database file that was created in the Database chapter of this book.

Six of the seven macros perform operations on the database. These macros are stored in a range named Menu. Together they constitute one large macro that creates a menu of the six database activities. The seventh macro uses the advanced macro command Menubranch to branch to the range containing the menu macro.

Follow the steps below to build to the menu.

1. Retrieve the database file.

First call up the database file. Once it appears, use the Range Erase command to erase the criterion range and the output range that are still in the file. The database should look like the illustration below.

```
A1: [W12]                                                        READY

         A          B    C       D       E        F        G        H
1                     Personnel Records
2
3        Name      Floor Office  Dept.  Status   Salary   Start
4   Nodine             2     21   Adm      FT    $34,680  Jun-81
5   Klein              3     12   Mkt       C    $31,000  Sep-80
6   Falke              2     14   Adm      FT    $28,950  Feb-82
7   Teal               3     13   R&D      FT    $26,600  Jan-82
8   Saddler            3     11   Mkt       C    $24,500  Apr-83
9   Sloane             2      8   Mkt      FT    $23,450  Jun-81
10  Wilder             4     17   Adm       C    $21,800  Jan-84
11  Carlson            4      7   R&D      PT    $16,500  Oct-81
12  Heineman           4     14   Mkt      FT    $14,800  Aug-82
13  Byrne              2     18   R&D      PT     $8,000  Nov-83
14  Martyn             3     14   R&D      PT     $7,600  Mar-84
15
16
17
18
19
20
```

2. Create a column width macro.

Create and invoke a macro to set the column widths of columns J, K, L, M, N, and O to 35 characters wide. Place the macro in column Q.

Suggested name: \Q
Macro: /wcs35~

3. Name the Menu range.

Name the range that will contain the six menu items and the individual macros that will perform those operations.

Location: cell J4
Name: Menu

4. Add the menu items and descriptions.

Enter the labels that will represent menu options and one-line descriptions of each item.

Move to: cell J4
Type: Datasort [▶]
Graph [▶]
Salaries [▶]
Macros [▶]
File [▶]
Quit [↵]
Move to: cell J5
Type: Sort names alphabetically [▶]
Create a graph of salaries [▶]
Display the salaries graph [▶]
Move to the macros section of worksheet [▶]
Save the amended file [▶]
Quit macros menu and return to worksheet [↵]

The entries in cells J4 through O4 constitute the menu that appears in the control panel. The entries in cells J5 through O5 serve as the explanations of each menu item and appear in the control panel when the applicable menu item is highlighted.

5. Create the macros for the six menu items.

For the first menu option, Datasort, create a macro to sort the database alphabetically. The macro below allows you to specify the data range to sort. You want to be able to specify the range when necessary as the database may increase in size.

Location: cell J6
Macro: /dsd{?}~
pA4~a ~g

For the second menu item, Graph, enter a macro to create a graph of salaries grouped by status. This macro has two parts. The first part, occupying the first line of the macro, sorts the database by status (Primary-Key) and by salary (Secondary-Key). The second part, comprising the rest of the macro, creates the graph.

Location: cell K6
Macro: /dspE4~~ sF4~ ~g
/grgqtb
x{?}~a{?}~
olaSalary~
tfSalaries by Status~
qv
ncsalaries~q

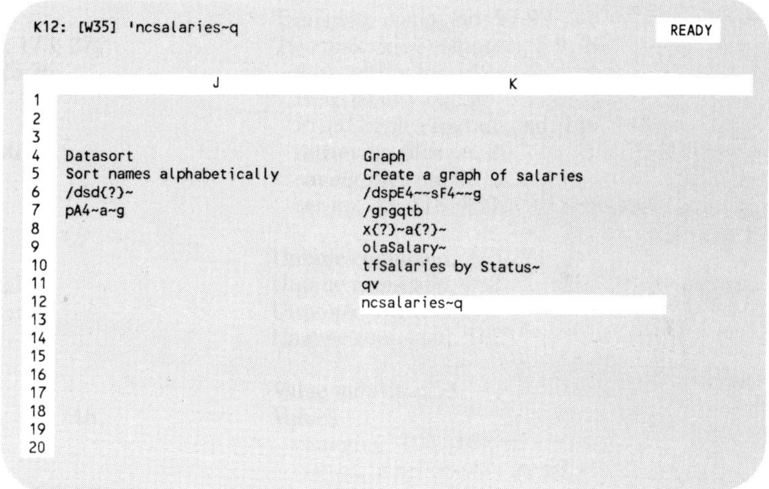

```
K12: [W35] 'ncsalaries~q                                              READY

                      J                                K
1
2
3
4   Datasort                            Graph
5   Sort names alphabetically           Create a graph of salaries
6   /dsd{?}~                            /dspE4~~sF4~~g
7   pA4~a~g                             /grgqtb
8                                       x{?}~a{?}~
9                                       olaSalary~
10                                      tfSalaries by Status~
11                                      qv
12                                      ncsalaries~q
13
14
15
16
17
18
19
20
```

This macro allows you to specify the X and A data ranges so you can adjust them when the database expands. To start, you can specify the Status field (E4..E14) as the X range and the Salary field (F4..F14) as the A range. The graph will display as part of the execution of the macro. Press Esc when you have finished viewing the graph to complete the macro.

For the third menu item, Salaries, enter a macro to view the graph just created.

Location: cell L6
Macro: /gnusalaries~q

For the fourth menu item, Macros, enter a macro that moves the pointer to the macros section of the worksheet.

Location: cell M6
Macro: {goto}menu~

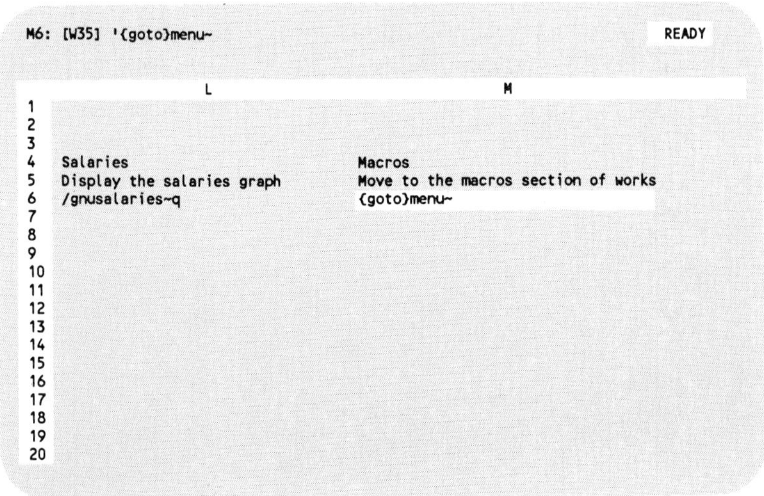

For the fifth menu item, File, enter a macro to save the amended database file.

Location: cell N6
Macro: /fs~r

For the last menu item, Quit, enter a macro to move the pointer to cell A1 and leave the menu macro.

Location: cell O6
Macro: {home}
{quit}

```
O7: [W35] '{quit}                                             READY

                  N                                    O
 1
 2
 3
 4   File                                 Quit
 5   Save the amended file                Quit macros menu and return to worksheet
 6   /fs~r                                {home}
 7                                        {quit}
 8
 9
10
11
12
13
14
15
16
17
18
19
20
```

6. Name the range for the seventh macro.

Name the range that holds the macro containing the command Menubranch. When this macro directs 1-2-3 to move to the Menu range, a menu is displayed in the control panel.

Location: cell J2
Name: \M

7. Create the seventh macro.

Add the macro command that will create the menu.

Location: cell J2
Macro: {menubranch menu}

Copy the command to cells J8, K13, L7, M7, and N7 at the end the five macros you created earlier. This way, when each individual macro finishes executing, it branches back to the beginning of the menu macro. The menu is displayed in the control panel. (The Quit item concludes with the {quit} command and should not loop to the beginning of the macro.)

```
J2: [W35] '{menubranch menu}                                      READY

                    J                                  K
1
2   {menubranch menu}
3
4   Datasort                             Graph
5   Sort names alphabetically            Create a graph of salaries
6   /dsd{?}~                             /dspE4~~sF4~~g
7   pA4~a~g                              /grgqtb
8   {menubranch menu}                    x{?}~a{?}~
9                                        olaSalary~
10                                       tfSalaries by Status~
11                                       qv
12                                       ncsalaries~q
13                                       {menubranch menu}
14
15
16
17
18
19
20
```

8. Invoke the menu macro.

Press: MACRO - m

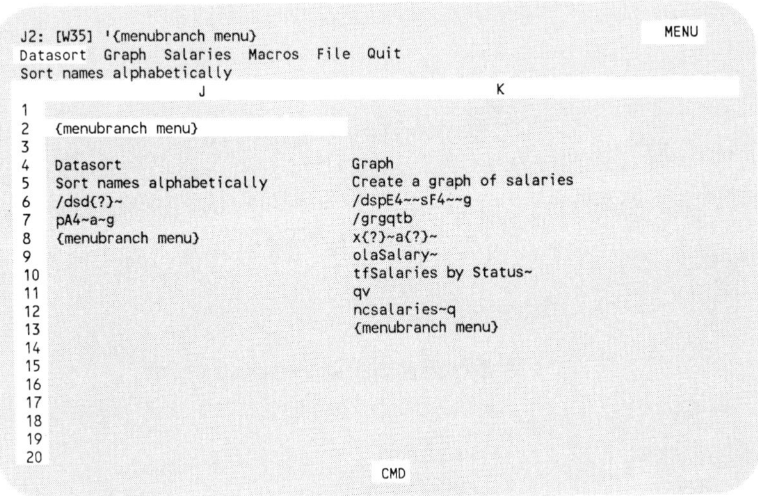

Your screen should look like the illustration above.

Test the various menu options. As with a worksheet menu, make a selection either by typing the first letter of the option, or by highlighting the option and pressing Return.

A Macro to Create Mailing Labels

A frequent question about 1-2-3 is whether it can create and print mailing labels. This kind of operation shows clearly the beauty of macros. Once you have built a database that contains a mailing list, you can enter a macro on the worksheet to create and print mailing labels automatically. This macro does not affect the use of the worksheet in any way, because it extracts data from the main area of the worksheet and transforms the data into mailing labels elsewhere.

There are many different ways to construct a macro to accomplish the same task. The macro in this example is large and somewhat complex, but once it is entered it does all the work involved in creating and printing mailing labels from a simple database.

This macro has been built using specific cell addresses. Build it exactly as it appears, and then modify it to fit your needs.

Follow these steps to build the mailing labels macro.

1. Prepare the database.

Enter the field names as shown, and adjust the column widths to accommodate the entries. To make sure the macro will work properly, place the field names exactly in the cells as shown.

```
G5: [W6] '93577                                                    READY

        A         B         C               D                E          F   G
1   Last      First     Co              Addr             City       St  Zip
2   Cooper    Madeline  Rogers Rainwear 100 Wet Road     Scarsdale  NY  10023
3   Mandler   Peter     DemSA, Inc.     Thomas Street    Princeton  NJ  08464
4   Graves    Nina                      2 Trevor Avenue  St. Paul   MN  55102
5   Collings  Vincent   China Corp.     90 Sarasota Way  Sarasota   FL  93577
6
7
8
9
10
11
12
13
14
15
16
17
18
19
20
```

Enter the sample records as shown. Be sure to leave the blank cell (it will demonstrate certain principles). Also, be very careful to enter all the records as labels only (even the zip codes); the macro stops if it encounters a value.

2. Name and document the ranges.

This macro uses two named ranges. Assign the first name to the first cell of the macro. The second range will serve as an argument for a Branch command at the end of the macro: the print command in the macro will be repeated for as many addresses as you have in the data range.

Assign the following names to ranges:

First range Name: \X
Location: cell B18 *(the first cell of the macro)*

Second range Name: LOOP
Location: cell B26

Document these ranges by typing \X in cell A18 and LOOP in cell A26.

3. Enter the macro.

Type the macro exactly as shown. Enter the first cell of the macro in the cell you named \X. (Notice that you can copy some of the entries to other cells and adjust them to match.) Remember to enter apostrophes before the non-label characters.

Macro:

```
{home}/rt.{right 6}~k1~
{goto}k1~/rnlr{end}{down}~
{goto}i1~/wcs25~
+first&" "&last~{down}
@if(@iserr(@length(CO))=1,ADDR,CO)~{down}
@if(@iserr(@length(CO))=1,CITY&", "&ST&"
  "&ZIP,ADDR)~{down}
@if(@iserr(@length(CO))=1,"",CITY&", "&ST&"
  "&ZIP)~
{home}/ppri1.i7~oouqq
{down}/rncTEMP~{bs}~
{if TEMP=0}{quit}
/rt.{right 6}~l1~
/ppagq{branch LOOP}
```

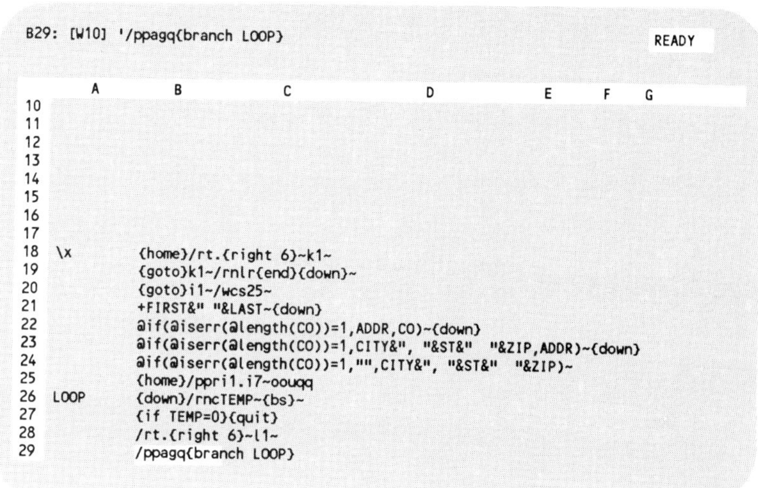

4. Invoke the macro.

Press Macro-X to print out the labels. Make sure the printer is on and the paper is aligned. During the first run of the macro, the screen shows the data being rearranged and the ranges being established.

5. Modify the macro.

You can modify the macro to suit your needs. You might choose to change the cell addresses, adjust the number of spaces between labels, and otherwise adapt it to your own database.

The meaning of each portion of the macro:

{home}/rt.{right 6}~k1~: Transposes the field names of the database and places them in column K.

{goto}k1~/rnlr{end}{down}~: Creates a set of ranges, each one named with one of the field names in column K, and locates each range to the right of its related field name.

{goto}i1~/wcs25~: Widens column I.

+FIRST&" "&LAST~{down}
@if(@iserr(@length(CO))=1,ADDR,CO)~{down}
@if(@iserr(@length(CO))=1,CITY&", "&ST&" "&ZIP,ADDR)~{down}
@if(@iserr(@length(CO))=1,"",CITY&", "&ST&" "&ZIP)~: These formulas are placed in cells I1 through I4; they test for blank cells in the company field, and convert the data into mailing label format prior to printing the labels.

{home}/ppri1.i7~oouqq: Specifies the print range and requests an unformatted printout.

{down}/rncTEMP~{bs}~
{if TEMP=0}{quit}: Names the range TEMP and tells the macro to quit if the cell is blank (equal to 0).

/rt.{right 6}~l1~
/ppagq{branch LOOP}: Transposes the entries in the data record into column L; after the entries print as a label the macro branches back to LOOP and repeats the print procedure for the next data record down.

Note: To move through the macro step by step, use 1-2-3's single-step mode, described earlier in this chapter.

/X Macro Commands

In previous releases of 1-2-3, macros can be created using a series of /X programming commands. All /X commands have corresponding advance macro commands in 1-2-3 Release 2. The new advanced macro commands offer greater flexibility and functionality in designing 1-2-3 macros. To maintain compatibility with previous releases, 1-2-3 Release 2 also contains all of the /X commands. The /X commands are:

/X Command	Corresponding Keyword	Function
/XIcondition~	{if}	If-then
/XGlocation~	{branch}	Go to
/XClocation~	{routine-name}	Call a subroutine
/XR	{return}	Return from subroutine
/XQ	{quit}	Quit macro execution
/XLmessage,location~ /XNmessage,location~	{getlabel} {getnumber}	Display a message in the control panel and accept a label entry (/XL) or number entry (/XN) from the keyboard and place it in a cell
/XMlocation~	{menubranch}	Construct a user-defined menu

7

1-2-3 Tips

This chapter presents shortcuts and tips to some of the more advanced 1-2-3 operations. The tips are organized into five sections: Worksheet, Functions and Formulas, Database, Printing, and Graphics. Feel free to read through the whole chapter at once, or simply refer to the individual tips as you need them. They should prove informative, and set you on the road toward mastering 1-2-3.

Worksheet

The following are a number of useful 1-2-3 worksheet tips.

1. Recalculation Modes: Manual and Automatic

1-2-3 has an initial setting for automatic recalculation. This means that every time you enter a new value or formula onto a worksheet, 1-2-3 stops to recalculate all the figures. This process takes very little time in smaller worksheets, but it takes longer and longer as the size of a worksheet increases.

If you find that you are waiting more than a few seconds for recalculation when building a worksheet, you can switch the setting to manual recalculation.

To set recalculation to manual:

Press: [/]

Select: Worksheet
Global
Recalculation
Manual

With this setting, press the CALC key each time you want the worksheet to recalculate. 1-2-3 reminds you to do this by displaying the word CALC in the status indicator whenever a change is made to the worksheet.

```
B6: (C0) 250                                                      READY

                A                   B          C          D          E
1                                 Income Statement
2                                 July-1-86  July-31-86
3
4   000's omitted                   PROD.1     PROD.2     PROD.3     TOTAL
5   ==================================================================
6   Gross Sales                       $250       $200       $200      $500
7     Sales Allowance                  $20        $80        $60      $160
8   Net Sales                          $80       $120       $140      $340
9     Cost of Goods Sold               $30        $60        $70      $160
10  Gross Margin                       $50        $60        $70      $180
11    Marketing/G&A Expenses           $35        $30        $30       $95
12  EBIT                               $15        $30        $40       $85
13    Interest                          $1         $2         $2        $5
14    Taxes                             $7        $14        $19       $40
15  Net Income                          $7        $14        $19       $40
16
17  % Total Net Sales                  24%        35%        41%      100%
18
19
20
                                                  CALC
```

In the worksheet illustrated above, a new value has been entered in cell B6 but the worksheet has not been recalculated. Notice that the numbers do not add up correctly and that the status indicator reads CALC.

2. Setting Horizontal and Vertical Titles

It often happens that labels identifying columns and rows are placed at the top or left edges of a worksheet and that these labels scroll off the screen as you move around the worksheet. The Titles command enables you to freeze the rows or columns (or both) of labels at these edges. The labels stay in place when you move around the worksheet. For example, on a worksheet with the months of the year entered as the top row of the worksheet, setting the top row as a title would keep the labels visible no matter how far you moved down.

Before setting the titles, locate the pointer in a cell just to the right of the column you wish to set as a vertical title, or just below the row you wish to set as a horizontal title. If you want to set both horizontal and vertical titles, place the pointer in the cell to the right of the column and below the row to be set.

To freeze titles at the top or left edges of the worksheet:

Press: [/]

Select: Worksheet
Titles

The command menu on the second line of the control panel gives the options **Both Horizontal Vertical Clear**. After you have made your choice, the menu disappears and the titles are frozen.

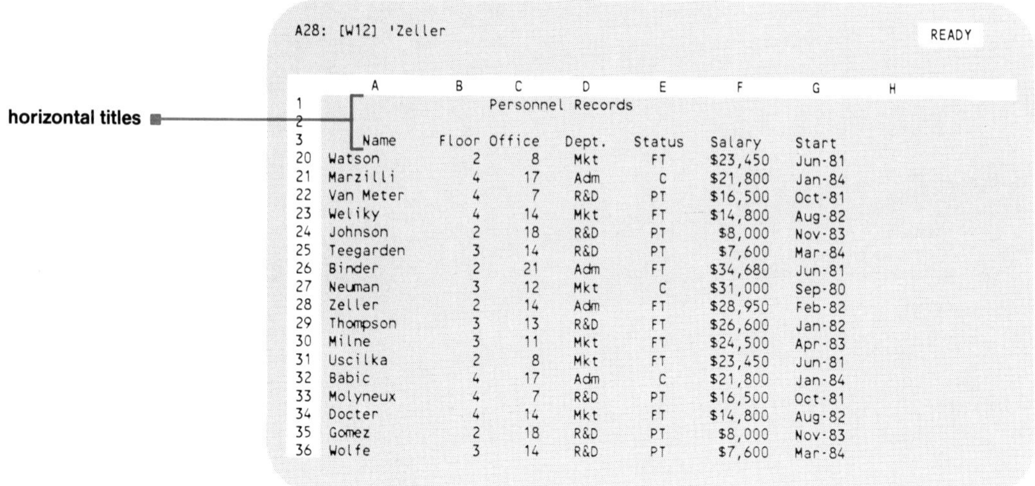

A28: [W12] 'Zeller READY

	A	B	C	D	E	F	G	H
1			Personnel Records					
2								
3	Name	Floor	Office	Dept.	Status	Salary	Start	
20	Watson	2	8	Mkt	FT	$23,450	Jun-81	
21	Marzilli	4	17	Adm	C	$21,800	Jan-84	
22	Van Meter	4	7	R&D	PT	$16,500	Oct-81	
23	Weliky	4	14	Mkt	FT	$14,800	Aug-82	
24	Johnson	2	18	R&D	PT	$8,000	Nov-83	
25	Teegarden	3	14	R&D	PT	$7,600	Mar-84	
26	Binder	2	21	Adm	FT	$34,680	Jun-81	
27	Neuman	3	12	Mkt	C	$31,000	Sep-80	
28	Zeller	2	14	Adm	FT	$28,950	Feb-82	
29	Thompson	3	13	R&D	FT	$26,600	Jan-82	
30	Milne	3	11	Mkt	FT	$24,500	Apr-83	
31	Uscilka	2	8	Mkt	FT	$23,450	Jun-81	
32	Babic	4	17	Adm	C	$21,800	Jan-84	
33	Molyneux	4	7	R&D	PT	$16,500	Oct-81	
34	Docter	4	14	Mkt	FT	$14,800	Aug-82	
35	Gomez	2	18	R&D	PT	$8,000	Nov-83	
36	Wolfe	3	14	R&D	PT	$7,600	Mar-84	

In the database illustrated above, the top three rows (containing the title of the database and the field names) have been made a horizontal title. Since these rows are frozen at the top of the screen, it is possible to scroll down the worksheet (in this case to see the records in rows 20 through 36) and keep the field names in view at the same time.

In order to clear the set titles, you have to call up the Titles command again and select Clear.

3. Initial Settings and the Status Screen

When you start up 1-2-3, many variable aspects of the worksheet's appearance and function are already determined. The worksheet format is set so all the columns are the same width, the cells have a specific format, and so on. In addition, the program is set to do such things as save files on the disk in drive A. These preset specifications are called the initial settings.

As you know, you can change the initial settings to your own default settings to meet your needs. You can alter the worksheet settings in countless ways, and you can customize 1-2-3 to your hardware.

The Status Screen

When you're in the process of building a worksheet, you have the option of changing any of the initial settings. It is helpful to see information on the current status of the worksheet first. At any point, 1-2-3 enables you to look at such information on the status screen.

To call up the status screen:

Press: /

Select: Worksheet
Status

```
                                                            STAT

Available Memory:
  Conventional..... 356032 of 357856 Bytes (99%)
  Expanded......... (None)

Math Co-processor:  (None)

Recalculation:
  Method........... Automatic
  Order............ Natural
  Iterations....... 1

Circular Reference: (None)

Cell Display:
  Format........... (G)
  Label-Prefix..... '
  Column-Width..... 9
  Zero Supression.. Off

Global Protection:  Off
```

The status screen informs you of worksheet characteristics such as initial settings for the cell format, the column width, and so on. It presents the settings for the entire worksheet—known as global settings—rather than for the cell that is currently highlighted; there may be many different settings and formats in various cells on the worksheet, but the status screen lists only the global settings for the entire worksheet.

The status screen also lists information on the status of the program. It tells you how much memory is left, whether there are circular references in the worksheet, and so forth.

You cannot actually gain access to the status screen to change any of the settings. To change the settings, you have to return to the worksheet and call up the Global menu. Each of the setting items on the status screen corresponds to an item on the Global menu.

To call up the Global menu:

Press: any key *(to make the status screen disappear)*
[/]

Select: Worksheet
Global

The Global menu appears, giving you the opportunity to change any of the global worksheet settings.

4. Copying and Moving

a. Copying Cell Formats

When you copy the contents of one cell to another, you are also copying the format of the first cell to the second. The new format overrides any previous format of the second cell.

In general, this is a helpful feature. If the first cell has been formatted to display its contents as a percentage with two decimal places, it would be disconcerting to see the same value, when copied to another cell, displayed as an integer. However, you should be careful to remember this feature when copying; you may want a different format in the new cell.

b. Specifying TO and FROM Ranges

When you are copying or moving one range of cells to another range, you should be careful about specifying the TO and FROM directions.

First, when copying or moving FROM a range, it's a good idea to specify only one cell as the TO range. 1-2-3 regards this single cell as the upper-left corner of the range to be copied or moved to, and fills in the range with the new cell contents.

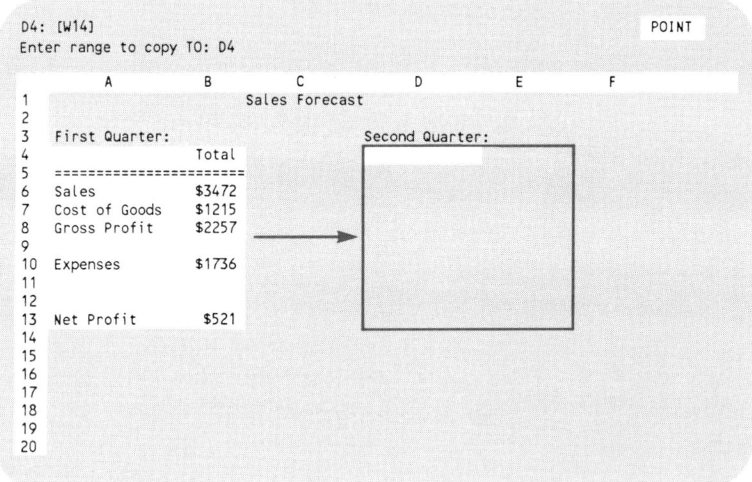

Second, make sure that the two ranges do not overlap at any point when copying. If they do, some of the original cell contents will be erased.

c. Overwriting Cell Contents

Finally, be aware that copying and moving data to a range of cells always erases the previous contents of the cells. There is no way to recover the contents. Formulas that refer to these cells are still valid, but the calculated values may change to reflect the new contents.

Always check a range before copying or moving new data into it. If it contains information you want to keep, move the old data somewhere else before proceeding.

5. Highlighting a Range

As you know by now, there are two ways to indicate a range of cells when using such 1-2-3 commands as Copy and Move. You can either type the cell addresses (e.g. E3.F6), or you can highlight the range on the worksheet. When highlighting a range, there are a few tips to keep in mind:

– The range is anchored if the prompt in the control panel displays a range of cells, e.g. E3..E3; it is not anchored if the prompt displays a single cell address, e.g. E3.

— If the range is not anchored, press the period key to anchor it. To release an anchored range, press Esc.

— After the range is anchored, use the Arrow keys to extend the highlight if necessary.

— You can change the free corner of the highlighted range, designated by the small blinking cursor in the lower-middle of the cell, by pressing the period key. Each time you press the period key, the free corner cell moves to a different corner of the range. You can then expand the highlight in the direction of the free corner.

— Use the End key along with the Arrow keys to highlight various ranges in the active area of the worksheet. If the pointer is on a blank cell, it moves in the direction of the arrow either to the first filled cell or to the edge of the worksheet. If the pointer is on a filled cell, it moves in the direction of the arrow either to the last filled cell before a blank cell or to the edge of the worksheet.

— To highlight the entire active area of the worksheet when specifying a range for a command:

Press: [HOME]
[.]
[END]
[HOME]
[↵] *(to enter the range)*

6. Planning and Documenting a Worksheet

Before you actually start to build a worksheet on the screen, take the time to plan it out and write down all your assumptions.

First, think about what the worksheet will contain. Do you want to create separate sections for different groups of data? How will these sections relate to each other? For example, will formulas link them? How large do the areas need to be, and will they need room to expand?

Next, given the answers to the questions above, map out a worksheet on paper. You do not have to be exact in your allocation of rows and columns, but sketch out the general locations of groups of data and how big an area each group will occupy.

Next, make a record of the assumptions involved in building the worksheet. You can do this either on the screen or on paper. Record such things as dates, numbers used in formulas, and so on.

Finally, after you have built the worksheet, print out a document that lists only the cell contents line by line. (See the Tip on "Printing Cell Contents.") This printout will give you information on all the material in each cell—formula, label, format, and so on—and will provide a reference for any questions you may have.

7. Protecting the Worksheet

When you create a new worksheet, all of the cells are unprotected; you can enter data into any of them. It's a good idea to protect the final version when you have finished building and modifying a worksheet. This will prevent you from inadvertently modifying or erasing important cell contents (labels, formulas or values).

1-2-3's protection feature is global: it protects all the cells in the worksheet. Once global protection is enabled, you can then unprotect specific ranges of cells that you want to be able to access and change.

To protect the entire worksheet:

Press: [/]
Select: Worksheet
Global
Protection
Enable

After enabling global protection, you will not be able to change any of the cells on the worksheet. In order to alter specific cells, unprotect the exact range of those cells.

To unprotect a range of cells:

Press: [/]
Select: Range
Unprotect

The second line of the control panel reads `Enter range to unprotect:`. You can either type in the range or highlight it.

```
B8: (CO) PR +B6-B7                                                  READY

          A                     B          C          D          E
1                          Income Statement
2                          July-1-86  July-31-86
3
4   000's omitted             PROD.1     PROD.2     PROD.3      TOTAL
5   ==================================================================
6   Gross Sales                 $100       $200       $200       $500
7     Sales Allowance            $20        $80        $60       $160
8   Net Sales                    $80       $120       $140       $340
9     Cost of Goods Sold         $30        $60        $70       $160
10  Gross Margin                 $50        $60        $70       $180
11    Marketing/G&A Expenses     $35        $30        $30        $95
12  EBIT                         $15        $30        $40        $85
13    Interest                    $1         $2         $2         $5
14    Taxes                       $7        $14        $19        $40
15  Net Income                    $7        $14        $19        $40
16
17  % Total Net Sales            24%        35%        41%       100%
18
19
20
```

In the worksheet illustrated above, the unprotected cells have been highlighted; on the screen, the unprotected cells actually appear brighter than the others on the screen. In this worksheet, the cells containing labels and formulas have been protected; the cells containing numbers are unprotected, allowing you to enter data at any time. A U appears in the first line of the control panel next to the contents of an unprotected cell; PR appears in the control panel by the contents of a protected cell.

In order to re-protect a range of cells you have unprotected, use the command Range Protect. (Note that you cannot simply use this command to protect a range on an unprotected worksheet. The 1-2-3 global protection feature applies to the entire worksheet; the Range Protect command can be used only to re-protect ranges that have been unprotected.)

8. Range Names

The ability to name a range of cells is one of 1-2-3's most helpful features. With a little practice, you can easily learn to use range names in most commands that call for ranges. Referring to the names can save you the time and trouble of remembering and pointing to the actual cell addresses.

The Range Name menu gives you a number of choices, providing a great deal of flexibility in the creation and manipulation of the ranges. The following are some tips to keep in mind.

— When choosing a name for a range, use only one word. If you want to use two words, connect them with a hyphen.

— To modify the named range, select Range, Name, Create, and then the name. The currently defined range of cells will be highlighted; use the Arrow keys and the period key to change the range and then press Return.

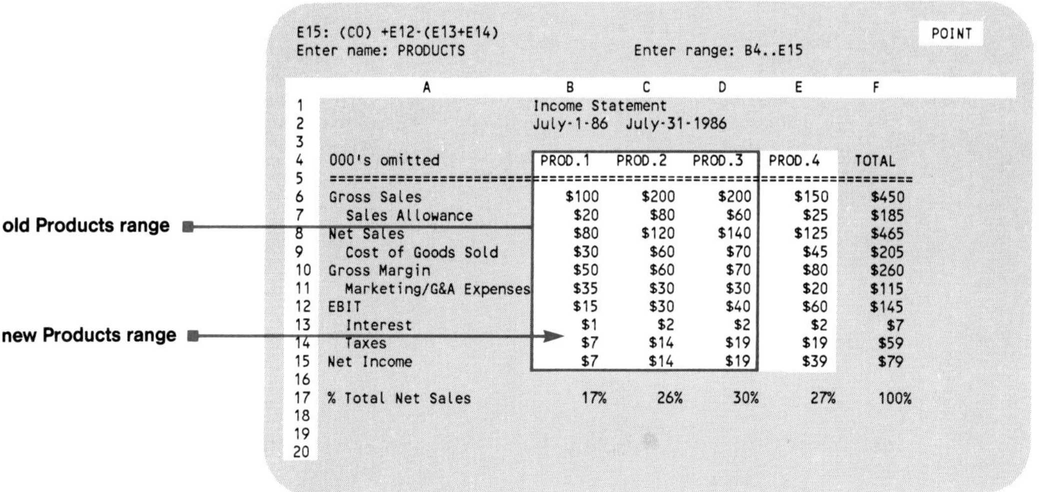

— When you change the range of cells assigned to a name, any references to the original range are transformed into references to the new range. For example, if you change a range that is named and used in a formula, the formula will now refer to the new range assigned to the name. In addition, if you name a range that is already used in a formula, that formula will display the range name—instead of the range itself—in the control panel. The references are modified whether they were originally made by cell addresses or by name.

— You can delete all the range names by selecting Range Name Reset. You can delete single names by selecting Range Name Delete.

— Using the Delete or Reset commands to eliminate range names does not cancel references to the range. The range name simply ceases to be associated with the range. Formulas previously referring to the range name now refer to the range itself.

— To rename a range, select Range, Name, Create, and then the name. Press the Edit key; the highlighted range is frozen, and you can now edit the range name itself. When you have changed the name and pressed Return, the old name will be deleted and the new name will define the original range.

9. The Name Key

The Name key makes it possible for you to see a good deal of information about the data disk currently in the computer and the worksheet currently on the screen. Pressing the Name key while executing certain commands calls up a screen which can supply complete lists of the files on the data disk or of the range names in the current file. This screen also offers additional information on the files and the range names.

Try calling up a list of the files on the data disk:

Press: [/]
Select: File
Retrieve
Press: [NAME]

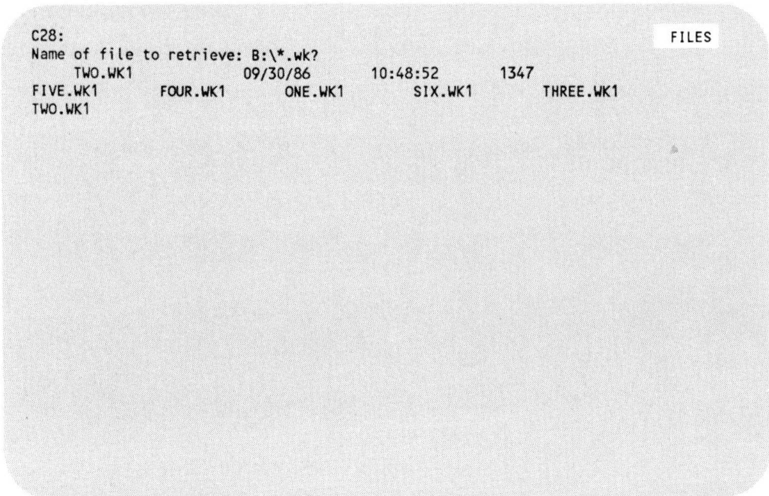

A new screen appears. The top two lines of the control panel remain the same, but the third line now lists information on the file name highlighted on the screen—information which includes the date and time the file was created and the size of the file. The rest of the screen is occupied by the names of all the worksheet files on the disk, including the highlighted file. Use the Arrow keys to move around the list; notice that the information on the third line changes as the cursor moves. To select a file, highlight it and press Return. The Name key offers the same facility in the File Save operation as well.

You can view lists of other types of files on the data disk as well. To see the list of .PIC files, execute the Graph Save command and then press the Name key. The list appears in a similar screen.

Finally, the Name key calls up a list of all the range names in the current worksheet.

Press: /

Select: Range
Name
Create

Press: NAME

A screen appears listing all the range names. The third line of the control panel now displays the name of the currently highlighted range and the cell addresses of the range.

The Name key works as a toggle key: pressing it makes the screen appear and then disappear. You can always make a choice from the screen when it is displayed by pressing Return.

10. Hiding Columns

1-2-3 Release 2 features commands that hide (and unhide) one or more columns on a worksheet. This facility enables you to view otherwise separated columns next to each other, and to print otherwise non-adjacent ranges next to each other as well. It makes it easier to compare certain ranges of values.

To hide columns on a worksheet:

Press: /

Select: Worksheet
Column
Hide

At this point the second line of the control panel reads `Specify column to hide:`; the mode indicator reads POINT. You can either type in the cell addresses of the range of columns you wish to hide, or you can press the period key and use the Arrow keys to extend the highlight to the right or left. You can include as many columns as you like, and you can execute these commands as many times as you like on different areas of the worksheet.

When you have specified the range, press Return. The selected columns disappear and the pointer rests on the column to the right of the hidden range.

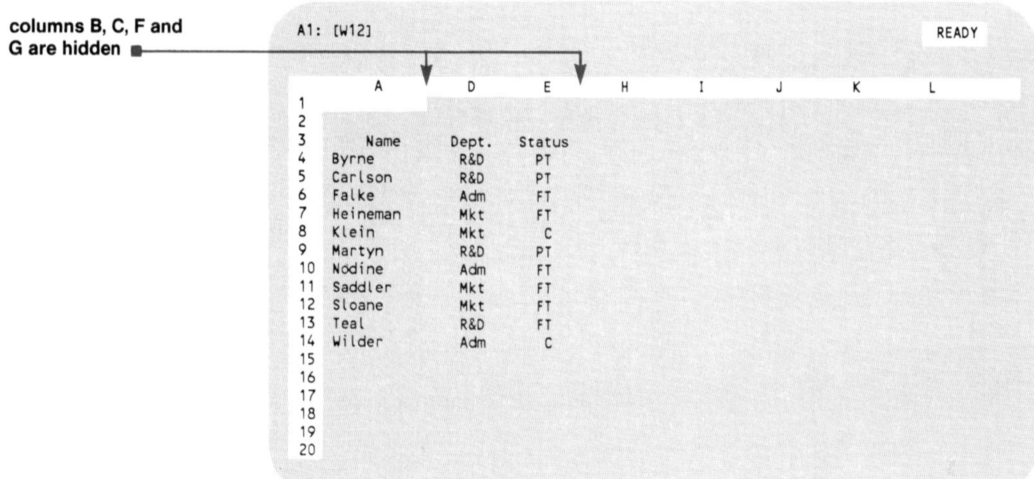

In the database illustrated above, columns B, C, F and G are hidden. The column containing the Dept. listings is now directly adjacent to the column containing the names, thus making it easier to compare those two fields.

Hidden columns are not displayed in the READY mode, nor are they accessible—you cannot enter data in them. The existing contents of the columns still figure in the worksheet; for example, formulas that refer to the cell contents calculate correctly.

Hidden columns are displayed whenever you are in the POINT mode. Therefore you can see those columns when you select commands that call for a range, or when you're entering a formula and pointing to the cells. Columns that are temporarily unhidden are marked by an asterisk placed after the column letter on the top border of the worksheet.

To unhide the hidden columns:

Press: [/]

Select: Worksheet
Column
Display

Again, you can type the cell addresses or highlight the range containing the columns you wish to redisplay. Note that you can expand the highlight over unhidden columns to reach non-adjacent ranges if you like. Once you have specified the range, press Return.

11. The Insert Key

When you press the Edit key to begin editing cell contents, the insert mode is automatically on. The insert mode allows you to add new characters without displacing the old ones in the cell. You can switch to the overstrike mode while editing by pressing the Insert key. This enables you to overwrite the current cell contents.

When you press the Insert key during in the EDIT mode, the status indicator reads OVR. You can overwrite the contents in the cell—value, formula, label. Pressing Return enters the edited cell contents and turns off the overstrike mode.

Functions and Formulas

1. Rounding Off Numbers

You can control the number of decimal places displayed on the worksheet in three ways: with the Range Format Fixed command, the @INT function, or the @ROUND function. However, each of these procedures affects the values displayed on the worksheet in a different way.

The Format Fixed command determines how a number is displayed, but it does **not** affect the actual value of the number. No matter how many decimal places are displayed on the screen, the number is stored at its full value in the cell. The @INT function, on the other hand, actually deletes all decimal places from 1-2-3's memory and leaves only an integer (a positive or negative whole number). The @ROUND function rounds a value up or down to the specified number of decimal places.

You can see the different effect of each of these procedures by entering the same numbers in all three ways. See the table below.

Column A	Shows the values exactly as they are entered on the keyboard.
Column B	Contains the values from column A, but the cells have been formatted with the Format Fixed command to display 0 decimal places.
Column C	Contains the values from column A, entered with the @INT function (e.g., @INT(2.33)=2), which deletes any decimal places.

Column D	Contains the values from column A, entered with the @ROUND function (e.g., @ROUND(2.33,0)=2), which rounds the value up or down to the specified number of decimal places.

	A	B	C	D
	Values	/RFF0	@INT(value)	@ROUND(value,0)
	2.33	2	2	2
	55.111	55	55	55
	12.66	13	12	13
TOTALS	70.101	70.101	69	70

Notice that the totals for columns A and B are exactly the same; this is because the Format Fixed command does not change the actual values of the numbers. Since the @functions do change the values, however, the totals for columns C and D are different.

2. The Absolute Key

Pressing the Absolute key changes the nature of a cell address. You can control whether the cell address will be mixed, absolute or relative by striking the key a specific number of times. In Release 2 of 1-2-3, the Absolute key works both when you point to a cell or a range and when you type the address.

Press Abs	Result
first time	$A$1 (absolute cell address)
second time	A$1 (relative column address, absolute row address)
third time	$A1 (absolute column address, relative row address)
fourth time	A1 (relative cell address)

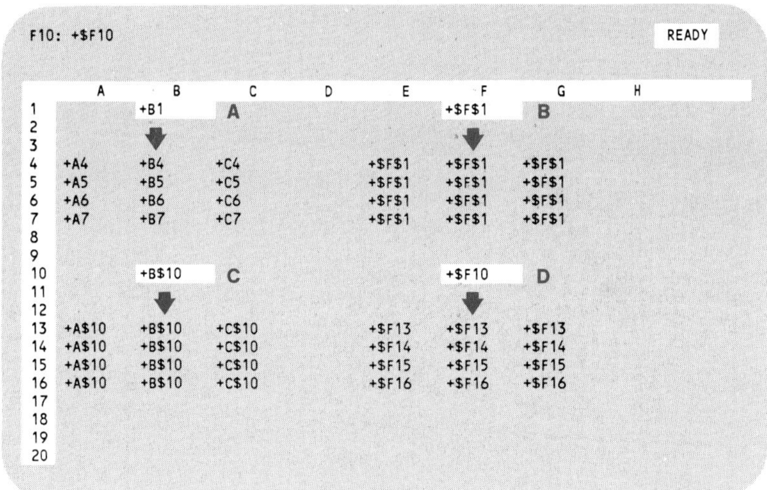

The illustration above shows the four different combinations for relative and absolute cell addresses. When the cell address in cell B1 (*A*) is copied, both the row number and the column letter change because the address is relative. Since the cell address in cell F1 (*B*) is absolute, neither the row number nor column letter change when the cell address is copied. The cell address in cell B10 (*C*) has a relative column address and an absolute row address; only the column letter changes when the cell address is copied. And since the cell address in cell F10 (*D*) has an absolute column address and a relative row address, only the row number changes when that cell address is copied.

3. Editing Formulas

Sometimes after entering a formula in a cell, you find that the formula is not working as it should, especially in the case of long and complex formulas. Rather than retyping the entire formula, you can use a simple process to debug it.

You want to take a look at the formula, and try different combinations of cell addresses and operators—but you want to leave the original entry intact to avoid forgetting it. To do this, convert the formula to a label, copy the formula to another cell, and then test the various options. By converting the formula to a label, you preserve the cell addresses, which, being relative cell addresses, would change if the formula were copied to another cell.

To convert the formula to a label:

Move to: the cell containing the formula

Press: EDIT

HOME *(to move to the beginning of the entry)*

Type: ' ↵ *(apostrophe)*

If the new label is longer than the width of the column and if there is data in the cell to the right, only a portion of the label will display in the cell. If you need to see the entire label, widen the column.

Now copy the label to another cell on the worksheet. Then, after editing the label, convert it back to a formula: press Edit, Home, Delete, and Return to eliminate the label prefix. Check the resulting calculation from the formula, and, if necessary, repeat the editing process until the formula works.

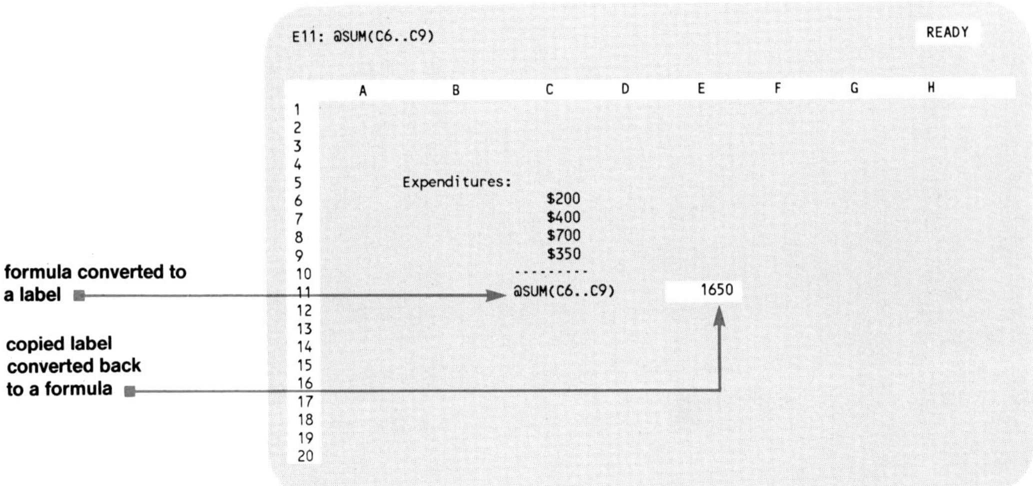

In the worksheet illustrated above, a simple formula was converted into a label and copied to another cell, where it was converted back to a formula and then tested. This process enables you to keep all the cell addresses the same in the original and the copied versions. (In the example the formula is actually correct, but you can see the value of this method for longer formulas.)

When your copied formula is correct, you may convert it into a label and copy it into the original cell, replacing the label there.

To convert the original entry back to a formula, move back to the cell, press Edit, Home, Delete, and Return to get rid of the label prefix.

4. Dates for the Years 2000 to 2099

When the @DATE function is used, 1-2-3 assigns a value to a date that represents the number of days from the beginning of this century (January 1, 1900) to the date. For example, the entry @DATE(1,2,4) stands for February 4, 1901; 1-2-3 assigns it the value 401, which stands for 401 days from January 1, 1900. (The value appears in the cell until you format the cell to display its contents as a date.)

1-2-3 can display dates for any year from 1900 to 2099. For years after 1999, you simply identify the year as a number between 100 and 199—this just means adding 100 to the last two digits of the year. For example, to enter the date October 31, 2042, you type @DATE(142,10,31).

C2: (D1) [W13] @DATE(142,10,31) READY

	A	B	C	D	E
1		Income Statement			
2		01-Oct-2042	31-Oct-2042		
3					
4	000's omitted	PROD.1	PROD.2	PROD.3	TOTAL
5	=========================	============	============	============	============
6	Gross Sales	$100	$200	$200	$500
7	Sales Allowance	$20	$80	$60	$160
8	Net Sales	$80	$120	$140	$340
9	Cost of Goods Sold	$30	$60	$70	$160
10	Gross Margin	$50	$60	$70	$180
11	Marketing/G&A Expenses	$35	$30	$30	$95
12	EBIT	$15	$30	$40	$85
13	Interest	$1	$2	$2	$5
14	Taxes	$7	$14	$19	$40
15	Net Income	$7	$14	$19	$40
16					
17	% Total Net Sales	24%	35%	41%	100%
18					
19					
20					

Years from 2000 to 2099 display as four digits when the cell is formatted to display dates, so be sure the cell is wide enough to accommodate the longer entry.

5. Changing Formulas to Values

It's possible to change a formula in a cell to a value. This prevents the value from changing when the worksheet is recalculated. The Range Value command converts formulas into values, and then gives you the option of copying the converted value to another part of the worksheet (thus preserving the original formula) or replacing the formula permanently.

To change a formula into a value:

Move to: the cell containing the formula
Press: [/]
Select: Range
Value

You will be asked for the FROM range and the TO range. If you want to preserve the original formula or formulas, specify a TO range in another area of the worksheet; the values appear in that area and you can then decide whether to leave them there or to copy them over the original range. If you simply want to replace the formulas with the values, specify the same range of cells for both the FROM and the TO ranges.

Database

The following are a number of tips that are useful when you are working in a 1-2-3 database.

1. Wildcard Characters in Criterion Range

When setting up the criterion range in a database, you usually have to make sure that the word or words in the range match exactly the word or words you are trying to find in the database. Any incorrect characters will throw off the search.

There are three wildcard characters that enable you to search for records that do not match exactly. The characters ?, *, ~ and tell 1-2-3 to look for more than one specific label.

? — Matches any single character; "t?p" will match "tap" and "tip" (but not "tips"). You can use more than one ? in a label; "s??r" will match "sear" and "sour" (but not "soul").

* — Matches all characters to the end of the label; "dum*" will match "dumpling" and "dumb" (but not "drum").

~ — The tilde at the beginning of a label is the equivalent of "not equal": It instructs 1-2-3 to accept any label **except** the one following the tilde. For example, ~ Milne will select all records that do not have Milne in that field. You can place labels beginning with tildes in several fields of the database at once.

```
A17: [W12] 'S*                                                          READY

          A         B     C       D        E         F        G        H
3         Name    Floor Office  Dept.   Status    Salary    Start
4    Nodine          2     21    Adm      FT      $34,680   Jun-81
5    Klein           3     12    Mkt      C       $31,000   Sep-80
6    Falke           2     14    Adm      FT      $28,950   Feb-82
7    Teal            3     13    R&D      FT      $26,600   Jan-82
8    Saddler         3     11    Mkt      FT      $24,500   Apr-83
9    Heineman        2      8    Mkt      FT      $23,450   Jun-81
10   Wilder          4     17    Adm      C       $21,800   Jan-84
11   Carlson         4      7    R&D      PT      $16,500   Oct-81
12   Sloane          4     14    Mkt      FT      $14,800   Aug-82
13   Byrne           2     18    R&D      PT       $8,000   Nov-83
14   Martyn          3     14    R&D      PT       $7,600   Mar-84
15
16        Name    Floor Office  Dept.   Status    Salary    Start
17   S*
18
19        Name    Floor Office  Dept.   Status    Salary    Start
20   Saddler         3     11    Mkt      FT      $24,500   Apr-83
21   Sloane          4     14    Mkt      FT      $14,800   Aug-82
22
```

In the database illustrated above, an entry has been made in the Name field of the criterion range using the letter S and an asterisk. Since this criterion matches all entries that begin with the letter S (it does not matter what follows the first letter), the data records for all those personnel whose names begin with S have been extracted to the output range.

2. Editing in the Find Operation

The Find operation enables you to locate in a database those data records that match specified criteria. In addition, you have the ability to edit those records once you have found them.

When in the FIND mode, 1-2-3 highlights each data record that matches the conditions in the criterion range. The cells in the row containing the record are marked with an extended pointer. Within that pointer, the current cell is identified by the blinking cursor; the current cell contents are displayed in the first line of the control panel. If you simply want to locate the other records that match the criterion range, you use the Up and Down keys to move the pointer to the next matching record.

If you want to edit one of the cells in the highlighted record, you can do so. First, you use the Right and Left keys to move the blinking cursor along the cells in the record; notice that the cell contents in the first line of the control panel change.

Second, during the Find operation 1-2-3 treats the current cell as it does in the READY mode. You can either type in new data and press Return; or you can press Edit, modify the cell contents, and press Return. In both cases, 1-2-3 returns to the FIND mode and the pointer remains where it was. Simply pressing Return while in the FIND mode exits the Find operation and returns you to the Data Query submenu.

A5: [W12] 'Falke EDIT
'Falke

	A	B	C	D	E	F	G	H
1			Personnel Records					
2								
3	Name	Floor	Office	Dept.	Status	Salary	Start	
4	Byrne	2	18	R&D	PT	$8,000	Nov-83	
5	Falke	2	14	Adm	FT	$28,950	Feb-82	
6	Nodine	2	21	Adm	FT	$34,680	Jun-81	
7	Sloane	2	8	Mkt	FT	$23,450	Jun-81	
8	Klein	3	12	Mkt	C	$31,000	Sep-80	
9	Martyn	3	14	R&D	PT	$7,600	Mar-84	
10	Saddler	3	11	Mkt	FT	$24,500	Apr-83	
11	Teal	3	13	R&D	FT	$26,600	Jan-82	
12	Carlson	4	7	R&D	PT	$16,500	Oct-81	
13	Heineman	4	14	Mkt	FT	$14,800	Aug-82	
14	Wilder	4	17	Adm	C	$21,800	Jan-84	
15								
16	Name	Floor	Office	Dept.	Status	Salary	Start	
17					FT			
18								
19								
20								

The database illustrated above shows the pointer resting on the first record located by the Find operation, in this case, the first record containing FT in the Status field. The first cell in that record is cell A5, and its cell contents are listed in the first line of the control panel. Pressing the Edit key has moved the contents of that cell to the second line of the control panel; it is now possible to modify the contents. Then press Return to complete the step and return to the FIND mode.

Printing

1. Printing Today's Date in Headers and Footers

You can instruct 1-2-3 to print today's date in the header or footer of a printout. Assuming either that your computer has an internal clock or that you entered the date correctly at the DOS prompt, the @ character specifies today's date in the Print command.

After you have specified the range to be printed, follow these steps to print today's date in a header:

Press: [/]
Select: Print
Printer
Options
Header
Type: @ [↵]
Select: Quit
Align *(to align the top of the page)*
Go

Today's date will be printed as a header. 1-2-3's initial setting justifies the date with the left edge of the page. If you prefer to center the date, type ¦@¦; to align the date with the right edge, type ¦¦@.

Follow the same steps to print the date as a footer. (For more details on printing footers, see the next Tip.)

2. Printing the Footer on the Last Page

When you are printing a document of more than one page, you will notice that the footer is not automatically printed on the last page. However, after the document has finished printing, you can issue the Page command: this feeds the last page down to the bottom so that the footer does print.

To print the footer on the last page of a document, wait until the document has finished printing, then select Page from the Print menu. 1-2-3 will feed the paper down to the bottom of the page and print the footer.

3. Printing Cell Contents

When attempting to identify and isolate problems in a worksheet, it's very helpful to see all the cell contents (especially formulas) listed in full. With the Cell-Formulas option on the Print menu, you can get a printout of all the literal cell contents.

The printout lists one cell per line and runs down the left side of the page. Each line gives the cell address, the cell format and column width (if other than 1-2-3's initial settings), and the actual contents of the cell (label, value, or formula).

A portion of the cell contents printout of the Income Statement created in the worksheet chapter is illustrated below.

```
C9: (C0) 60
D9: (C0) 70
E9: (C0) @SUM(B9..D9)
A10: W24 'Gross Margin
B10: (C0) +B8-B9
C10: (C0) +C8-C9
D10: (C0) +D8-D9
E10: (C0) @SUM(GROSS-MARGIN)
A11: W24 ' Marketing/G&A Expenses
B11: (C0) 35
```

To get a printout listing the cell contents of the worksheet:

Press: [/]

Select: Print
Printer
Options
Other
Cell-Formulas
Quit
Align
Go

Be aware that this version of the printout takes up many more lines than a regular version. Also notice that the Cell-Formulas setting remains on the Print menu until you restore it to As-Displayed.

4. Printing Column and Row Borders

a. Column and Row Borders

When 1-2-3 prints a large worksheet, it automatically breaks up the printout into smaller chunks to fit on separate pages. One result of this is that you may lose important row and column labels from the top and left borders of the worksheet on the second and all following pages.

You can use the Borders command to print certain columns, rows, or both at the top and left edges of every page of the printout. So, for example, if the labels for the months of the year are located at the top of the worksheet, you can print that row at the top of every page of the printout in order to keep track of related data more easily.

To print column and row borders on every page of the printout:

Press: [/]

Select: Print
Printer
Options
Borders

Make your choice and specify the rows and/or columns that you want printed. Note that you can choose any rows or columns from the worksheet—they do not have to be from the top or left edge. Be aware that the columns you choose must be located somewhere in the rows designated in the print range. Likewise, the rows specified as borders must be in the same columns as those in print range.

b. Column Letters and Row Numbers

Using the commands mentioned above, you can set up a situation where the printed row and column borders actually label the worksheet with column letters and row numbers. This process requires a little work, but it's very helpful to be able to refer to specific cells when looking at a printed worksheet.

Essentially, you create a row and a column that match the top and left borders on the 1-2-3 screen, and then specify them as the borders to print out. The first step is to number the rows. Use the Data Fill command to create a column of consecutive numbers that match the left border.

As you follow the steps below, 1-2-3 asks you first for the Fill range; specify the column and use the Arrow keys to extend the highlight until it reaches the bottom of the active area of the worksheet. Then you will be asked for the Start, Step, and Stop values; 1-2-3 offers initial settings that start at 0 and fill the range in steps of 1. You want to start at 1 and step by 1.

Move to: a cell in row 1 in a column to the right of the active area of the worksheet

Press: [/]

Select: Data

Fill

Press: [.]

[▼] *(until the highlight reaches the bottom of the worksheet)*

[↵]

Type: 1 [↵]

Press: [↵]

```
I1: [W4]                                                          EDIT
Enter Fill range: I1..I16
Start: 1              Step: 1                 Stop: 8191
        A           B      C        D        E        F        G        H     I
1                        Personnel Records
2
3        Name      Floor Office   Dept.   Status   Salary    Start
4    Nodine            2     21    Adm       FT   $34,680   Jun-81
5    Klein             3     12    Mkt        C   $31,000   Sep-80
6    Falke             2     14    Adm       FT   $28,950   Feb-82
7    Teal              3     13    R&D       FT   $26,600   Jan-82
8    Saddler           3     11    Mkt       FT   $24,500   Apr-83
9    Sloane            2      8    Mkt       FT   $23,450   Jun-81
10   Wilder            4     17    Adm        C   $21,800   Jan-84
11   Carlson           4      7    R&D       PT   $16,500   Oct-81
12   Heineman          4     14    Mkt       FT   $14,800   Aug-82
13   Byrne             2     18    R&D       PT    $8,000   Nov-83
14   Martyn            3     14    R&D       PT    $7,600   Mar-84
15
16
17
18
19
20
```

Press: [↵]

When you have specified the range and all the values, numbers from 1 to the number of the last row of the active area appear in the column.

Now change the width of the column to be as narrow as the left border (the column prints out as it appears, so if there are spaces around the numbers, the spaces appear on the printout).

Press: [/]

Select: Worksheet
Column
Set-Width

Type: 4 [↵]

The next step is to create a row of letters that will match the top border. Choose a row below the active area of the worksheet, and type in letters to correspond to the letters in the top border. The letters in the row must be centered in their cells.

Move to: a cell in column A in a row below the active area of the worksheet

Type: ^A

Press: [▶]

Type: ^B

Press: [▶]

Continue labeling the columns across the row until you have covered all the columns containing data. The worksheet illustrated below shows the border column and row in place.

```
I1: [W4] 1                                                          READY

          A          B    C       D       E        F         G      H    I
1                       Personnel Records                                1
2                                                                        2
3            Name    Floor Office  Dept.   Status   Salary    Start      3
4      Nodine            2    21    Adm      FT    $34,680   Jun-81      4
5      Klein             3    12    Mkt       C    $31,000   Sep-80      5
6      Falke             2    14    Adm      FT    $28,950   Feb-82      6
7      Teal              3    13    R&D      FT    $26,600   Jan-82      7
8      Saddler           3    11    Mkt      FT    $24,500   Apr-83      8
9      Sloane            2     8    Mkt      FT    $23,450   Jun-81      9
10     Wilder            4    17    Adm       C    $21,800   Jan-84     10
11     Carlson           4     7    R&D      PT    $16,500   Oct-81     11
12     Heineman          4    14    Mkt      FT    $14,800   Aug-82     12
13     Byrne             2    18    R&D      PT     $8,000   Nov-83     13
14     Martyn            3    14    R&D      PT     $7,600   Mar-84     14
15                                                                      15
16                                                                      16
17        A          B    C       D       E        F         G
18
19
20
```

columns border

rows border

Set up the row and column just created as the borders of the printout.

Press: [/]

Select: Print
Printer
Options
Borders

Specify the row and then the column containing the labels you just created.

Select: Quit
Align
Go

5. Inserting Page Breaks

Previously, 1-2-3 printed documents in a continuous flow. The printout broke only in order to fit the document onto the separate pages. Using 1-2-3 Release 2, you can choose to break the printout at specific points. You might want to start a new page after the end of a section or the beginning of a memo.

The procedure to insert a page break is very simple.

Move to: the row where you want the new page to start

Press: [/]

Select: Worksheet
Page

```
A17: [W24] |::                                                       READY

              A                   B          C          D          E
1                          INCOME STATEMENT: 1986 By Month
2
3   JANUARY                    PROD.1     PROD.2     PROD.3      TOTAL
4   ================================================================
5   Gross Sales                  $100       $200       $200       $500
6     Sales Allowance             $20        $80        $60       $160
7   Net Sales                     $80       $120       $140       $340
8     Cost of Goods Sold          $30        $60        $70       $160
9   Gross Margin                  $50        $60        $70       $180
10    Marketing/G&A Expenses      $35        $30        $30        $95
11  EBIT                          $15        $30        $40        $85
12    Interest                     $1         $2         $2         $5
13    Taxes                        $7        $14        $19        $40
14  Net Income                     $7        $14        $19        $40
15  % Total Net Sales             24%         35%        41%       100%
16
17  ::
18  FEBRUARY                   PROD.1     PROD.2     PROD.3      TOTAL
19  ================================================================
20  Gross Sales                  $110       $185       $170       $465
```

page break

1-2-3 inserts a new row above the pointer; it contains the label ::. If you look at the cell contents in the first line of the control panel, you will see that the cell actually contains ¦ ::. When 1-2-3 encounters this series of characters while printing, it automatically advances to the next page and continues printing.

To clear a page break, locate the pointer in the row containing the page break, and select Worksheet, Delete, and Row.

Graphics

1. Graphing in Color

In order to view color graphics, you need an RGB monitor. You choose the Color option on the Graph menu, and the current graph displays in color.

You can choose the color option if you have a black and white monitor. The graph will still display and, depending on your hardware, may have a variety of different shadings to distinguish the ranges (or it may make all the ranges look the same).

The only way to change the colors that 1-2-3 uses to draw the graphs is actually to reassign the data ranges to different ranges on the graph. You can modify the colors on a color printer or color plotter.

When you save a graph, 1-2-3 assigns a different color to each data range. PrintGraph can then draw the graph in color, even if the graph was created with the B&W option.

2. Skipping Labels on the X Axis

If the X axis of a graph contains several labels, you may find that the labels overlap and the graph is hard to read. This often happens if the X data range contains long labels.

You can usually solve this problem by using the Skip option on the Graph Options menu. You instruct 1-2-3 to skip labels at a certain interval.

To skip labels on the X axis of a graph:

Press: [/]
Select: Graph
Options
Scale
Skip

The second line on the control panel reads Enter skip factor (1..8192): 1. The number you enter, up to 8192, will determine which labels are printed. For example, an entry of 5 means that every fifth label will be printed. The entry 1 is the initial setting, and means that all labels are included. To print every other label, enter 2.

Type: 2 [↵]
Select: Quit
View

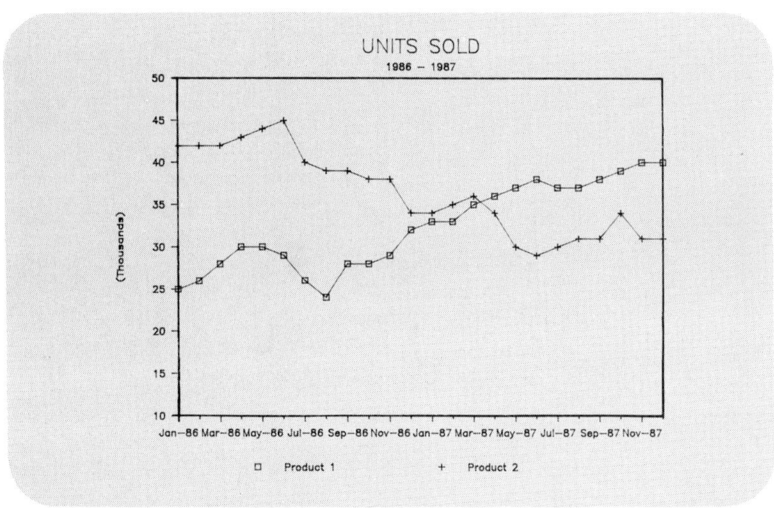

In the graph illustrated above, only every other label is included on the X axis (a skip factor of 2). The best time to use this option is when the labels are sequential (as with the months) and you can easily determine what the missing labels are.

3. Suppressing the Scale Indicator

When applicable, 1-2-3 automatically places a label next to the Y axis that indicates the scale of the numbers shown. The label is shown in parentheses and reads Thousands, Millions, and so on.

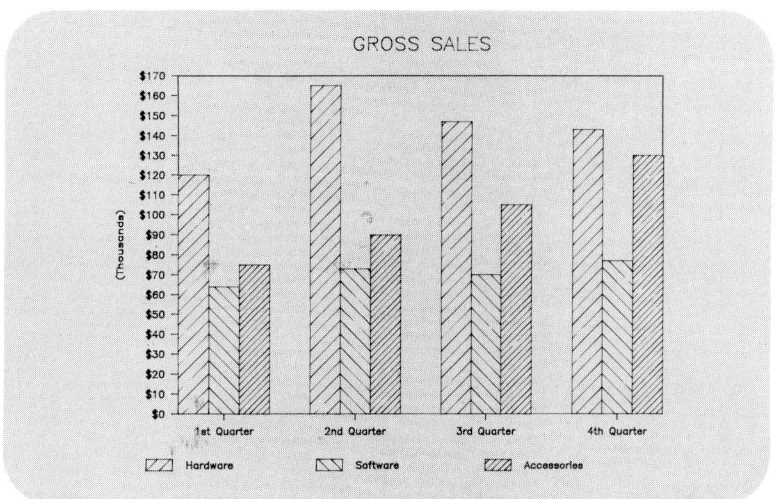

In the graph illustrated above, the indicator informs you that the Y axis is actually graphing numbers in the hundreds of thousands ($100 stands for $100,000, and so on).

Using 1-2-3 Release 2, you can change the initial setting and suppress the scale indicator. To suppress display of the label:

Press: [/]

Select: Graph
Options
Scale
Y Scale
Indicator
No
Quit
Quit
View

The label is suppressed, but the actual scale of the Y axis does not change—the numbers look the same.

4. Adding Data Labels to Graphs

1-2-3 has a feature that enables you to add data labels to a graph. The labels appear on the graph itself, next to the data points.

Data labels are drawn from a range on the worksheet. A range of data labels is matched against a range of data being graphed; each label corresponds to a value in the data range. You can specify a different range of labels for each range of data being graphed. The labels can be values or words.

To add data labels to a graph:

Press: [/]

Select: Graph
Options
Data-Labels

You are prompted to choose the data range against which to place the labels (range A through F). Once you have made your choice, the second line of the control panel reads `Enter label range for A range data:`. Use the Arrow keys to point to the range you wish to use as labels. Note that if you select a range that has more or fewer cells than the data range, only the first corresponding labels will be used.

After you have specified the range of cells to be used as labels, the command menu reads `Center Left Above Right Below`. For line and XY graphs, 1-2-3 lets you determine where the labels are placed in relation to the data points. For bar and stacked bar graphs, the labels are automatically placed above the bars. Once you have selected the position of the labels, view the graph.

Select: Quit
Quit
View

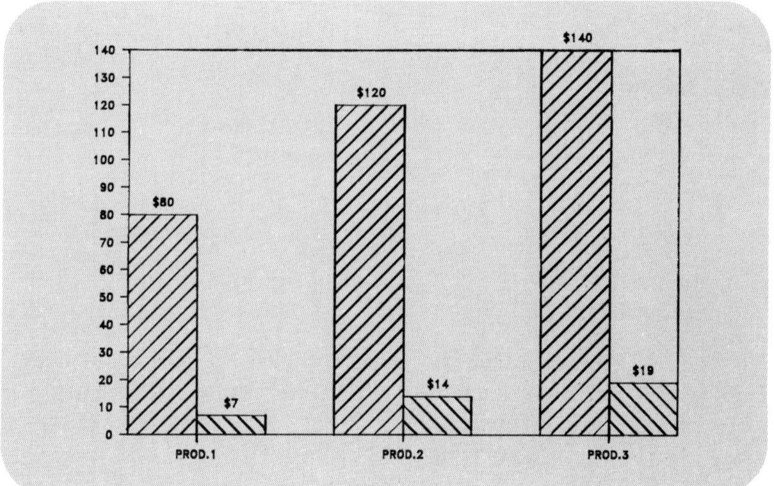

In the graph illustrated above, the ranges used for the data labels are the same as the ranges used for the data points themselves. You can see the actual values being graphed above the bars.

Pie charts do not accept data labels because they plot only one data range. However, note that the data in the cells specified as the X range are used as labels next to the pie slices. Simply specify an X range that contains the labels you want for the slices (again, you can label the slices with the numeric quantities they represent by specifying the same cells for the X and A data ranges).

INDEX